Boozang from the Trenches

Learn Test Automation with Boozang in an Enterprise Environment

Gianni Pucciani

Apress®

Boozang from the Trenches: Learn Test Automation with Boozang in an Enterprise Environment

Gianni Pucciani
Meyrin, Geneve, Switzerland

ISBN-13 (pbk): 978-1-4842-9009-5   ISBN-13 (electronic): 978-1-4842-9010-1
https://doi.org/10.1007/978-1-4842-9010-1

Managing Director, Apress Media LLC: Welmoed Spahr
Acquisitions Editor: Aditee Mirashi
Development Editor: James Markham
Coordinating Editor: Aditee Mirashi

Cover designed by eStudioCalamar

Cover image designed by Freepik (www.freepik.com)

Distributed to the book trade worldwide by Springer Science+Business Media New York, 1 New York Plaza, Suite 4600, New York, NY 10004-1562, USA. Phone 1-800-SPRINGER, fax (201) 348-4505, e-mail orders-ny@springer-sbm.com, or visit www.springeronline.com. Apress Media, LLC is a California LLC and the sole member (owner) is Springer Science + Business Media Finance Inc (SSBM Finance Inc). SSBM Finance Inc is a **Delaware** corporation.

For information on translations, please e-mail booktranslations@springernature.com; for reprint, paperback, or audio rights, please e-mail bookpermissions@springernature.com.

Apress titles may be purchased in bulk for academic, corporate, or promotional use. eBook versions and licenses are also available for most titles. For more information, reference our Print and eBook Bulk Sales web page at http://www.apress.com/bulk-sales.

Any source code or other supplementary material referenced by the author in this book is available to readers on GitHub via the book's product page, located at www.apress.com/978-1-4842-9009-5. For more detailed information, please visit http://www.apress.com/source-code.

Printed on acid-free paper

Dedicated to my extended family, for their support and unconditional love.

100% of the author royalties will be sent to EMERGENCY, an Italian NGO. EMERGENCY provides free, high-quality healthcare to victims of war, poverty, and landmines, alongside building hospitals and training local staff.

Table of Contents

About the Author

Gianni Pucciani is a simple guy from Livorno (a beautiful port city in Tuscany) who never thought he would end up with a Ph.D. at CERN (European Organization for Nuclear Research, cern.ch) and then working for a prestigious company in Switzerland. But he always knew that at some point in his life, he would have written a book.

In his early career as a software developer, he built some C/C++ code, but, pretty soon, debugging null pointer exceptions drove him crazy. He then decided he would be better off testing software rather than building it.

Wherever he worked, he tried to push for automating tests. Because manual testing, let's be honest, is not fun, and it can be dangerously repetitive. People at work must have fun, if possible. At Touring Club Suisse, he defined an IT Test Policy stating "Test automation is developers' stuff" until he discovered Boozang. And then, in his first two hours of using this tool, he thought, "Man, this is fun!"

Thus, he finally found a good topic for his book.

About the Technical Reviewer

Santhosh Kumar Srinivasan, a.k.a San, is a Professional Cloud Architect helping clients all over the globe on their digital transformation journey. He has expertise in Software Engineering, DevOps, and SRE. He is certified in multiple Cloud technologies (GCP, AWS, Azure, and Hashicorp Terraform). He is an expert in architecting highly available, fault-tolerant workloads in the Cloud to solve complex problems.

San is passionate about teaching. He is a mentor for Advanced Certification in Software Engineering for Cloud, Blockchain, and IOT offered by IIT Madras and GreatLearning. He has trained hundreds of developers on Full Stack Development in Python using web frameworks like Flask, Django, and FastAPI. He creates and maintains open-source teaching materials on various software engineering topics such as Python, Docker, Cloud, Terraform, and RegEx on his GitHub (`https://github.com/sanspace`).

San has a bachelors's degree in Computer Applications from Bharathiar University, Coimbatore. He started his career as a test engineer with Infosys in the late 2000s. Though he switched to development and then moved on to DevOps and Cloud Architecture, Test Automation has always been a part of the work. He has experience with Selenium, jMeter, and Puppeteer tools.

He is currently working with Google as a Cloud Engineer on the Google Cloud Platform. He lives in his hometown Coimbatore, India, with his wife Vishnu and daughter Aruvi. He plays chess, table tennis, and badminton. To know more about San, please visit his website `https://sanspace.in` or follow him on Twitter @2sks (`https://twitter.com/2sks`).

Acknowledgments

Every book is a journey. This journey was possible first of all thanks to my family that supported this effort and the time I took away from being a husband and a father; I'll pay you back. ;)

Then, the Boozang team, especially Mats and Wensheng, who supported the project by constantly improving the tool and fixing issues incredibly quickly.

A special thanks to Franck and Amin who have been the main force behind our E2E automation suite, and for their constant support to improving our automation approach.

Thanks also to Thomas and Olivier who trusted my intuition and supported our Boozang journey.

Thanks to Romain for his help in building our current pipeline in Jenkins.

Thanks to Joe Colantonio and his podcast who made me discover Boozang in the first place.

Thanks to Amol who was the first person I got in touch with for a reference on this new tool, and his availability to share his experience.

Thanks to Patrick for his initial input, and to Santhosh for his technical review.

And finally, a big thanks to the Apress team, especially to Aditee and her team, always present to answer my questions and moving the project forward.

Foreword 1

Mats Ljunggren
CEO, Boozang

Boozang was built on the belief that there must be a better way to automate software testing. Over-reliance on unit tests and manual testing prevented the companies we worked with from embracing the true benefit of practicing continuous integration. When Gianni reached out to us, he described a slightly different challenge. His team's use of several off-the-shelf solutions wasn't yielding the results they had hoped for. On the other hand, the alternative of using Selenium was simply too time consuming to consider.

I rushed out to Switzerland to perform a proof of concept, which for lack of a better word was stressful. Could Boozang really deliver a solution that could compete with the giants in this space?

As a testament to this book, we were successful. Having a company like Touring Club Suisse onboard with our testing philosophy was a win worth writing home about. We approached the relationship as a partnership, and Gianni opened our eyes to embracing the likes of Xray and supporting Cucumber syntax to scale our Test Automation vision. He also introduced new ideas, like test auditing and root-cause analysis, to further make our solution scale.

There are few greater honors than Gianni taking the time to write a full book about this partnership. *Boozang from the Trenches* is much more than a tip of the hat to our work together; it's about realizing Test Automation at enterprise scale. In practice, budgets will have constraints, and you will encounter limitations rooted in reality. This book will explore the types of scenarios you could already find yourself in.

Gianni shines a light in this book on how you can achieve Test Automation in a challenging environment. Regardless if you'll use Boozang or not, consider it a blueprint for those wanting to elevate their Test Automation game and unlock the true potential Test Automation can do for your software delivery pipeline.

Foreword 2

Cristiano Cunha
Solution Architect and Testing Advocate at Xray by Xblend

In this book you can find a detailed description of the author's journey to redefine his testing automation strategy and how tools like Boozang, Jenkins, and Xray have helped.

It is, as we can find in the title, a description from the "trenches," not just theoretical content but a real-life example of how the author and his team manage a transformation into a better Test Automation strategy using those tools.

The stage is set up with detailed descriptions of the contexts and difficulties felt in their day-to-day work. Having these rich descriptions enables you to fully understand the choices described ahead and are easily relatable. At the end of the day, in one way or another, we all face similar challenges regarding Test Automation.

This book does a good job in making the reader understand how each tool is solving a particular challenge and how they all integrate into a full-blown solution that takes them toward the goal to have a stable and reliable automation strategy. You will find how the author is addressing each challenge, from strategies on how to define your tests, to the importance of having the results visible or how to deal with environments along the way. Every challenge is properly introduced with a context description stating the difficulties faced and the solution found for each issue.

Detailed instructions are provided on the strategies, tools, and processes used so that it is easily followed and applicable locally.

The book is very well structured with chapters written in such a way that you can switch between them, deep diving in some subjects, depending on your interest, or just follow the story along.

I'm a Solution Architect and Test Advocate, and I've been through similar automation challenges during my career that were addressed using different approaches. In this book you will find some of those approaches and their technical solution descriptions with step-by-step details to help you.

The content is not only focused on tools and technical descriptions, you will understand how strategies and tools play a big part in increasing visibility and fostering collaboration between teams and individuals and how this is crucial to having a healthy and maintainable system.

Nowadays, tools are not there just to solve a technical challenge, but they are socio-technical tools that bridge the gap between humans and machines, and so they need to be considered not only based on how they will help in solving a technical challenge but also on how they will integrate into the actual solution/process and leverage the interaction with humans.

If you are thinking of using Boozang, Jenkins, or Xray, this book is for you! You will learn the specifics on how each tool is important for different stages and how the combination of tools culminates into a solution that solves the challenges the team was facing. The book is filled with code examples and strategies that will allow you to apply this knowledge right away and enhance your process making the most of each tool.

Even if you are not using these tools, you can easily relate to the challenges and transpose the approaches to your own experience or ignite new ideas and approaches to your own challenges. Definitely a book to have on the shelf.

Introduction

Why This Book

End-to-End Test Automation is becoming increasingly important in today's world, where business processes are performed via several interconnected web applications. The team at Boozang understands this and has created a Test Automation tool that solves many of the issues other competitors are not addressing.

Boozang is quite new in the Test Automation tools arena, and as an early adopter, I was lucky enough to be in the right place at the right time.

At the time of this writing, Boozang is still not nearly as popular as it should be. I hope this book will create awareness of what this tool can do and help those professionals struggling to find an appropriate Web Test Automation solution, like I was.

This is a technical book that tells a real story, like *Lean from the Trenches* by Henrik Kniberg. Kniberg's book is one of the IT books I have enjoyed reading most. I hope the title transmits the idea of a real experience that people can learn from and at the same time enjoy some reading time.

All too often, testing books describe the theory as if we are all working for IT giants or start-up software development companies, building flashy apps with microservices architectures, following all the latest trends in the industry. This is not the reality for most of us. Many IT professionals work in enterprises where IT is a unit that is considered an "enabler" that does not produce direct financial gains but rather costs. The goal of these IT units is not to build new software from scratch. They rather try to find the most appropriate solution to business problems, and usually prefer to buy COTS (Commercial-Off-The-Shelf) solutions, with some configuration or customization capabilities. These applications are then integrated into an existing IT ecosystem, made of several other applications, hosted both on-premise and in the cloud, legacy and not.

In these cases, the challenges are quite different; the focus is on automating End-To-End business processes rather than unit tests, since access to the original codebase is hard to come by.

Very few books in IT (*Lean from the Trenches* is the great exception), and none in Test Automation, present an approach or tool with real examples, from real-life projects. Therefore, I felt the need to fill this gap and present not only the Boozang tool but also why I chose it, the way I set it up in my environment, and how I use it in a real project. I describe the Test Automation challenges we went through in the project and how we addressed them, including the setbacks and speed bumps along the way. Still, I try to keep the context in this book general enough so that most readers can relate to it.

Finally, I wanted to write a book where the ending is not known from the beginning.

I bet on Boozang, and I bet on the TCS project. But I still don't know if I won this bet. In any case, if I win or lose, the reader will learn a lot from this experience.

Who This Book Is For

This book is mainly for software test and quality assurance professionals who want to know more about Web Test Automation (GUI and API) and learn how to master the Boozang tool.

The book is filled with examples that also go beyond the Boozang tool, and cover the setup of a Test Automation project in a real context, with practical solutions as well as open points for which we are still looking for new ideas. We show, for example, the integration with JIRA and XRay, as well as other plugins used to manage effectively our project.

Therefore, I believe this book can also appeal to IT project, release and delivery managers, developers, and business analysts.

A minimal IT background can simplify the reading, but I will provide references whenever possible for the reader who needs to fill some gaps.

What This Book Is Not

This book is not a reference for learning Boozang from scratch; the tool has its own documentation and training courses on Udemy to get started with.

This book is not a reference of widely accepted best practices in Test Automation, but rather a set of practical solutions applied in our project with our specific context, which I am sure many will relate to. I will nonetheless cover common Test Automation best practices, and challenge their application in our enterprise context.

This book is also not a beginner's guide to testing or Test Automation. Several books are already available to get started with software testing, and also for Test Automation. Unfortunately, Test Automation books for beginners are often far too generic, or tend to use a coded approach, mostly based on Selenium Web Driver. We won't be doing any of that here.

How I Discovered Boozang

By accident, one day, I went on Joe Colantonio's website, maybe from a Google alert on software quality I had set a long time ago and now rarely follow. Joe provides very helpful resources via his website and podcast "Test Automation Guild." I tuned into a podcast where Joe interviewed Mats Ljunggren, CEO and co-founder of Boozang. The tool sounded interesting enough for me to visit their website boozang.com.

Free trial, clear pricing, okay let's sign up and try it out.

I was impressed by the tool's simplicity and clean user interface. I recorded a simple test scenario on SalesForce in just a few minutes. I cross-checked the features on the website and then found the Udemy free video courses, clear and to the point.

What happened next is the basis for this entire book.

What I Like About Boozang

Their team of highly skilled people is agile by nature. The company's clear vision and ownership of the solution gives them the ability to fix issues and introduce new features at an incredible speed.

The tool is easy to learn, yet extremely powerful.

I also like the fact that it focuses on Web Test Automation, GUI and API, and leaves the requirements and release management features to other tools with which it easily integrates. But for Web GUI and API testing, you can do almost everything a production user would do in the browser.

PART I

Testing Web Applications in an Enterprise Context, Why Boozang

Not everyone works at Google or Spotify...

Yes, it's definitely true that not everyone works for large and famous software development companies.

These kinds of companies use all of the latest trends in IT. Many popular new practices and tools are also created in-house. Some of them can even afford to roll-out new releases for their internal users with little End-To-End testing; in case of issues they can quickly fix them without too much business impact. Hence they invest a lot in Unit, Service, and API automated tests and much less on functional End-to-End tests, like the automation pyramid of Test Automation of Mike Cohn teaches us.

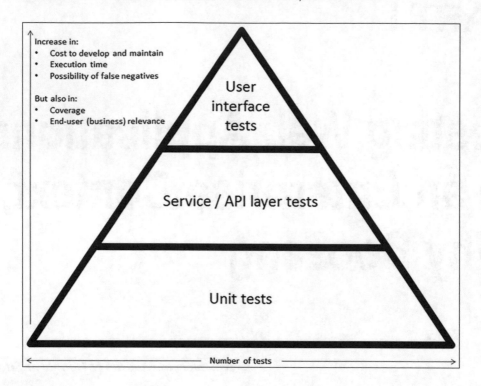

The large majority of IT people work in environments (finance, insurance, retail, healthcare, etc.) where the agile transition is still in progress and DevOps practices are not yet established. Most use a mix of technologies, legacy and not, self-hosted or on the Cloud. These IT units have limited budgets and are usually constrained by lack of resources and internal skills.

In these settings, End-to-End Test Automation becomes more and more relevant, and Boozang can step-up as a great fit.

This part is setting up the stage with context and a sort of business case for adopting Boozang in your work.

This is the smallest part of the book, so if you are in a hurry and want to jump into learning Boozang, skip ahead to Part 2. However, make sure to come back here to fully appreciate the rest of the book and the practical examples.

Chapter 1, "Web Test Automation in an Enterprise Environment," defines the context and terminology for the practical parts of this book. I also cover aspects that may be of interest to readers with management responsibilities like Return on Investment (ROI) analysis.

Chapter 2, "Selenium: Best Practices and Pain Points," covers some aspects of classic coded approaches to Test Automation and highlights some specific practices and challenges when using Selenium.

Chapter 3, "Meet Boozang," talks about the PoC (Proof of Concept) and Pilot phases I have done before selecting Boozang and highlights the strengths of this tool.

Chapter 4, "The TCS Project," presents the TCS project that will be used to explain the Boozang features applied to real use cases.

Chapter 5, "How Boozang Was Born," tells the story of Boozang from its very early stages. This section comes directly from the founders of Boozang.

CHAPTER 1

Web Test Automation in an Enterprise Environment

Before playing, let's set the table with a few rules.

This chapter introduces basic Test Automation concepts that will be used throughout the book. Besides ISTQB[1] standard terminology, I'll also cover the constraints typical of an enterprise environment that might not be the same for small startups and IT giants.

---

[1] International Software Testing Qualifications Board, `www.istqb.org/`

© Gianni Pucciani 2023

G. Pucciani, *Boozang from the Trenches*, https://doi.org/10.1007/978-1-4842-9010-1_1

Common Test Automation Challenges

If you are reading this book, you know why we automate tests, and I don't need to convince you of the value of moving from manual testing to Test Automation. If you still have doubts, there are lots of great resources on the Web. My favorite read on this topic is *Continuous Delivery* by Dave Farley and Jez Humble. It was published in 2010 but is still, in my opinion, one of the must-reads for IT professionals trying to improve their delivery process. That book will certainly convince you that you should automate many more manual activities than just tests.

While automation is great, common sense should always prevail. Some automation initiatives are more profitable than others (see section "Test Automation ROI, Theory and Practice").

My personal view is that manual testing, besides being error-prone and time-consuming, is boring. Test Automation can be fun and we should always try to have fun at work.

Certainly we can agree on the fact that you will never be able to (and should not aim to) automate all testing activities. There are still situations where human beings do a better job than robots. For example, exploratory testing and testing non-functional requirements like usability are better suited to manual tests.

I'd also like to clarify that testing, especially Test Automation, is very context-dependent. In Chapter 4, "The TCS Project," I will spend time clarifying the context for the project in this book. Organizational structure, business domain, technologies, culture, and background are to be considered when applying Test Automation and selecting a tool.

The next section lists the four main challenges that organizations can face when trying to get management buy-in or implementing Test Automation. This is not a comprehensive list, but one that shines a light on the most common, all of which we will provide practical solutions for in this book.

Challenge N1: Culture

The challenges encountered when promoting or applying Test Automation might be less about technologies and tools than you would expect.

In my professional experience, for example, I've worked in two types of environments: one where Test Automation was part of the company's culture and one where every cent spent in Test Automation was challenged and had to be justified.

In an enterprise environment, projects and budget approvals have key gates where Test Automation is either promoted or killed before it starts.

You might benefit from learning how to advocate Test Automation and prove its benefits (see section "Test Automation ROI, Theory and Practice").

Another challenge you may face requires soft skills to manage opposing views on Test Automation. You might work in a context where developers and QA are on opposite sides. One is responsible for implementing features, and the other is responsible for ensuring that features work as expected. Thankfully this situation is less and less common these days since agile and lean practices are being adopted.

These two cultural challenges are especially important when Test Automation is done by an off-shore team, or by a team which is not part of the main organization.

Challenge N2: Skills and Resources

Let's assume your organization uses agile principles, and you overcome the first challenge. The next challenge you might face is about people skills and resource availability.

Even if your team supports Test Automation, you may lack the resources and skills necessary to conduct conventional coded Test Automation.

I was in this situation, and here a tool can help. As long as the tool is easy to use, more people can use it. Better yet, if the tool allows you to be efficient without needing developer skills, you can get more work done, making it easier to scale up your automation initiative.

If your tool and the process driving it fit well into your organization, you will not need to waste time begging for buy-in, convincing stakeholders, and training expensive resources.

Challenge N3: Technology

Less often than you think, technology will represent a challenge for Test Automation in today's world. Web, API, desktop, and mobile applications are the four main categories supported by functional Test Automation tools. Some tools are better than others in each category. A few commercial tools try to support all of the above, but they end up being hard to use and difficult to integrate into your delivery process.

In my case, which I believe is quite representative, our main objective is to automate web applications (GUI and API), for the critical End-to-End business processes. No mobile and no desktop applications. Therefore a functional web automation tool would cover our primary requirements.

Additionally, the project affords us the luxury of ignoring some edge cases that are difficult to automate. For those cases we still rely on manual testing as part of User Acceptance Tests (the section on "Test Levels" later in this chapter covers UAT and other test levels and types).

Challenge N4: Long-Term Maintainability

A last common challenge worth mentioning is an automation framework that is hard to maintain, with flaky tests which rarely provide the expected value of Test Automation.

Even when you have the right organizational culture, in-house skills, and no specific technological challenges, you might still have problems in the long run, where Test Automation initiatives often tend to be abandoned. This normally happens when Test Automation is made without any previous experience and tests are built with little modularity and reusability. In these cases, a simple UI change might become very costly to address if it impacts many tests. Test Automation projects built without modularity can be more costly to maintain than manual testing.

Even with a great automation tool, if best practices are not applied, success is less than guaranteed.

If any of these challenges sound familiar to you, then this book is for you, keep reading!

Test Automation can be applied at several test levels. Therefore, it is important to understand the concepts of test level and also test type. We will discuss these two concepts at length in the next sections.

Test Levels, Test Types, and Testing Roles

Since the early 2000s, the Standard Software Testing Qualification Board (ISTQB) provides a common vocabulary and certification path for professional testers and test managers, as PMI does for Project Management and ITIL for Service Management.

An advantage to following these standards is the adoption of a common vocabulary. When dealing with partners located in different countries, referring to the same thing when discussing "unit testing" or "UAT" is fundamental.

Let's briefly review some important taxonomy that will help you better understand the later chapters of this book. We will start with test levels, test types, and test environments. You will then see how they apply to Test Automation and Boozang.

Test Levels

The four most common test levels are

- **Unit and component tests**: These tests are normally implemented by developers for small software units, like classes and functions. *xUnit* frameworks are used to implement and run these tests. They are dependent on the development language. Boozang does not apply here.

- **System tests**: Here we test a single system or application. Boozang can certainly play an important role at this level.

- **Integration tests**: Testing multiple systems to validate how they interact and provide a certain user functionality. Boozang definitely helps here with its GUI- and APIs-based End-to-End capabilities.

- **User Acceptance Tests (UAT)**: At this level, Boozang can replace manual tests. This is especially true when automated tests are part of a fully automated delivery pipeline.

In reality, few organizations can deliver to production environments without the validation of real users. Therefore, in most cases, I say Boozang can reduce the manual effort needed. This allows end users to focus on usability issues rather than regression tests.

Test Types

Test types are a transversal classification to test levels. In fact, the following test types can be applied to almost all levels. We'll cover each type and how Boozang handles them.

- **Functional and non-functional testing**: Functional testing is definitely where Boozang shines. For non-functional tests, Boozang provides some interesting features for performance testings, while for things like usability and security[2] testing, other tools are certainly better suited. Boozang can measure the performance of any actions (UI and API), but it is not made to generate load with different patterns.

- **Testing related to changes**: In a classic release management process, for each new release, we need to test new features while making sure existing ones didn't break. Regression testing is essential, and automating regression tests is key to keep down application maintenance costs and provide confidence with frequent releases. Regression testing is definitely where Boozang fits, and, depending on the process, it can also be used to test new features before they are shipped.

- **White vs. black box testing**: Boozang can be used in a black box approach,[3] meaning that you do not need to know how your System Under Test (SUT) is built to be able to test it. White box testing is usually done at the unit test level, often using tools like Sonar Cube (`www.sonarqube.org/`).

Testing Roles

Since the early 2000s, the profession of test engineers has gained popularity, and certification paths are more available than ever for professional testers. Besides the advantage of having a common dictionary, as I already mentioned, testing and test management techniques have become widely consolidated and adopted.

In 2012 the book *How Google Tests Software* was published, and with its gain in momentum, so did the profession of Software Engineer in Test (SET) or Software Development Engineer in Test (SDET). Today SDET professionals are highly sought after and an integral part of performant agile teams.

As the name suggests, an SDET is a software developer that has basic development skills and is able to apply these skills specifically to software testing. Besides knowing

---

[2] I prefer to consider security as non-functional even if this is not always the case.

[3] We consider API Testing (covered later in the book) as black box when designing tests based on an API contract.

Test Automation tools, an SDET should also be able to set up and use tools like GIT, Maven, Jenkins, and Sonar to build CI/CD pipelines.

They should also have the necessary soft and hard skills to build effective Gherkin[4] scenarios with business users and/or product owners. Most of all, they should stay curious, with the quizzical attitude and desire for quality typical of test engineers.

In agile contexts, however, the separation between developers and testers can be fuzzy. In an ideal world, a cross-functional team can assign implementation and testing tasks to any member, so that efficiency is maximized.

We covered test levels, test types, and testing roles. To wrap up, the next section will cover test environments and discuss which environment category is suitable for each test level, test type, and type of users.

Test Environments

In terms of test environments, each organization has its own policies. Here we will show a classification that I consider quite common, even if the naming can certainly change.

- **Production**: This is the environment used by business users to perform operational work. Despite current trends to shift-right, that is, testing in production, most enterprise companies are not comfortable allowing tests in production. Hence, no Boozang tests here, unless you know what you are doing. The only testing activity you may want to perform in a production environment is normally called a "sanity check." Sanity checks are used to validate that deployments have been executed correctly and the environment is up and running.

- **Pre-production/acceptance/staging**: This is the environment used by business users to perform User Acceptance Tests. This environment should be feature equivalent to production and similar in terms of sizing. You can certainly run Boozang non regression tests on this environment, and let business users focus on validating new features.

---

[4] Gherkin is a Given, When, Then syntax to define scenarios, and we will cover this in more details in the following chapters.

- **Test/quality assurance**: This is an environment where most of the testing activity should take place. It can be functionally equivalent to production and pre-production but less "powerful" in terms of sizing.[5] This is the main environment where we design, run, and troubleshoot Boozang tests before running them in pre-production.

- **Development and integration/DevInt**: One or more environments can be used to develop and integrate code. Normally, in these environments, developers run unit and component tests. Nothing prevents you from running Boozang tests here; in our project we wanted to implement tests in a more stable environment, like the previous two.

This covers the most common environments you will find, but others are possible depending on the specific needs of each project or organization (e.g., training, migration purposes, or for executing load and performance tests).

How We Manage Test Environments

Effectively managing test environments is important for every IT project. In our project (see Chapter 4, "The TCS Project"), we put in a considerable effort early on to outline the delivery chain and make sure the entire team was aligned on which environment must be used for each type of activity. This work is crucial when working with remote teams and integrating COTS[6] solutions.

In the following picture you can see a template that we normally use for describing the delivery process and the test environments. We highlight which environments are locally hosted and which remotely.

---

[5] CPU and cores, RAM, and disks size.

[6] COTS is an acronym of commercial/consumer off-the-shelf.

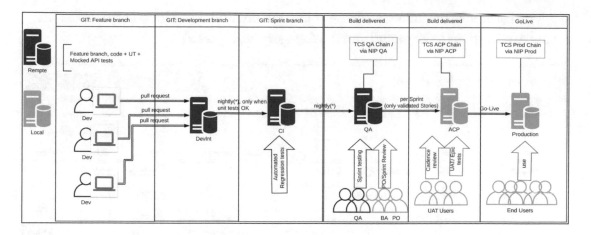

A TCS model for test environments

We also noted which test activity is performed where, and the frequency of deliveries from one environment to the next. In this example, developers work on a local machine while developing on a feature branch. A pull-request based approach integrates all the developers work into the main branch, deployed on the DevInt on which unit tests are run. On a nightly basis the code is deployed on a CI environment where the automated regression suite is run. With a frequency that can be nightly or ad hoc, the build tested in CI with success is promoted to the QA environments, where in sprint testing activity can be performed. At the end of the sprint, the validated Stories are delivered on the ACP environment (pre-production) for end users validation.

The QA, ACP, and production environments are fully integrated with other systems via an API management layer that we called NIP.

In Chapter 4, "The TCS Project," where the project scope and organization are described, we will see how we implemented this model in more detail.

Managing Test Environment in JIRA with the GoLive Add-on

At TCS, we use a JIRA add-on called GoLive from Apwide[7] that is very handy for managing test environments. Each application environment has an entry in JIRA, and deployments are recorded so that each stakeholder knows, at any time, which build is deployed on any given environment. This information is key for testing since it should be clear whether a certain Story or Bug fix is present and can be tested.

---

[7] www.apwide.com/

As an example, the following figure shows our environments inventory with a filter on the Applications (APP prefix) and the Category (CAT prefix).

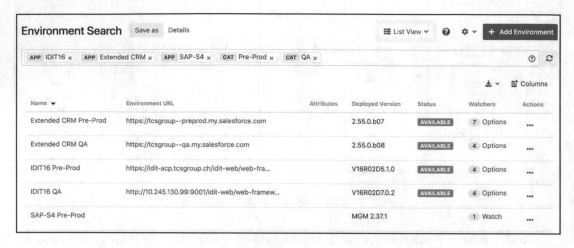

Environments page

A common challenge is that environments are often shared resources, used for different kinds of activities: security scans, load testing, infrastructure changes, etc. Since you don't want someone to reboot your application in the middle of a business demo, you need to schedule those activities carefully. Apwide GoLive helps us avoid booking conflicts, thanks to a powerful timeline editable featuring a convenient drag-and-drop interface.

The following figure shows how we use the GoLive Timeline to schedule activities on the different environments of the CRM application.

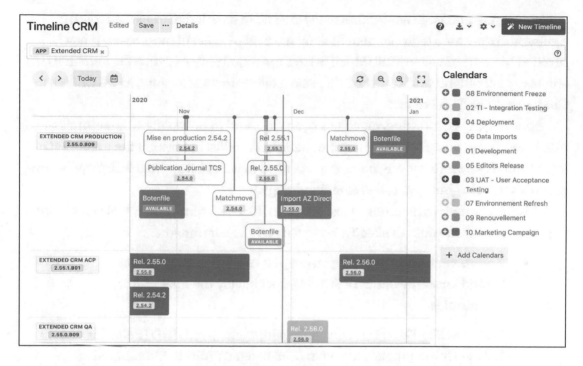

Timeline environments

Apwide GoLive goes way further than our basic use case, by allowing the integration of deployment events and environment statuses into a Continuous Delivery pipeline using the GoLive RestAPI (a Jenkins Shared Lib is also available). Thanks to Webhooks, JIRA users can also trigger deployments and/or environment provisioning.

In the "Application Environments" section, we will cover how Boozang manages Environment Categories and application URLs.

At the time of this writing, the entries in JIRA are duplicated with the ones in Boozang since no direct integration is available. Given the frequency this information changes, this is not too bad after all.

Test Automation in Agile Development

Agile development is widely adopted these days. Even the most conservative enterprises are adopting some of the principles found in the Agile Manifesto (`https://agilemanifesto.org/`). On the other end of the spectrum are the organizations that adopt agility at the enterprise-scale with frameworks like SAFe (Scaled Agile Framework `www.scaledagileframework.com/`).

Most small and large enterprises today are still in a period of transition toward Agility, and they tend to implement their own brand of agile. In most cases, it has resulted in a sort of Water-SCRUM-fall, where the requirements gathering and final UAT still take a considerable effort. The TCS project falls into this category, as we will see in Chapter 4, "The TCS Project."

About Agility and Testing, much has been said, and in my opinion, sometimes too much. Testing in an agile project requires additional skills, but overall the transition to agile should not scare test engineers that are used to waterfall approaches. Good testing practices remain good regardless of methodology.

Despite changes in planning of test activities, here are some additional skills a test engineer should consider to effectively work in agile environments.

- **Framework knowledge:** If you are part of a SCRUM team, you should know the basics of SCRUM, specifically the roles and ceremonies.

- Practices like **TDD** (Test Driven Development[8]) and **BDD** (Behavior Driven Development[9]) are often used in agile projects. One should learn the basics of them.

- **Soft skills:** Collaboration and communications are more important than ever in an agile team. If you are used to receiving detailed scenarios and working alone at your desk, you should prepare to work directly with developers and product owners while tolerating not having a detailed long-term project plan.

One thing you will face while testing in an agile project is the constant evolution of your SUT (System Under Test). Automated tests developed in one sprint might need to be adjusted in the following sprints. Even worse, some might need to be completely redone or thrown away.

In Chapter 13, "Gherkin and Behavior Driven Development," we will cover Gherkin and BDD which are key parts of testing in agile contexts.

---

[8] TDD is a development practice part of XP (Extreme programming) where unit tests are prepared before the code is fully developed.

[9] BDD brings the TDD's ideas further. We will present BDD and Gherkin in Chapter 13, "Gherkin and Behavior Driven Development."

In most agile initiatives automated tests are included from the very beginning, ideally with practices like TDD and BDD. There will be times where your pursuit of Test Automation might be challenged by managers questioning the effort and the benefits. We all know that Test Automation projects have a high failure rate, and many have bad memories of their last automation effort that cost a fortune and was abandoned before producing any real benefits.

In the next section, you will see how to calculate an ROI analysis for a Test Automation initiative, if you really have to. ;)

Test Automation ROI, Theory and Practice

Test Automation, like any initiative that requires investment, must prove to be profitable.

ROI analysis is one of the common methods used when quantitative data needs to be provided to justify the budget needed to acquire a Test Automation tool. Luckily, the pricing for the Boozang tool is very reasonable, and most medium to large organizations can easily afford it.

In an enterprise environment, you might have to deal with legacy applications, where the automation effort was not part of the development process from the beginning. In these cases justifying the costs of automating tests can be a challenge.

On Legacy Applications

In a webinar hosted by software test professionals (https://www.softwaretestpro.com/) and titled "BDD, Gherkin and Happiness," Bas Hamer defined a few precise characteristics of a legacy application.

What makes a software become legacy? The fact of not having the correct up-to-date information to support it. Correct, not 10 or 20 years, but pure information.

We need to consider as well that today developers' turnover is much higher than it used to be a while ago. Therefore the need of having this information is higher. But here is the thing, when you read "information" you should not think about word documents but rather living documentation. And living documentation means executable Gherkin (we discuss Gherkin in detail in Chapter 13, "Gherkin and Behavior Driven Development").

I liked a lot how Bas represented the impact of developers' understanding of how the system is supposed to behave. A legacy system is therefore a system without living documentation that becomes hard to maintain because of the lack of clarity and alignment.

From my experience, objective ROI analysis for Test Automation initiatives is a minefield. Assumptions must be clearly stated, and numbers can easily be changed to make a good initiative look like a bad investment. The opposite is also true. Without an honest discussion about the assumptions, you can present a very bad initiative as a worthy investment.

Many ROI analyses start from an initial situation at t1, when the Test Automation initiative starts. At t2 the automated tests start to bring benefits[10] and reduce manual testing. At t3 the automation is complete and only a minimal part of manual testing is left. At t4 on the timeline, we will end the ROI analysis.

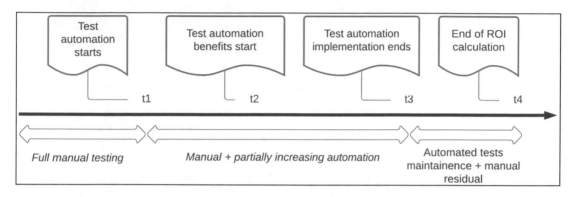

Timeline for ROI calculation

There are some peculiarities with ROI estimations for Test Automation.

First of all, between t1 and t2, you should consider both the cost of the initiative and the cost of manual testing. From t2 on, the benefits can be added, but without forgetting that manual testing costs are reduced although still present. Moreover, automated tests need to be maintained, and this is a cost you should not forget to include. Maintenance cost estimation is very important and difficult to do. A solid and modular approach can be easy to maintain, while a poorly designed monolith, with lots of duplication can be very costly to maintain.

Another point to consider is that, once automated, tests will run way more frequently than if they were to run manually. Hence the comparison has to be "fair," and consider quality independently of test execution time. This is the case for defect counts and defect fixing costs. Having a comprehensive set of automated regression tests normally prevents major bugs from being shipped into UAT phases or even worse into production.

Finally, you should not forget to include other benefits of automating tests that can be hard to quantify like employee satisfaction. Implementing and maintaining automated tests, when done correctly, is much more fun and rewarding than running manual tests over and over again.

---

[10] Automated tests start bringing value from the moment they run according to their specification.

If you are interested in knowing more on how to perform an ROI analysis for a Test Automation initiative, in the Appendix section "ROI Example for a Test Automation Initiative," you find a detailed example with further considerations on this topic.

CHAPTER 2

Selenium: Best Practices and Pain Points

Thank you, you gave us a lot, but now it's time to move on.

This chapter presents the typical approach to testing web applications with coded solutions like Selenium and highlights the main pain points that could undermine a Test Automation initiative's success.

© Gianni Pucciani 2023

G. Pucciani, *Boozang from the Trenches*, https://doi.org/10.1007/978-1-4842-9010-1_2

On my side, the main reasons for moving away from Selenium were mainly two:

1. The skills required to master the Selenium-based framework: it
    was not easy to have developers with Selenium skills to maintain
    and extend the framework.

2. It was too difficult to test End-to-End business processes,
    spanning three or four web applications.

In the next sections, while presenting the main challenges of a Selenium-based
approach, I will state how you can address the same challenges with Boozang.

Locators and Page Objects Pattern

Locating elements is the art you need to master for building robust tests in Selenium.

The "Hello World" case where you locate your element with a fixed ID never works in
practice because today most of the IDs are dynamically generated.

Name and attributes, XPath locators, and CSS selectors, all these types of locators
need to be mastered to avoid flaky tests.

With Boozang, as we will see in Chapter 8, "Elements Location Approach," you can
most of the time forget about element location strategies.

The Page Object Pattern is recognized as one of the best practices when using
coded tools like Selenium. It was proposed in 2009 in the SeleniumHQ wiki page (`www.
selenium.dev/documentation/test_practices/encouraged/page_object_models/`)
and later promoted by Martin Fowler in a famous blog post (`https://martinfowler.
com/bliki/PageObject.html`).

Page objects are meant to abstract the physical structure of a web page and provide
an API that is more oriented toward that page's actual services. For each web page, you
usually build one or more page objects. You can also have a single page object for a
section of the page used multiple times within a website or application.

Page objects make your tests more robust: if an element of the page changes, you
don't have to modify all the tests using this element but rather a single page object.

Assertions should typically not be included in a page object, and in general,
good page objects should not contain any details of the business logic. Their sole
responsibility should be to locate elements and provide methods to interact with them.

With modern Web UIs and development frameworks like React[1] and Angular,[2] page objects can quickly become hard to maintain.

Writing good page objects is not straightforward, and it requires a good experience. But it is also a crucial aspect that can make the difference between a maintainable suite and an abandoned one.

On top of page objects, you usually define business actions as methods, which are low-level use cases on how users interact with your application to achieve a well-defined objective. These mini use cases are what Alistair Cockburn places at the "indigo" level (under the sea) in his *Writing Effective Use Cases* (Addison-Wesley Professional; 1st edition, October 5, 2000).

The good news is that with Boozang you can forget about page objects and focus directly on the mini use cases, removing one layer of complexity.

Browsers and WebDriver Compatibility

How many times did you find your scenarios all red in your nightly run and discovered that Chrome had just released an update which was not compatible with your WebDriver version?

You head up to `https://sites.google.com/a/chromium.org/chromedriver/downloads`, download and install the correct version, and you need to re-run all your scenarios.

Not too bad you might think, unless this happens the day before you scheduled a production deployment, when your tests have to give the green light.

Boozang, unlike other solutions, does not rely on the WebDriver API. This means that you can completely forget about browser and WebDriver compatibility!

Timing and Waits

Modern web applications use Ajax, Javascript components, and elements on the page can be loaded at different times. If you do not make proper use of explicit waits, you will get the infamous *ElementNotVisibleException*, with your screenshot on the failed tests clearly showing that the element you wanted to locate is clearly there.

---

[1] `https://it.reactjs.org/`

[2] `https://angular.io/`

With Selenium, the default implicit wait is 0, but depending on the SUT you can set it to 5 or 10 seconds. This means that Selenium will wait 5 or 10 seconds before throwing the *ElementNotVisibleException*.

Explicit and fluent waits allow you to instruct Selenium to wait for a specific condition, like an element to be visible or clickable on a page, until a timeout that you define. In the explicit wait, the polling frequency is fixed to 250ms, while in the fluent wait you can specify the polling frequency.

With Boozang, the implicit wait is possible on each action with the delay attribute. Explicit waits are then handled with timeouts. Moreover, you can specify a fail element to avoid lengthy timeouts (see more in Chapter 9, "Exit Conditions, Conditional Flows, and Timers").

Data Management

Data management is probably one of the most important aspects of a maintainable Test Automation framework. A good modular design means that your test suite is made of smaller and reusable parts. These parts are interconnected via

1. **Sequence flow**: The series of calls from high-level pieces to lower-level ones

2. **Data flow**: The set of data passed from one test to the other

When you build your automated tests relying purely on the WebDriver APIs, the framework's quality depends on the skills and experience of the developers who build and maintain it.

On the other hand, you have full control and flexibility over what you can do.

Same as for software development, the danger is to build something that ends up being hard to maintain. And the risk is higher when more people are involved in maintaining the tool. This is something you should consider, especially in an enterprise environment.

Proper data management is even more critical when you start running your tests in parallel.

Besides the fact that each test should create its own data set to avoid conflicts, each scenario should run independently from the others.

We dedicate an entire chapter to Data Management with Boozang (Chapter 9, "Exit Conditions, Conditional Flows, and Timers"). The advantage of using a tool like Boozang is that it comes with its own data management capability, and you just have to use it. It might feel constraining to developers, but the advantage of having a standardized way of working with data can make the difference in the long run. We will see how Boozang, with its powerful data management capabilities, addresses the flexibility needs of most developers and keeps it as simple as possible for non-developers.

Reporting and Script Readability

When a test fails, you want to be able to find out the root cause quickly.

The quality of the test reports directly influences the time needed to troubleshoot failed tests. And the time required to troubleshoot the failures is a direct measure of your test suite's quality.

A framework built with Selenium needs to provide its custom reporting system or produce reports in a standard JUnit or Cucumber format. All this takes time away from developing scenarios.

Tools like Boozang come with their reporting features, allowing you to focus on writing scenarios. Boozang has its custom reports, both for local and CI-based runs, but it also provides JSON cucumber reports that you can easily publish on Jenkins or other dashboards.

While troubleshooting, the first thing to look at is the action in error and its details, like an element not found or a failed validation. This information, together with a screenshot, gives you a good idea of the root cause.

If you want to dive deeper into what happened before the failure, the coded approach will give you the error in the form of a stack trace. This sequence of method calls can be quite hard for a non-developer to understand.

In Boozang, a test is a sequence of actions that are human-readable. The execution reports are a sequence of tests called within a scenario, and they are easy to understand. Most of the time, you don't even need to know the tool to understand what went wrong.

Development Skills

Locators, WebDriver, and browser compatibility, timing, data management, and script readability are just some of the most critical aspects of the complexity behind a Test Automation framework based on Selenium.

I honestly thought this was the price to pay for having a maintainable suite, until I discovered Boozang.

We already discussed the role of SDET in section "Testing Roles." The reality, though, is that we are not all like Google.

The learning curve of your Test Automation framework is a good indicator of its time resilience.

The harder your framework is to learn and maintain, the higher are the chances of being abandoned over time. The learning curve of Selenium is quite steep.

The WebDriver API supports different languages, from Java and JavaScript to Ruby and Python. You might find a person that already knows the WebDriver API in Python, but that won't help if you developed your framework in Java.

A key point I will stress later on for tools like Boozang is the shallow learning curve and the fact that only a general software development background is needed to use it effectively.

In particular, I believe that Boozang is very easy to learn thanks to its well-designed User Interface and pure focus on Test Automation.

CHAPTER 3

Meet Boozang

Tools, like friends, should be few and well-chosen.

This chapter introduces Boozang and how it addresses the pain points of a coded solution as described in the previous chapter. It also presents a possible selection approach for selecting an automation tool, particularly the one I followed before adopting Boozang.

© Gianni Pucciani 2023
G. Pucciani, *Boozang from the Trenches*, https://doi.org/10.1007/978-1-4842-9010-1_3

Proof of Concept Phase

Every organization has its own rules, means, and degree of flexibility when adopting new tools, and the same applies when selecting a Test Automation tool.

In any case, a typical selection process starts with a more or less clear need, and a list of criteria that the tool must satisfy.

When investments and risks are high, RFI (Request for Information) and RFP (Request for Proposal) phases can be applied, where software editors formally provide information based on an input document.

Otherwise, for small investments, this information can be taken directly from the editors' websites, where you usually find a list of features and supported technologies and integrations. But of course, from their own website, every tool is the best one :).

What I look for from the editors' website is a clear list of features, transparency in the licensing scheme, and links to documentation to see more details.

Another common source of information for medium to large enterprises is the Gartner Magic Quadrant reports, which give you a good idea of the best players for a particular topic and the specific market dynamics.

These preliminary phases allow you to do a shortlist and eliminate some candidates. But until now, you haven't tested them yet.

Here is where a Proof of Concept (PoC) phase typically comes into play. The PoC phase allows you to uncover hidden risks. In a PoC, you usually install the tool and implement real automated tests on a representative scenario. The scenario should be complex enough to challenge the tool, but not too much, so that you can implement it with a reasonable effort. In fact, within 1 or 2 days, you should already be able to make up your mind about the tool's strengths and weaknesses.

In my case, around September 2019, I started looking for a tool to cover functional tests on End-to-End business processes and mainly web applications. I could afford to keep Mobile and Desktop technologies out of the scope.

I decided to evaluate the top five automation tools as rated by Gartner.

With two of them, I wanted to pursue the PoC phase.

The first one, at that time leader of the market, was soon ruled out: besides being expensive (even for a PoC phase), I found it too invasive and hard to fit into my organization in terms of skills, integrations, and change of processes. I like how we manage releases and manual testing with JIRA (I will cover these aspects in the section "Using JIRA with XRay"), and I don't want to change our process because of a new automation tool.

The second one was a tool based on image recognition. I was initially skeptical. I thought the image recognition approach was not a good fit for our functional and business rules intensive tests, but I gave it a shot. In the first scenario, the validation on a text would fail when the window was smaller and the text broken into two lines. This was enough for me to rule it out.

Not convinced with the "big players," I looked into smaller and newer solutions. Here Google searches, blogs, and word of mouth are the main channels.

I came across Boozang via the TestGuild podcast (`https://testguild.com/podcast/`). The podcast caught my interest and convinced me to give Boozang a closer look. After following the Udemy courses,[1] I played with it for a couple of hours and decided it was worth doing a PoC scenario.

Luckily, our Digital Services team (responsible for maintaining the eCommerce tcs.ch site and mobile app), just a few weeks before, had defined 10 critical Use Cases as scope for a potential automation effort. All these Use Cases had clearly defined steps and also screencasts to understand well the UI interactions.

I selected one of these Use Cases (number 6) as scope for the PoC. This case was a tough one, covering the e-Commerce site, a backend user activation system, and SalesForce (the CRM).

Use case description

UC06 - Acquisition PJ Privée IND by a member identified by inline eCare login

Prerequisite: *identify a Salesforce account and its eCare account. Portfolio contains membership but no PJ Privée*

---

[1] See, for example, `www.udemy.com/course/advanced-test-automation-using-boozang/`, or search for Boozang in the Udemy catalogue. These courses are all free by the way, which is always appreciated.

- *Go to PJ Privée product page*

  - *Insured persons?* **Individual**

  - *Press continue → Modal "Are you a member already?" appears*

  - *Press yes → "enter membership information" appears*

  - *Enter identified eCare login + password*

  - *Press 'add to basket' → Shopping cart appears*

- *Press continue → Personal data page appears*

  - *Data is already pre-filled with identified account data*

- *Continue → Payment page appears*

  - *Select an **activation date in the future***

  - *Select **Mastercard** as payment method*

  - *Check the legal checkboxes*

- *Continue → Six payment modal appears*

- *Finalize → Confirmation page appears → Confirmation email appears in the mailbox*

In a Gherkin format (Gherkin syntax will be covered in Chapter 13, "Gherkin and Behavior Driven Development") would be something like this:

Given an existing client with an active <existing_product>
And an active eCare account
When the client buys a <product> with option <option>
And the payment method is <payment_method> with <payment_option>
Then the confirmation page appears with <final_price>
Examples:

```
| existing_product | product | product_option | payment_method | payment_option | final_price |
| TCS Soc. Ind. | PJ privée | none | MasterCard | future activation | 255
```

The "Given" part was quite tricky since it included the account creation in Salesforce and its activation on the Web Site via the backend system.

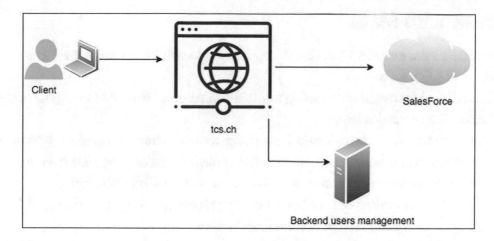

System interactions in the PoC scenario

During the PoC, what impressed me about Boozang was the ease of use. The UI is self-explanatory, and recording the first scenarios was very easy.

Being able to perform a PoC at no cost, at my own peace, and without having to deal with salespeople was also a good point. Boozang has a free version unlimited in time that allows you to perform a PoC smoothly.

Pilot Phase

After the PoC phase that should last a few days, the next step is to perform a Pilot phase.

A Pilot phase is usually longer, it should involve more people, and it should be complex enough to stress the tool in all the needed functionalities that can be important in the long term.

In this case, you may need a certain budget and editor support.

In my case, I had planned around 20 man-days of effort.

During this time, I had also planned to involve the Boozang team to make sure I would start on the right track.

Having a Pilot phase was very important. It allowed us to anticipate many issues we would otherwise have experienced in a real project, where time constraints are different.

We found and promptly fixed some Boozang bugs, and we found ways to deal with application issues like SalesForce pages with slow loading iFrames and hard to automate popups from the backend application.

A Week with Mats

As part of the Pilot activity, I had the pleasure to work with Mats Ljunggren, Boozang co-founder and CEO, for a week.

We set the objective of automating the 10 e-Commerce Use Cases using the brand new Cucumber scenarios feature.

When we started, early on Monday morning, we could have jumped straight into the automation work, but instead, we decided to have a chat over breakfast where I presented to Mats our organization and short-term automation challenges.

After that, Mats figured out the basic building blocks to set up in Boozang. This approach gave us a good start with solid foundations.

In Boozang terminology this means a good separation of Modules and Sub Modules.

Each day we would start with some planning over coffee and pain au chocolat, and then hands-on work until the end of the day.

It became immediately clear that the critical aspect for us was the data management. When debugging a test, it must be clearly visible how the data flows from a Gherkin scenario down to tests. This part was definitely the number one improvement for Boozang.

At the end of the week, we had completed two Use Cases and most of the rest. Overall, I would say 80% of the automation code was done because a lot of tests were re-used among Gherkin scenarios.

We also managed to have our first Jenkins job running via the Docker container.

During Mats' stay a couple of times, we made our priorities clear, and every time we were agreeing on the most important thing: robustness over features. As the principles in the Agile Manifesto, it does not mean that features are not important. But when compared to overall robustness, they have lower priority. There is nothing worse in Test Automation than mistrusts toward the tool; hence robustness should come before any new feature request.

What we did not manage to do during our week together, as initially planned, was a thorough time tracking per scenario. With each scenario saved in JIRA (I will cover our JIRA setup in detail in Chapter 14, "JIRA with Boozang via XRay"), we wanted to precisely track the implementation effort. But the fact is that the construction of the tests was not done on a per-scenarios basis, but rather on application modules. Therefore, we only tracked the time for translating the initial scenarios into proper Gherkin, which ended up being almost one and a half day.

Here is how it was done using the Structure add-on for JIRA.

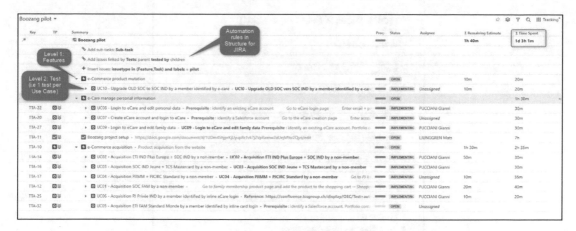

JIRA Structure page with features and scenarios of the Pilot phase

Pilot Results

During the Boozang pilot, I was suggested to evaluate another codeless tool, Testim,[2] which seemed to have a similar approach. The Testim PoC was successful enough to deserve a Pilot phase against Boozang.

In the following figures, you can see the results of the two pilots. Since the pilot execution time many improvements were done on Boozang, I will report them below.

The reader should be aware that the comparison results are based on my personal criteria and experience, and at a specific time. Testim is an excellent tool, and during my pilot their support team was very friendly and helpful.

---

[2] www.testim.io/

Testim vs Boozang

(score 1-low, 2-medium, 3-good)

Color scheme:

| GREEN | : Better |

| YELLOW | : Worse |

| RED | : Possible blocker |

Score (higher better)

	Sum of Testim	Sum of Boozang
Total	64	84

Details

> Click here to expand...

Topic	Testim	Boozang
Recording	3	3
Technology support (web)	2	2
Versioning	3	2
Data handling	2	3
Code extension	3	3
Conditional statements	2	3
Copy/paste, drag&drop, test extract...	1	3
Auto-completion for entering data	1	3
Disable step	1	3
Dropdown dynamic elements	1	3
UI responsiveness	2	3
Run test y if test x fails	2	3
See upstream tests impacted	3	1
Pop-Up handling (UAPS)	2	3
Bug capture	3	2
Cloud Grid	3	1
Concurrent work	2	3

Parallel execution	3	2
Cucumber integration	1	3
Single step execution	1	3
Execution speed	tbd	tbd
Documentation	3	2
User Experience	1	3
Easy to learn	2	3
Easy debug/troubleshooting	1	3
Environments management	2	3
Test re-use	3	3
Modularity and re-use simplicity	3	3
Company size	3	1
Roadmap influence	1	3
Trial version limits	1	3
PoC implementation issues	2	2
Pricing	1 (but*)	3

Boozang Updates

- **Versioning**: Boozang now provides a branching system to manage concurrent work. I will cover this in section "Branching and Merging."

- **See upstream tests impacted**: This functionality is now present in Boozang.

- **Cloud Grid**: With the docker workers, it is now possible to set up your local or cloud-based grid for test execution.

- **Documentation**: Boozang has a good documentation section and a forum for users to discuss new features.

- **Parallel execution**: Support for parallel execution is now present in Boozang; see section "Tips to Keep Execution Time Low."

- **Company size**: The Boozang team is growing. Today it still cannot be compared to other top of the market tools, but I bet it will keep growing. Moreover, many times, having a small but highly skilled team has been quite an advantage in terms of agility and delivery time.

Why Boozang

In this section, I will summarize some key elements for choosing Boozang as your Test Automation tool. First of all, it has to be clear what Boozang is not for.

Boozang is not a Test Automation tool for desktop applications: in this case tools like Sikuli (free and open source, `http://sikuli.org/`) or commercial tools like Ranorex and Tosca are more suited.

Boozang is not a Test Automation tool for native mobile applications. In this case I would go with Appium (`http://appium.io/`) for a coded, free, and open source approach, or other commercial tools.

Boozang is not a release and manual test management tool, where you can manage in an integrated way Requirements, Tests, and Bugs and have release readiness reports. In this case, tools like JIRA and its add-ons ecosystem are to be preferred.

Boozang is also not a load and performance testing tool. If you need to test the performance of your application and generate a load with thousands or more users, tools like JMeter (`https://jmeter.apache.org/`) and NeoLoad (`www.neotys.com/`) are more suited. Nonetheless, Boozang offers some interesting performance insights while running your tests (see Chapter 11, "Reporting and Troubleshooting") that can spot basic performance issues.

If your focus is to automate functional tests and End-to-End scenarios on web applications that run within the browser, Boozang is definitely a good choice. Here are the main reasons, which we will cover in detail in the rest of the book.

Ease of Use

This is the first thing that you will probably notice while using Boozang. You can create a simple test without even looking at the training material.

The GUI is made in such a way that both technical and non-technical people will quickly find what they need. The SaaS approach means that setting up a project is a matter of a few clicks (see Chapter 6, "Starting Up with Boozang").

Focus on Test Automation

Most organizations today have in place their own tool (or tools ecosystem) to manage requirements, manual tests, create and track Defects, and produce advanced reporting on release readiness.

Boozang's smart approach is to focus on Test Automation and provide all the necessary solutions to integrate with your existing tools rather than duplicating these features.

Simple and Solid Language-Based Element Recognition

As we will see in Chapter 7, "Elements Location Approach," Boozang does not rely on Selenium Web Driver to locate elements, removing a lot of complexity as we mentioned in Chapter 2, "Coded Approaches and Selenium Pain Points." It instead uses an efficient language-based location strategy that allows you to build stable locators, and maintain them easily in case your application changes.

Data Management

Data management is probably the most important piece of functionality of every Test Automation tool. Boozang offers you the possibility to store data at three different levels: project, module, and test. Tests can also receive and pass parameters. Each of these options has its own peculiarity, as we will see in Chapter 10, "Data Management."

Gherkin and BDD Support

More and more organizations apply Gherkin and sometimes pure Behavior Driven Development in their agile development. Boozang supports Gherkin and the BDD approach, making it a good fit for agile projects where people with different skills can participate in the automation effort.

We will cover BDD and Gherkin in Chapter 13, "Gherkin and Behavior Driven Development."

Concurrent Development

Boozang can effectively manage concurrent automation implementation with solutions that have been used for decades in software developments: branching and merging. But you do not need to master GIT or SVN since the Boozang GUI hides a lot of the complexity that is behind VCS features.

Support and Vision

Last but not least, Boozang support is timely and eager to listen for improvement coming from users.

Their roadmap is well centered around common automation issues and keeps the focus where it is needed: easily build long-lasting automated scenarios.

Codeless Approach: How Important Is It?

I admit I was more than skeptical about this concept in Test Automation.

I had practiced tools based on the image recognition approach, then object recognition with HP Quick Test Pro, and then Selenium Web Driver. I appreciated a lot the flexibility that Selenium Web Driver offers, mainly due to the fact that within a development environment you can do almost anything, from GUI to API and Database access. In terms of modularity, you have no limits, and CI/CD integration is like for any other development project.

I assisted to lots of demos from tools claiming that they can be used by "Business Users," without any need of a development background. But when you dig in a bit more, you realize that the typical Business User is not familiar with modularity concepts, refactoring, and reusability. Without considering the skills needed to accurately manage your HTML selectors. Even though they can easily record monolithic test cases, if you want your automation project to sustain the effects of time, avoiding good design and modularity is not an option.

If you ask companies who have applied such tools with success in most of the cases, you will find that they rely on a team of automation engineers certified on the tool.

Boozang is no exception, let's be clear. Yes, it is indeed codeless in 80% of the cases, which is not bad at all, and it does not close the doors to programmatic solutions with JavaScript.

Good design and modularity are still of primary importance in Boozang. For this reason, I would suggest anybody to have at least one person in the team with programming or automation experience that can act as an architect and keep things in order.

A cool feature that Boozang provides to help in these housekeeping tasks is the quality checks, which I will cover in the section "Quality Control."

Therefore, codeless is certainly important, but it is not at all the final goal. The goal is to easily build long-lasting automated scenarios. And I find that Boozang keeps this concept at its heart. It always strives to simplify your work, but it does not hide away from dealing with complex issues.

A similar reasoning can be applied to recording. The recording feature is very important, but you are not going to build a large and stable suite of automated tests just with recording. Recording is there to save you time while initially building your tests.

CHAPTER 4

The TCS Project

Clarity is easier to achieve with a narrow context.

This chapter presents the context of the TCS project used all along the book to provide practical examples. I believe that there is no one-size-fits-all solution for software testing and tools. Therefore, clarifying the context is very important to better understand the examples and consider possible adaptations one will have to make for a different context.

© Gianni Pucciani 2023
G. Pucciani, *Boozang from the Trenches*, https://doi.org/10.1007/978-1-4842-9010-1_4

TCS Organization and Test Automation History

Founded in 1896 by a group of cyclists in Geneva, Touring Club Suisse (TCS, www.tcs.ch) is the leader in the mobility sector in Switzerland, with more than 1.5 million members. TCS provides services beyond insurance and road assistance, including education and driving courses, vehicle equipment tests (child car sits, tires, etc.), and juridical assistance. It is also active in the tourism sector, managing campings all around Switzerland.

Many of us with good experience in the IT sector have seen at least one IT project that, like a skeleton in the closet, stayed in the company's memory. I arrived at TCS while the company was undertaking this type of project. The project lasted 2 years (pure waterfall approach) but needed 2 more years to be "stabilized." The objective was to replace the old ERP developed on the IBM AS400 platform with a modern cloud solution based on Salesforce.

It went "so wrong" that after a few months from the go-live, the company mandated an external audit to assess the technical debt and define a stabilization plan. The audit, among other things, discovered that the manual testing effort was way too big and that tests had to be automated.

As part of the stabilization program, I was in charge of filling the Test Automation gap. I hired one of the most skilled developers I knew to build a Test Automation framework using Selenium and Cucumber. We managed to build something quite solid: Gherkin tests defined in JIRA via XRay, implemented via Selenium Web Driver with the Page Objects approach, and a Jenkins job that executed the tests nightly and reported back results to JIRA. This project also had unit tests for testing the testing code. At the end of the mission, we handed over the testing framework to the internal developers with no previous experience with Selenium.

Nice job in the end, but not the easiest thing to maintain. The biggest constraint was that only two internal developers were trained to work with it. Over time, their availability for maintaining and extending the framework was too low compared to the time allocated to fixing bugs and developing new features.

The framework covered most of the main business processes. However, the heavily customized Salesforce instance, with heavy web pages and slow background batch processes, made some of the automated tests flaky. Nonetheless, we managed to address most of the random and timing related issues, sometimes in the test code, sometimes directly on Salesforce.

Feature	Steps						Scenarios			Features	
	Passed	Failed	Skipped	Pending	Undefined	Total	Passed	Failed	Total	Duration	Status
Login SFDC	5	0	0	0	0	5	2	0	2	21.545	Passed
	92	8	40	0	0	140	6	8	14	3:17:10.246	Failed
Acquisition of products on prospect	561	1	0	0	0	562	45	1	46	7:38:23.977	Failed
Mutation of new products	386	22	31	0	0	439	19	22	41	10:52:57.379	Failed
Account management	234	0	0	0	0	234	12	0	12	1:23:56.438	Passed
Kids Help	22	0	0	0	0	22	2	0	2	30:58.868	Passed
Resiliation	80	0	0	0	0	80	8	0	8	1:43:56.934	Passed
Invoices payments	63	0	0	0	0	63	7	0	7	57:19.321	Passed
Creation opportunity	180	0	0	0	0	180	14	0	14	1:25:26.390	Passed
	1623	31	71	0	0	1725	115	31	146	1 3:50:31.102	9
	94.09%	1.80%	4.12%	0.00%	0.00%		78.77%	21.23%			66.67%

Jenkins Cucumber reports for the Selenium-based framework

Code repository of the Selenium-based framework

I also managed to involve business analysts and developers and have them take ownership of the framework. Nightly runs were checked every morning, and production deployments were accepted only with the green light from the automated regression tests.

The feedback I received from the developers maintaining this framework was pointing at the technological stack complexity as the number one pain point. The dependency from WebDriver was also an issue, especially when tests failed due to a UI element change that is not visible to the end users (see also Chapter 2, "Selenium: Best Practices and Pain Points").

New Roadmap, New Challenges

In 2018, the IT department of TCS defined a roadmap to make its Information System more "rational," avoiding redundancy and reducing maintenance costs.

Several IT projects originated from this roadmap, most of them aiming at introducing COTS solutions with a well-defined scope and replacing one or more of the internal legacy systems.

The roadmap included introducing an API lifecycle management platform to manage all the interfaces among internal and external applications in a secure and scalable way.

One of the first and most important projects of this roadmap was named NIS (New Insurance Solution), which will be the project used in this book.

NIS Project Introduction

The General Director of TCS is the sponsor of the NIS project. The project goal is to provide TCS with a standard Policy and Claim Administration System (PCAS) to speed up the time to market and build products aligned with our customer's needs. At the same time, the management wanted to align TCS systems and adopt international industry standards.

The new PCAS system will replace all the custom code developed in Salesforce to manage the product catalog and the logic related to the sales process and contract life cycle. Claims management is also part of the project's scope.

The PCAS is a COTS solution built in Java and running on a JBoss server with an MS SQL Server database.

SalesForce will stay as master for all customers' data (CRM), and all these data will be pushed to the PCAS.

In addition to the out of the box GUI provided by the PCAS, the project will introduce a new GUI system to allow contact center agents to perform quick sales operations and respond effectively to customer requests.

Integration and interfaces will be one of the main topics because, besides SalesForce, the PCAS will interface with SAP, the tcs.ch website, the TCS mobile app, and other systems, internal and external. All these integrations will be based on REST APIs developed in the IBM API Connect platform. API testing will be crucial for the success of this project.

The following picture shows a high-level architecture diagram of the project's scope, with more than 40 interfaces to systems within and outside the TCS domain.

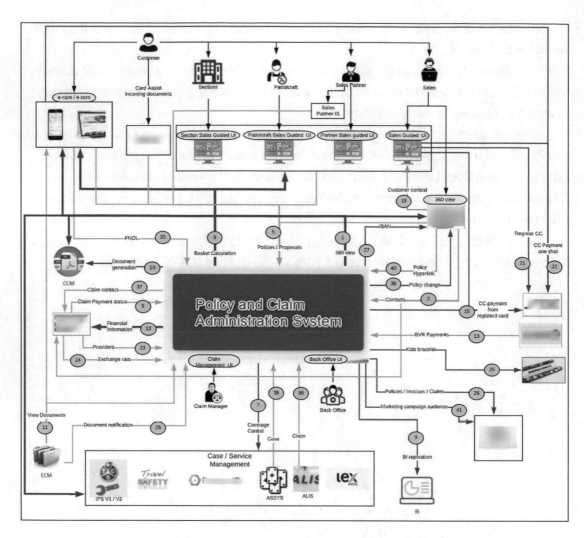

High-Level Architecture View of the NIS Project

This NIS project started after a pilot phase where we became familiar with the new system and evaluated the pros and cons. During the pilot phase, where the PCAS went live with a single TCS product, the testing effort was an issue. The pilot project's relatively small team did not have enough capacity to test all the delivered features, and the UAT phase was quite intense. Many issues were found during UAT but promptly addressed.

During the NIS project, therefore, a small team for Test Automation was created. Besides myself in the role of Test Automation stream leader, we added to the team an experienced Test Automation engineer, and a senior business analyst with development and QA background.

To give a better idea of this project, let us see some practical numbers:

- We have six streams, organized by key domains: Products and Policies, Sales, Claims, Billing and Finance, Document Management, and Migration.

- Each stream has a product owner, a scrum master, and a team of business analysts (both from TCS and the PCAS editor) and developers (PCAS developers and TCS developers for the integration with our internal systems).

- The initial backlog had around 100 Epics and 1000 Stories. Everything is tracked in JIRA; not only Stories, Development tasks, and Defects but also project Risks and dependencies.

- The initial scope was divided into four Cadences (AKA Product Increments) of four Sprints, each Sprint being 3 weeks time. For a total of 48 weeks and a final 4 months UAT period.

- All the project governance documentation is hosted in Confluence.

Test Automation Stream, NISTA Setup

NISTA stands for NIS Test Automation, and it is the acronym we use for the Test Automation stream of the project.

When implementing Test Automation, and not doing pure TDD/BDD, there are two options:

1. Start late, when the SUT[1] is stable enough.

2. Start early, but with an unstable SUT.

With the first option, you have fewer refactoring risks, but you also lose parts of the automation benefits since you have to do more manual tests.

With the second option, you need to consider that the UI or the APIs are not ready yet, and are subject to frequent changes: therefore, higher refactoring risk. However, the automation scripts will be ready to be exploited sooner than with the first option.

---

[1] System Under Test.

We decided to go with the second option, but have one Sprint of delay with respect to the implementation sprints. This way, we would have time to practice and work with a more stable system, on the already implemented and manually tested Stories. Our main objective is to have sufficient coverage before the final UAT phase so that the UAT will focus on validating the delivered features more than finding bugs.

We defined our JIRA setup with a few simple rules:

- We use Sprints of 3 weeks as the implementation sprints.

- We build our backlog based on the implementation's progress and define which scenarios we want to automate during our Sprint planning sessions.

- Our Sprint planning sessions take place right after the implementation sprint reviews, so that we have fresh in mind the demo and the features we want to test.

- We create Tasks (and SubTasks if needed) in our JIRA backlog. We define our scenarios with Gherkin and group them in Features (more on this in Chapter 14, "JIRA with Boozang via Xray").

We do not have predefined coverage objectives; our primary goal is to cover all the main business processes on the GUI and at the API level. We are going to set our Sprint and coverage objectives along the way based on the delivered features

CHAPTER 5

How Boozang Was Born

You seem worried... don't worry. I will fix.

This chapter is a special one about the history behind Boozang. I believe it gives a great idea about this tool's strengths: the two key persons behind it.

This input has been kindly provided by Mats Ljunggren.

"I had been working in the Telecom sector for a little over ten years as a solution architect. This work often involved spending time at customer sites worldwide, delivering complex software solutions on a tight deadline. This time I was in the middle of a large integration project for a Tier 1 operator, and things weren't looking good. I had flown in to lead a specific part of the project: an E-commerce front-end. This work hadn't even started, and it was expected of us to have a prototype within six weeks.

Instead of designing the solution around legacy products that were the norm in that company, I had pushed for a vision with a more modern, user-friendly, Javascript front-end. Unfortunately, I only had access to junior Javascript developers. After being initially

© Gianni Pucciani 2023

G. Pucciani, *Boozang from the Trenches*, https://doi.org/10.1007/978-1-4842-9010-1_5

enthusiastic about the challenge, the week before the customer demo, enthusiasm changed to dread.

I looked at the code we had produced so far, and what we had wasn't nearly ready for demo. Even though only a couple of days remained, I started asking around for reinforcements to our development team to get a prototype ready for the demo. They suggested a contractor they have been working with that might be able to help, and I thought it was worth a shot. We got introduced, and he suggested that we should redo everything from scratch using AngularJS (this was in 2014, so Angular was all the rage), scrapping all the existing code.

A little aggressive as the upcoming demo was on Tuesday the following week. Considering that what we had was relatively useless, and the contractor was confident, I decided to scrap all the code and put all my faith in the contractor's ability. The current dev team got understandably annoyed when I told them we would refactor all their code (read: throw away), so I was basically without a platform the week before the customer demo.

I started getting stressed when my peers began telling me how crazy I was, and when I learned that the contractor wasn't working Friday, which meant he had the weekend only, I became a bit anxious.

I started sending all the hand-over material throughout the next day, hoping I would hear some signs of life, but nothing. I needed a plan B. What if I could fly in some developer friends from Sweden? Arrange a Hackathon? I got a case of beers and started brainstorming the best I could, but it looked like I was in deep shit.

At 11 pm on Friday, Skype lights up. It's the contractor. His first message was, 'you seem worried… don't worry. I will fix.' Suddenly, I was relieved. Maybe this could work out despite the crazy time-frame.

When I woke up the next morning, the contractor had already sent a fully working product that I could demo. What had taken us five weeks not to deliver, he delivered overnight. I had never seen a developer working so fast, providing code working well without any back-and-forth.

I continued working with the contractor throughout the project, helping out other project teams deliver on time, securing a big win for the company. What looked to be the worst project of my career turned out to be the best, thanks to the mystery developer I had found.

After almost a year, the project was coming to an end, and it was time to part ways. I met the contractor at a nearby restaurant, and even though we had become great friends, it's sometimes hard to continue to keep in touch as we get new project engagements.

He didn't seem sad at all; instead, he seemed excited. He had something he wanted to show me. During the last couple of years, he worked on a new type of test technology. The technology utilized an HTML-fragment to trigger client-side code that would open a new browser window. As the new browser window had control over the secondary browser window, it could be used to do Test Automation.

This story took place five years ago today, and the contractor is my co-founder Wensheng Li. The Test Automation technology he discovered is the base for the Boozang tool."

PART II

Boozang Main Concepts and Use Cases

Thanks for your patience, let the show begin!

In Part 1, we introduced some basic concepts of testing and Test Automation and the project we will use to learn Boozang. If you skipped Part 1, no problem, I trust you will go back to it if needed.

In Part 2, we now start diving into Boozang, how to set it up, and use it. In each chapter, I will show some practical examples of our NISTA project (see section "Test Automation Stream, NISTA Setup").

Part 2 is the biggest among the three parts of the book because we will see all the essential features Boozang offers for creating a solid Test Automation project.

In Chapter 6, "Starting with Boozang," we will see how to start a project and give access to a team. We will also see how Boozang works "behind the scenes."

In Chapter 7, "Main Concepts and Entities," we will go over the main Boozang entities so that you can start implementing, running, and reporting your first simple tests with good foundations.

In Chapter 8, "Elements Location Approach," we will take some time to understand the strategy Boozang adopts to locate web elements, one of the main aspects that sets Boozang apart from other Test Automation tools. If you are in a hurry, you can skip ahead to Chapter 9, "Exit Conditions, Conditional Flows, and Timers," and come back here when needed.

In Chapter 9, "Exit Conditions, Conditional Flows, and Timers," we will see some simple but powerful features you will need to implement some more advanced tests.

In Chapter 10, "Data Management," we will do another step up and introduce the data management options that Boozang provides to make your tests modular and your project robust. Data management is a crucial aspect; make sure you understand well all the possibilities you have to pass data among scenarios and tests.

Finally, in Chapter 11, "Reporting and Troubleshooting," we will close the circle and see how to produce and read test execution reports. We will also see how to analyze failures via root cause analysis and the Known Issues database.

CHAPTER 6

Starting Up with Boozang

A good beginning bodes well.

One of the advantages of a tool like Boozang vs. a coded approach is that setting up your first projects is really easy and fast. Nothing to install, no code or POM files to prepare.

This chapter will go over the registration process and the few steps needed to create a project. We will also see how to administer your account and projects and finally show how Boozang works behind the scenes.

© Gianni Pucciani 2023
G. Pucciani, *Boozang from the Trenches*, https://doi.org/10.1007/978-1-4842-9010-1_6

Creating Your First Project

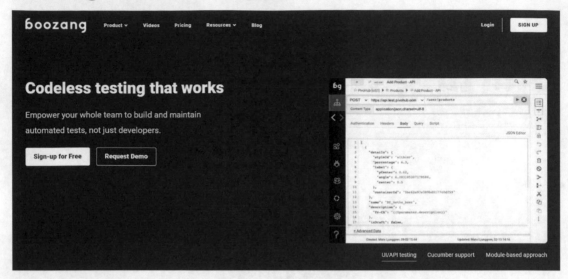

Boozang home page

The first step to do is to sign-up at the boozang.com site. This will bring you to the registration form where you can enter your information: email address, first name, and last name; nothing more, your privacy is important.

You can use the promotion code "*BFTT*" to have a 3 months access to a Team license.

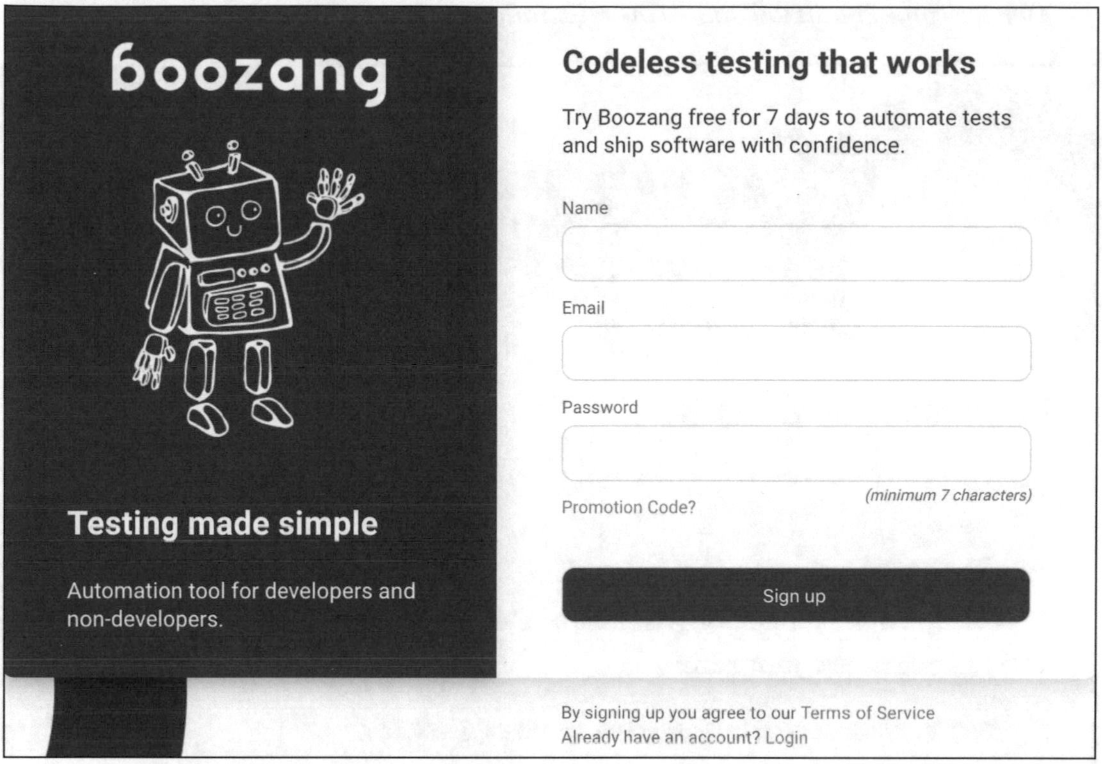

Registration page

After signing up, you will receive an email to confirm your address and complete the registration.

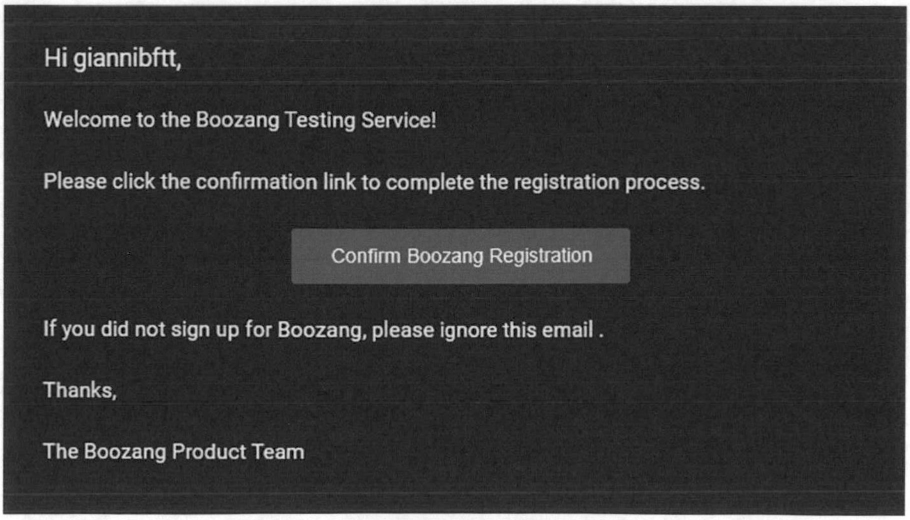

Confirmation email

Two welcome emails will follow the registration:

Welcome to Boozang! 🎉

Hi there,

At Boozang, our aim is to make user interface and API testing a piece of cake. That's why we created a unique testing tool that is:

Simple. You don't need to be an advanced developer to use it.

Flexible. Boozang's natural language scripting language adapts to all situations.

Powerful. It's more than a record and reply tool, we use AI to auto generate tests.

Maintainable. Our smart locators make tests resilient to code changes.

Start testing

Welcome email

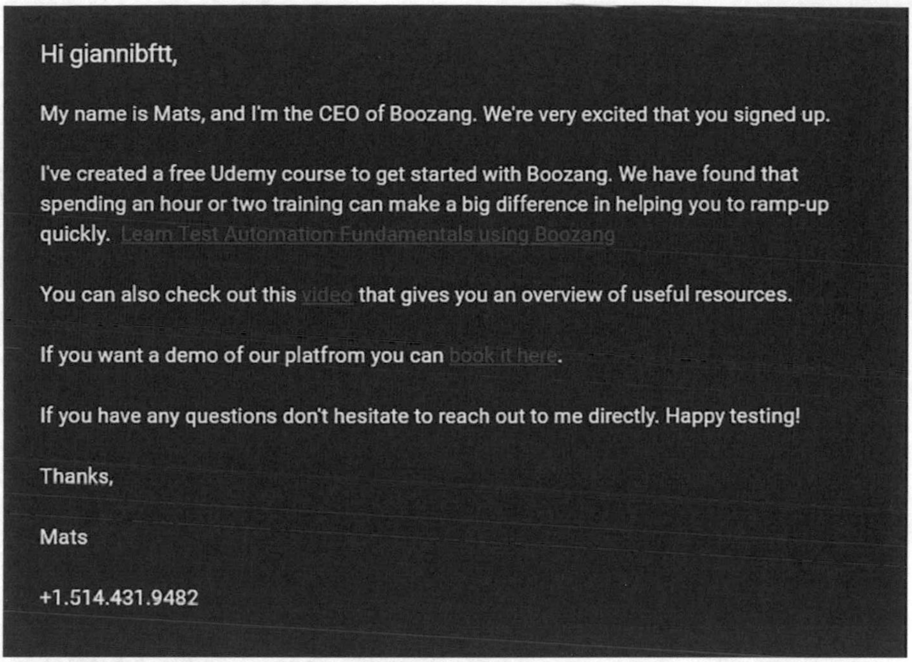

Hi giannibftt,

My name is Mats, and I'm the CEO of Boozang. We're very excited that you signed up.

I've created a free Udemy course to get started with Boozang. We have found that spending an hour or two training can make a big difference in helping you to ramp-up quickly. Learn Test Automation Fundamentals using Boozang

You can also check out this video that gives you an overview of useful resources.

If you want a demo of our platfrom you can book it here.

If you have any questions don't hesitate to reach out to me directly. Happy testing!

Thanks,

Mats

+1.514.431.9482

Email with useful links

Once the registration is complete, you can reach your account page where you can create your projects or use an existing demo project.

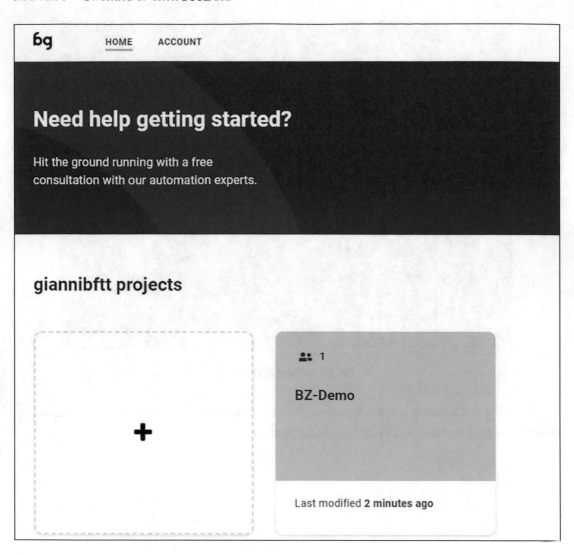

Projects dashboard

Let's go ahead and create a project.

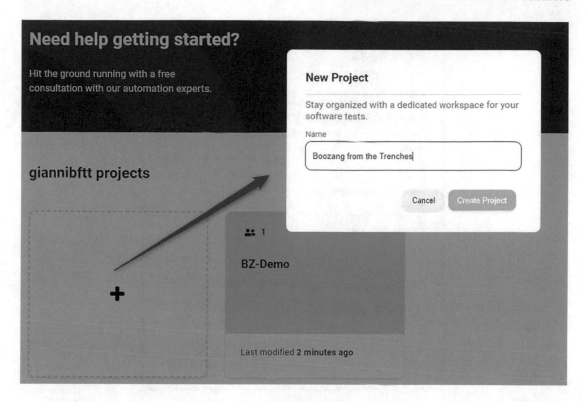

Project profile page

You can edit the project name, card color, and add a description. You can also decide whether to make the project public or not:

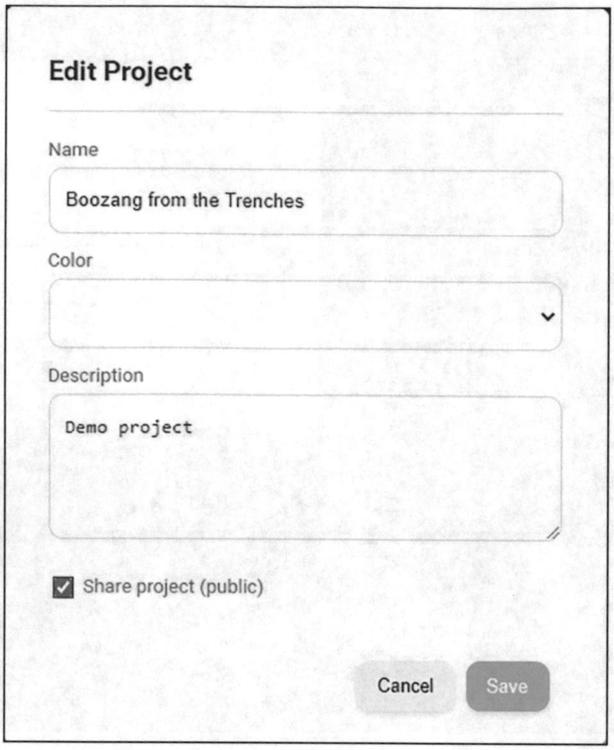

Edit Project

Name

Boozang from the Trenches

Color

Description

Demo project

☑ Share project (public)

Cancel   Save

Edit project details

I only used the sharing option for this book project; in reality, our projects at TCS are not public, as in most cases for enterprise settings.

A click on the project will launch the web client: make sure to allow the request to access images.

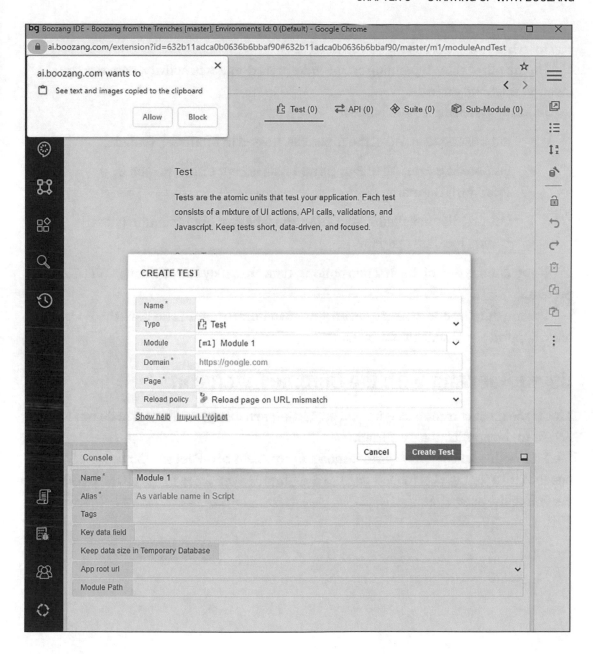

Where Are Your Data Stored?

Boozang is a SaaS solution; this means that you don't need to install anything: no setup scripts, no databases to maintain. Updates are regularly pushed, and you just need to refresh your browser to have new features and bug fixes.

SaaS solutions have several advantages in terms of maintenance and flexibility. You pay for what you need, as long as you need it.

On the other side, depending on the enterprise domain of activity, data storage location might be an issue.

Boozang offers three possibilities:

- ai.boozang.com: All of the Americas, hosted in Montreal, Canada.

- eu.boozang.com: All of Europe and Asia except China, hosted in Frankfurt, Germany.

- On-premise installation for China and whoever might require it due to data location restrictions.

If you choose one of the first two options, data are safely stored on the OVH Cloud provider.

For the third option, you can set up your own infrastructure and have the Boozang team support the installation process.

Using Boozang with the Chrome Extension

This is the most common usage if you are testing several applications and do not have access to the application's webroot.

Follow this link `https://chrome.google.com/webstore/detail/boozang-ai/bnaebcjlolajbgllgjlmlfobobdemmki` to the Chrome Web Store to install the latest version of the extension.

Chrome extension installation

Using Boozang with the HTML Fragment

If you have access to the application's webroot, you can work either with the previous method (Chrome extension) or install the HTML fragment.

The HTML fragment installation option is described here: http://docs.boozang.co m/#installation-options.

What are the advantages and disadvantages of these two installation methods?

The HTML fragment allows you to run Boozang with different browsers. However, if you want to test multiple applications, you must install the HTML fragment on each application's webroot folder.

If your focus is to test functionalities, and you can do it just with Chrome, the extension is probably the best option, simpler and quicker.

In our projects at TCS, we always rely on the first method, via the Chrome extension.

Managing Team Access

Granting access to other team members is done via the Team button in the left side bar of the IDE:

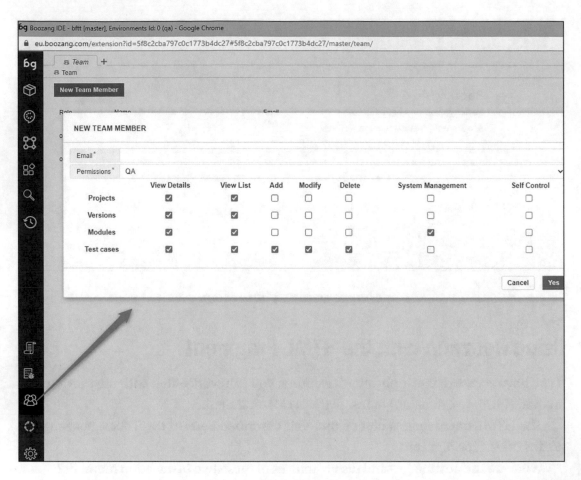

Team page

You need to specify the email address of the user so that he/she can receive the invitation and setup his/her account.

The pre-defined roles as QA or Owner come with a set of permissions, but you can easily adapt this to your needs. The permissions table is quite self-explanatory, with a sort of CRUD (Create, Read, Update, Delete) rules set for each object type.

In our projects, we are flexible with permissions: with a small team, you can afford to give the Owner role to everybody. On the other hand, when your team grows, and people have different skills, you can rely on the permissions to protect your project against unwanted changes.

Boozang Under the Hood

In this chapter, we describe some internal details of the Boozang architecture. This can help you fine-tuning how you are going to use Boozang within your organization's architectural constraints.

The following figure shows a typical deployment architecture.

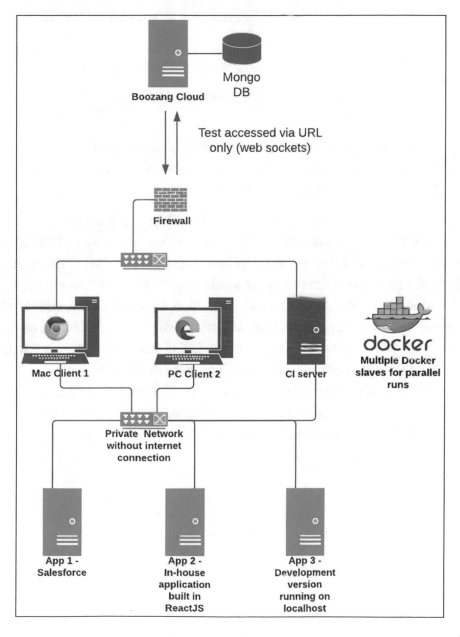

Boozang architecture

On the Boozang side, the two main components are

- **Boozang server**: This is a service deployed on the cloud whose main functions are to

    1. Load the IDE engine into the browser window

    2. Provision the IDE with the project data for the current branch[1] you are on

    3. Synchronize project updates among all the clients

    4. Handle asynchronous file saving operations (reports and screenshots)

- **MongoDB**: This is a document or no-SQL database used to permanently store all the artifacts you create via the client IDE. All these artifacts are stored in JSON format.

On the client organization side, behind the firewall, you find the personal workstations of the persons using Boozang. They can be Mac, Linux, or Windows stations. The Boozang client IDE runs in the browser of the personal workstations.

Within the organization's network, there will also be the Continuous Integration (CI) server like Jenkins, but you can also use a CI server on the Cloud, like Azure DevOps.

You then have several applications on which you will run your Boozang tests. These applications can be locally hosted or on the Cloud. The only prerequisite is that the application needs to have a Web GUI, or either be testable via APIs.

The most important thing to note here is that Boozang runs in your browser; therefore, you do not need any particular network configuration or firewall setting. If you can test your application from your browser, then Boozang can do it too.

---

[1] Branch management will be covered in Part 3.

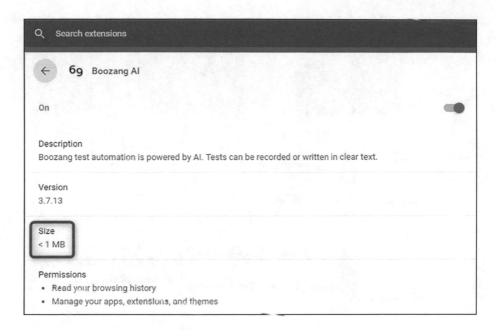

Chrome Boozang extension settings

The Boozang Chrome extension is extremely lightweight; the whole client takes 33KB!

What happens when you access Boozang from your browser, open the client IDE in your browser, and start designing your Tests?

The following sequence diagram shows the typical client-server interactions.

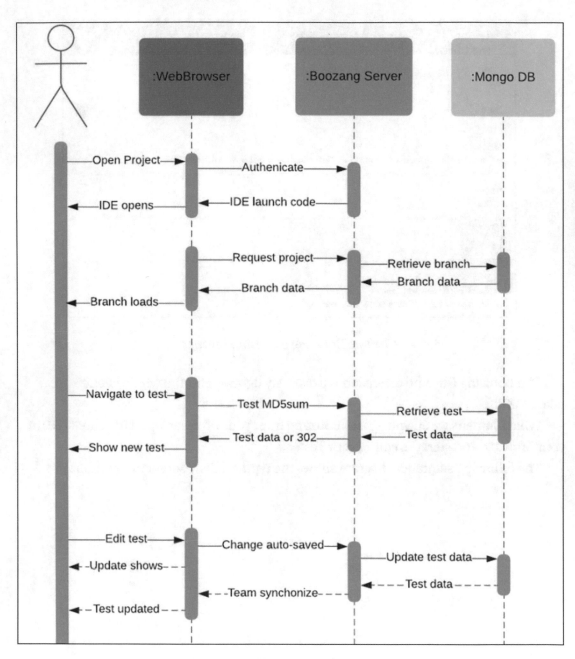

Sequence diagram client-server communication

Client-server communications use the WebSocket protocol[2] that provides bidirectional communication over a single TCP connection. The efficiency of the WebSocket protocol allows you to use the Boozang client IDE as any other locally installed application.

When you work in a team, and one person makes some changes, the other clients are immediately notified. This is a great collaboration feature, equivalent to collaborative editing in Confluence or Google Docs. When you need to work in isolation however, you can either create a different project or work with branches.

The Boozang team releases frequent updates: cloud deployments are automated with Ansible and tested with Boozang (how else ;). On the client side a simple refresh of the IDE is necessary to start using the new features after a server update. EU cloud deployments are normally scheduled outside working hours but before midnight to allow nightly executions to run smoothly.

Insight from the Trenches

Let's go into the trenches and see the setup of our automation project (see Test Automation Stream, NISTA Setup).

We created a single Boozang project where the three members of the automation team are working together.

In terms of permissions, we are flexible and we trust each other; we decided to give all permissions to all team members.

All of us use Boozang via the Chrome extension (see Using Boozang with the Chrome Extension).

We rely on a few basic JIRA and Confluence items that we describe one by one in the following sections.

---

[2]https://en.wikipedia.org/wiki/WebSocket

JIRA Agile Board

We define our Epics and Tasks in a SCRUM Agile board to prioritize the Backlog and manage the Sprints. We estimate the effort on Tasks via story points (even if we defined a story point equivalent more or less to an hour of work).

We rely on this board during the Sprint planning and the daily stand-up sessions.

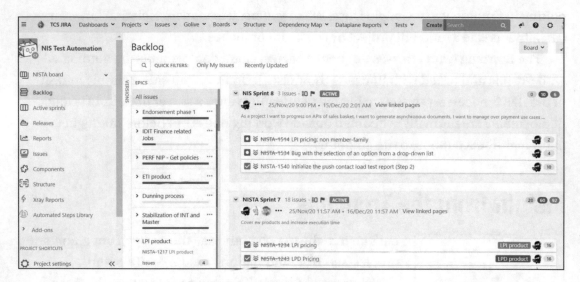

NISTA Agile SCRUM Board

On this Board, we also manage the automation Bugs. System Bugs are instead managed in another JIRA project and Board, the one used by developers to follow up on the implementation progress.

If you are not familiar with JIRA Agile Board, you can refer to the official Atlassian documentation.[3]

JIRA Dashboard

We use a classic JIRA Dashboard to present the progress of the automation team to external stakeholders.

---

[3] www.atlassian.com/agile/tutorials/creating-your-agile-board

In the following figure, we can see the three main sections:

1. **Text Execution reports**: We will see how from Boozang and Jenkins you can import execution results to JIRA, using the Xray Test Management add-on.[4]

2. **System Bugs**: Discovered via automation, with their Severity, Priority, Status, and Assignee.

3. **Tasks done since yesterday**: This is useful during daily stand-up meetings, for distributed teams or lockdown times where all meetings are held via videoconference.

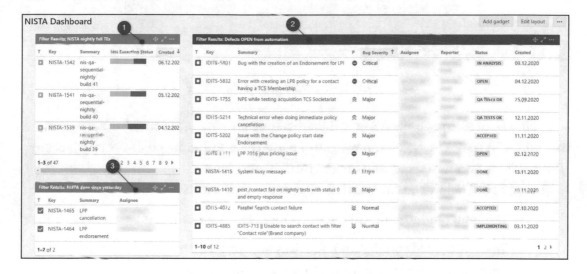

JIRA Dashboard

JIRA Structure

Via the Structure add-on,[5] we have created a page that shows our Gherkin scenarios organized by Features.

---

[4] Jenkins and JIRA-XRay integration is covered in Part 3. Until then, you can check out this blog post: https://boozangfromthetrenches.com/jira-xray-test-automation-with-boozang/

[5] https://marketplace.atlassian.com/apps/34717/structure-project-management-at-scale?hosting=cloud&tab=overview

In the following figure, you can see the automation statements used to build the structure.[6]

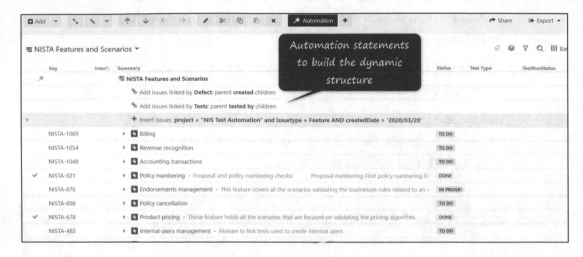

JIRA Structure page setup

In the structure page, each row is built dynamically via the automation statements that pull JIRA issues in the hierarchy. You can then customize the columns to select any JIRA fields you want to show, and organize them into views.

In the figure below you can see that we decided to show the

- Implementation status of the test (Open, In Progress, Done)

- Test Type (field coming from the Xray add-on) which allow us to see whether the test is an automated one or a manual one

- TestRunStatus (field coming from the Xray add-on) that shows the latest execution status

---

[6] If you are new to Structure for JIRA, head to their official documentation here: `https://wiki.almworks.com/display/structure/Structure+User%27s+Guide`

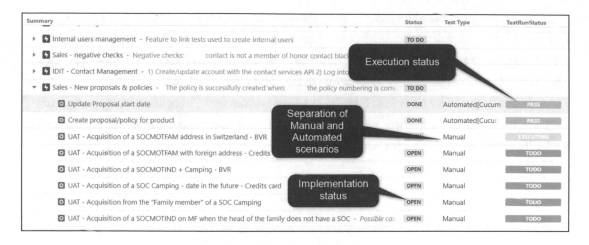

JIRA Structure fields

Confluence Pages

We rely on Confluence for all the internal documentation. We have one main page where we document the Impediments, JIRA and Jenkins setup, Boozang internal conventions, and any other information to simplify our coordination and onboard new team members.

Since all the project team is using Confluence, we can easily link to other pages where, for example, business rules used by our tests are documented.

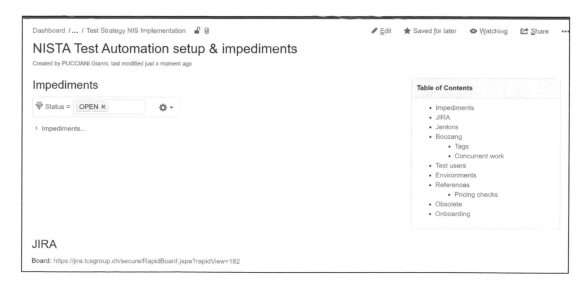

Confluence page for the Test Automation project Stream

Concerning Confluence, one major add-on that we use is the "Table Filter and Charts" add-on developed by StiltSoft.[7] This add-on allows us to filter and show only OPEN impediments. If you are using Confluence, this is one of the must-have add-ons, with one of the best support I have seen on the Atlassian marketplace.

Atlassian tools like JIRA and Confluence are widely used in many enterprises, but they are not the only ones. Boozang can be effectively used in combination with other tools, like GitLab[8] or Azure DevOps.[9]

---

[7] https://marketplace.atlassian.com/apps/27447/table-filter-and-charts-for-confluence?hosting=cloud&tab=overview

[8] https://about.gitlab.com/

[9] https://azure.microsoft.com/en-us/products/devops/

CHAPTER 7

Main Concepts and Entities

Solidity is all about building small and solid blocks.

This chapter describes the core objects available in Boozang and starts introducing the Integrated Development Environment (IDE).

As we mentioned in the previous chapter, the project is the topmost Boozang entity to organize your work. Each project has its own team and permissions set. In a project, you can define Modules, Submodules, and Features. In a Module, you can define Tests and Test Suites. In a Feature you can define Scenarios whose steps are implemented via Tests. Let's see each of these entities.

© Gianni Pucciani 2023

G. Pucciani, *Boozang from the Trenches*, https://doi.org/10.1007/978-1-4842-9010-1_7

Modules and Submodules

Modules and Submodules are used to organize Tests and Test Suites.

A good approach is to create modules according to the application's functionality.

The first button of the left side bar gives you access to the projects modules and lets you create new ones.

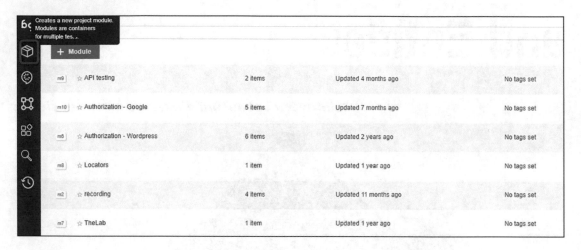

Modules page

When you click the *New Module* blue button, you get the following pop-up window to enter the module's information.

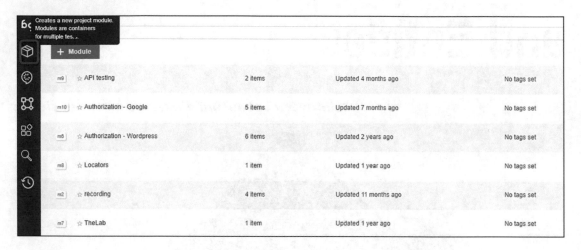

Creating a new module

The modules we created are application functionality like authorization, contacts, products, etc.

In the following picture, we see the root project page with three main parts:

1.   **The sections**: Modules or Features, with the number of items inside

2.   **Project and branch name** (we will see how branches work in detail in section "Branching and Merging")

3.   **The list of modules with some metadata**

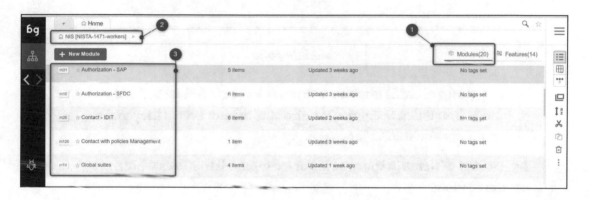

Modules page

It is good practice, when testing multiple applications, to name your modules with the name of the application as prefix.

When you click on a module name, you will see all the entities within that module.

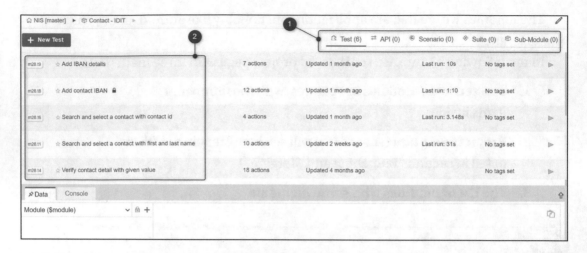

Module page

1. **The group of entities within the module**: Tests, API tests, Suite, and Submodules. Scenarios are also shown here even if they make more sense on the Feature page.

2. **The list of items in the group**: For example, all the Tests within the Module.

Modules and Submodules have their own id created automatically by Boozang: m1, m2, m3, and so on.

You will use these ids when searching for Tests or running Tests from a CI tool.

Application Environments

From the Setting menu on the left bar, you can access the Environments page.

This page shows the Environments of each application.

As mentioned in the section "Test Environments," having a good test environment classification is critical for testing activities.

In Boozang, an Environment is a category, like QA or Staging. In each category, you have one or more applications, each with its own URL.

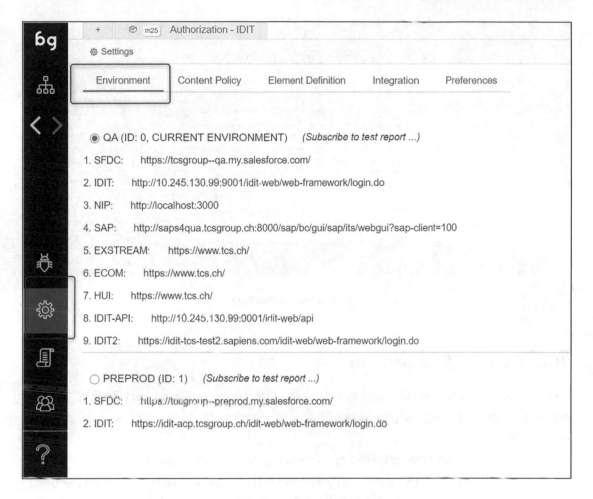

Environments page

When you click on the *New Environment* blue button, you have a pop-up window to create a new environment category.

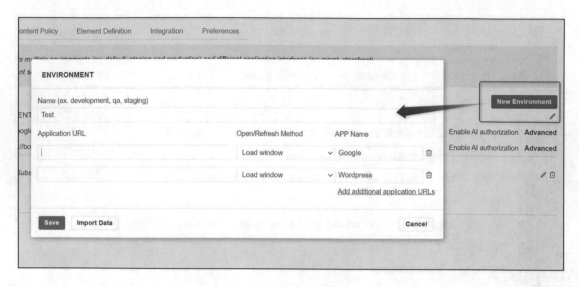

New Environment form

Tests and Test Suites

Finally, Tests! Yes, this is without any doubt the main Boozang item. You design, organize, run, and troubleshoot Tests. Therefore many features are built around this main item.

Test Suites are also essential to organize and group the execution of tests.

We are going to see here the main features and refer to later chapters when needed.

A Test in Boozang is built within a Module, it has a name, a unique id, and a specific URL, and it is made of one or several Actions.

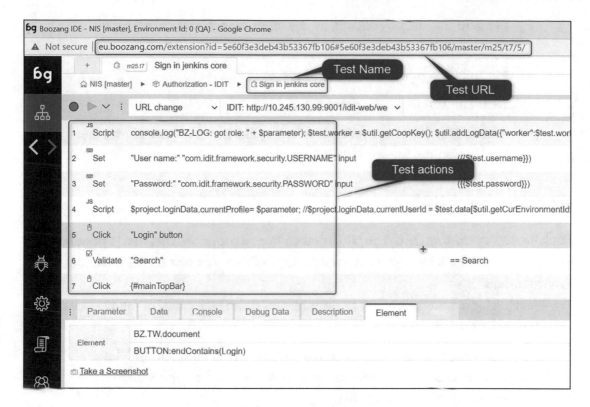

Sections of a Test page

Test URL

The Test URL has always the following format:

http(s)://<boozang site>/extension?id=<project id>#<project id>/<branch>/<module>/<test>

- **Boozang site**: Depending on where your account is located, boozang. com, eu.boozang.com, or something else (see section "Where Are Your Data Stored?")

- **Project id**: A unique id of 24 characters that identifies your project[1]

---

[1] You might have noticed that <project id> is repeated twice in the URL. This is not an error, but a legacy code issue. It might be removed in the future.

- **Branch**: "master" by default, or any other branch you are currently working on

- **Module**: The module id, for example, m25

- **Test**: The Test id, for example, t7

- **Action**: Only when an action is selected, like in the picture above, the id of the action, for example, 5

Environment URL

Each Test has a starting URL. The URL is taken from a dropdown list that is populated with the environments that you have previously defined (see section "Application Environments").

The URL load options are very important, and it can be a cause of many issues when not managed properly.

- **"Reload page on URL mismatch"**: This is the default option. The test will load the URL whenever it is executed if the application is currently on a different URL.

- **"Reload page on host mismatch"**: Same as above but only for the hostname.

- **"Never reload page"**: The Test will never change the application URL when being executed. You will want this option in most of the cases.

- **"Always reload page"**: Will always load the defined URL when the Test is executed.

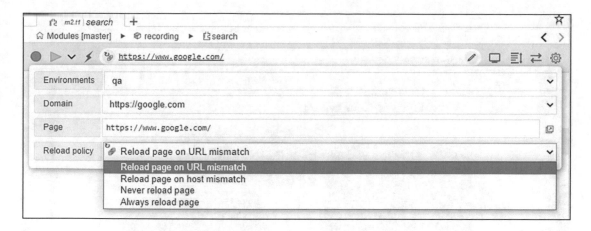

Test: Environment URL and options

Test Actions

The middle area of the Test page is where the logic of the Test resides.

This area is a table with four columns:

- **Action Id**.

- **Action type**: Many action types are possible; the most common ones are Click, Set, Validate, and Script. We will see these options later on.

- **Action description**: Boozang creates a default description based on the web element on which the action is performed. To maximize the readability, I suggest always ensuring that this description is clear and not filled with technical details.

- **Action value**: the value set or retrieved by the action.

Action details are also present in the "Details" panel. This panel can be placed on top of the actions or below. I prefer to position it below, but it is just a personal preference.

The following picture shows a higher-level view of the whole Test page, with left and side bars, the Details panel, and the metadata with the creator and last update on the footer.

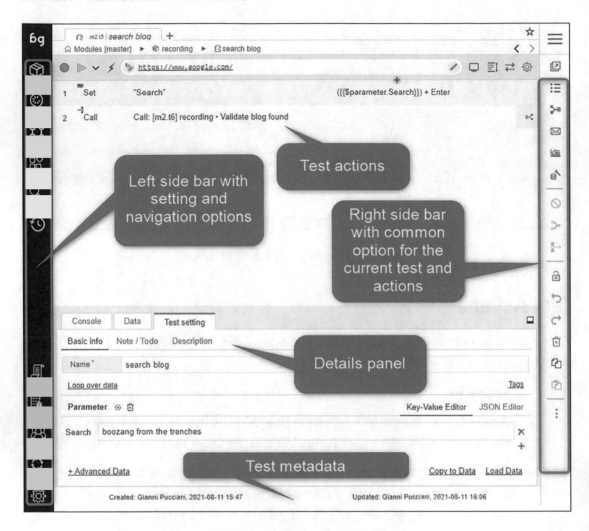

Test Page, high-level structure

Tests can call other Tests and pass and receive data via parameters, exactly like functions in software developments.

From many pages where tests are shown, you will see next to the Test name the green triangle to execute them.

The following picture shows the Module view, from which you can see and execute Tests.

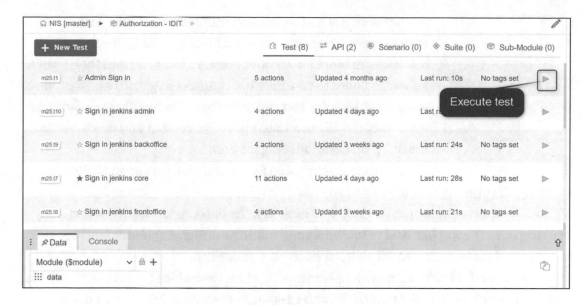

Module page

Keep It Modular, Avoid Monolithic Tests

What is the difference between a solid automated test suite, which minimizes maintenance and provides high value, vs. another one that is painful to maintain and provides little or no value? Certainly modularity.

In the first one the maintenance is reduced because each Test is not more than 10 or 15 Actions, has a clear scope, and it is easy to reuse. Tests call other Tests, exchange data, in a logical chain that is easy to understand. When the application changes, you rarely have to touch more than one Test.

In the second one, Tests are long, 20 or even more actions, and the same business logic is repeated in multiple Tests. Tests are rarely reused. When the application changes, you need to apply the same changes in many places.

Don't get me wrong, sometimes re-usability has a high cost, and some duplication is necessary. Finding a good compromise is key. In any case, the advanced search function is always a good help to locate specific actions in your project.

Keep your Project clean; use Modules wisely so that it is easy to find and reuse Tests. Choose meaningful names for Tests, and make your Tests readable by adapting the default Action description.

In Sprint 6, a bad regression was delivered in the test environment. The search contact function was broken. Since all our tests start with an account creation from API and then search for that account to continue the business scenario (e.g., a product acquisition), all the Tests were broken. The nightly run discovered this issue: at 8:15 am a Bug report was created and discussed in the daily "standup" meeting at 9 am.

The fix was scheduled for 12 am. That meant an entire morning lost since we could not run any test.

Luckily for us, the search function was broken from the contacts form but still working from the top bar. And thanks to a good modular design implementing the workaround for us meant modifying 3 actions on a single test.

At 9:30 am the workaround was operational, and we were able to continue our work, and then switch back to the original feature as soon as the fix got delivered in our test environment.

Test Suites

Test Suites are collections of Test or other Test Suites. Test Suites can be run locally in the IDE as well as remotely via the CI server.

You can define, for example, a "Smoke" Test Suite and a "Full Regression" Test Suite.

The first one may run a few basic Tests, while the second one will run all the Tests. On a large project, a full regression Test Suite can take several hours to complete. We will see in Chapter 14, "Jenkins and the Boozang Runner," how to reduce the execution time or large Test Suites.

When working with Gherkin Scenarios (more on this in Chapter 13, "Gherkin and Behavior Driven Development"[2]), each Feature has its own Test Suite. Having one Suite per Feature allows you to run only the Scenarios related to a particular functionality, very useful while troubleshooting application issues.

Test Suites can be created within Features or Modules.

---

[2] This chapter will be available in Part 3.

In our project, we created a Module called "Global suites" to host Test Suites that are executed via the CI server. The following figures show the Test Suites with the "Full regression" one made of 17 actions. These actions correspond to the call of 17 Feature Suites.

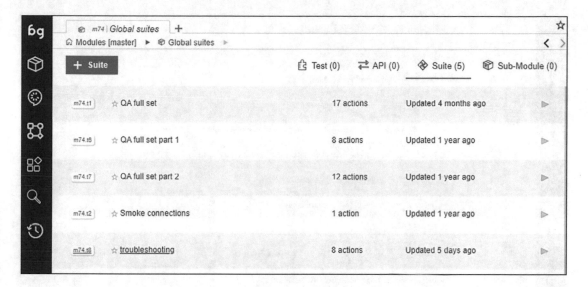

Global suites module

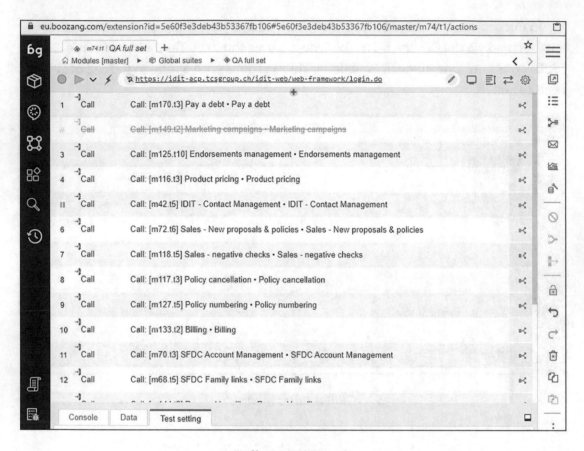

Full regression suite

The green play button appears when you select a Test Suite and it allows to launch the suite, even if most of the time suites are run via the CI server.

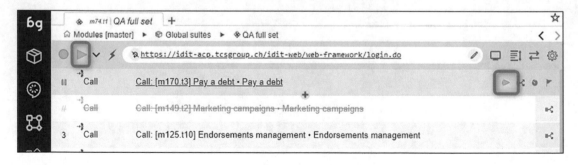

Execute whole or single suite

Features and Scenarios

Like Modules and Tests, Features and Scenarios are another way to organize your tests, especially when using Gherkin or doing pure Behavior Driven Development.

In Chapter 13, "Gherkin and Behavior Driven Development," we discuss more in detail about Gherkin and BDD.

For now, let's just say that Tests, as a sequence of actions, can be expressed in a business readable language based on the following format:

> ***Given*** *<an initial state or pre-requisite>*
>
> ***When*** *<certain actions are performed>*
>
> ***Then*** *<we can perform some validations on the expected results>*

This is the simplest form of a Scenario in Gherkin format.

In Boozang, this is a Scenario, and several Scenarios can be organized into a Feature, following the Gherkin language specification.

A Scenario is made of steps. In Boozang a step is nothing else than the phrase in one line of a Scenarios that starts with a Gherkin keyword (Given, When, Then, And).

In the following figure, we see the Features page with the list of all Features in the Project.

bg	© *Features* +		
	⌂ Features [master] ▷		
	+ Feature		
	m134 ☆ Accounting transactions	10 items	Updated 4 months ago
	m156 ☆ Batch executions	2 items	Updated 6 months ago
	m133 ☆ Billing	11 items	Updated 4 months ago
	m163 ☆ Blacklist management	3 items	Updated 7 months ago
	m171 ☆ Display portfolio in SFDC	3 items	Updated 3 weeks ago
	m125 ☆ Endorsements management	13 items	Updated 1 month ago
	m142 ☆ FNOL and Claim	3 items	Updated 6 months ago
	m42 ☆ IDIT - Contact Management	6 items	Updated 3 weeks ago
	m148 ☆ Incoming invoices	2 items	Updated 5 months ago

Features page

When you select a Feature from the Features page, you have the list of Scenarios included in that Feature.

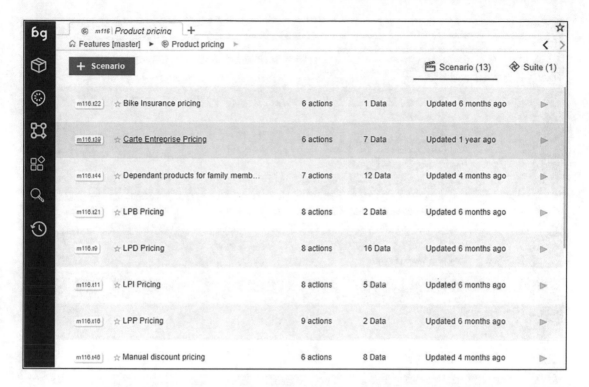

Scenarios page

Finally, when selecting a specific scenario, you see the description of the Scenario in Gherkin format.

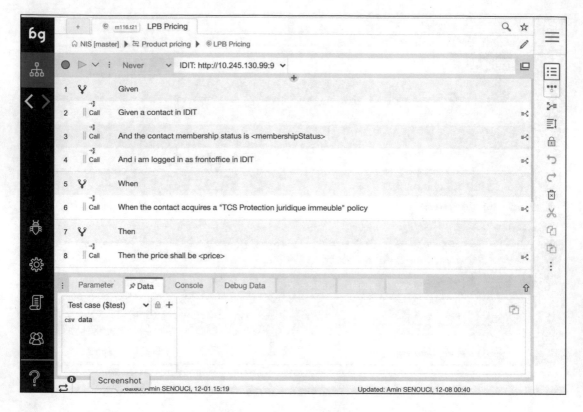

Scenario description

The Scenario in the picture above (as most of our Scenarios) is a specific type of Scenario, called Scenario Outline, where parameters are passed in the Steps via an Examples table, stored in csv data. All this will be much clearer in Chapter 13, "Gherkin and Behavior Driven Development."

You now have an understanding of all the main Boozang items. In the following sections, we will start using all these concepts to build and execute real tests.

Searching and Bookmarks

Wherever you are within the IDE, for example, from any test or module page, you can always use

1. **The navigation tree panel**: It allows you to see all the objects in a tree-like view, just like most development tools. This view is available for both modules-tests and features-scenarios:

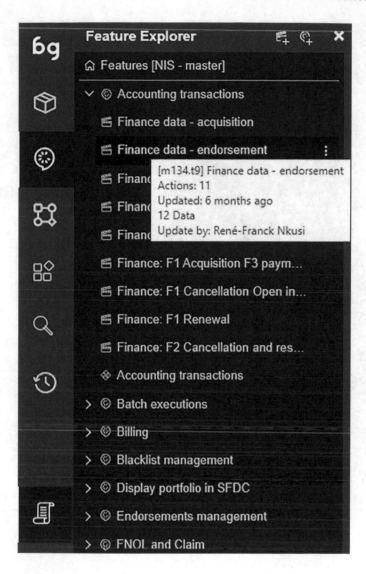

2. **The Search engine**: This is a powerful tool that allows you to search items by name or by ID in the navigation tree panel:

Search on the tree view

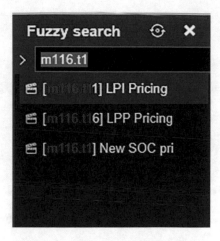

Searching by ID

3. **The Bookmarks**: You can bookmark, for example, any Test with
    a click on the star so that you can quickly access it from wherever
    you are. The bookmarked items will show up when you mouse
    over the star icon, with the possibility to un-bookmark.

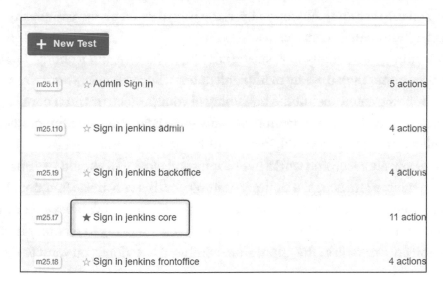

Bookmarking a Test

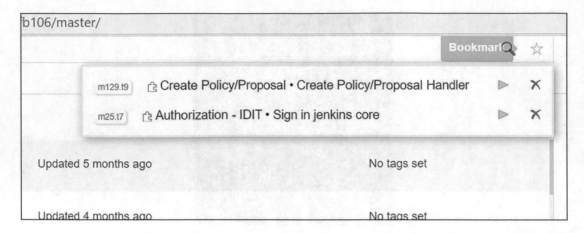

Bookmarked items

Recording

Recording in Test Automation has a bad reputation, mainly among those with a developer background. This is because of some marketing slogans in commercial tools that presented the recording functionality as the way to avoid all the complexity of implementing automated scenarios.

The recording functionality in Boozang is a crucial feature, but it should be seen as an accelerator rather than the way to implement tests. Recording is where you should start when building a new test, at the beginning of your project, or when covering new flows in your application GUI. The more you advance in your automation project, the less you will use recording. You will, instead, plug and re-use existing tests.

Let's see how the recording works in Boozang and what you should pay attention to. Please bear with me and accept a dummy example for this very basic functionality.

Starting from a new empty Test, the URL of the environment you have set will be used to open a new browser window. At this point, you are ready to record: just hit the record button and execute in the application window the actions you want to record.

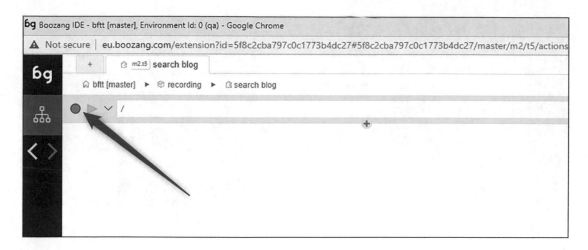

Recording, start

The application window will open at the set URL and a short pop-up window will tell you that the actions will be recorded.

In this dummy example, I headed to the Google site, entered a text in the search box, and clicked on a search result.

A small window on top of the application window will allow you to stop/start the recording and add validations on the go. If you click on the plus sign, this small window will extend to show more controls. If you leave the "Bind data" checked, the text you enter will automatically be mapped to a parameter:

Recording controls window

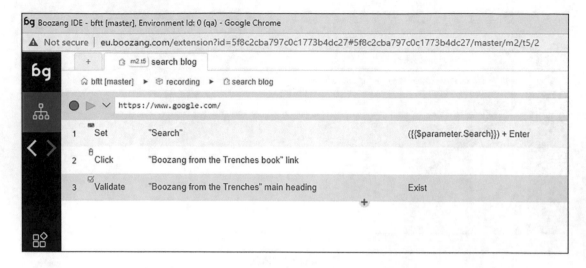

Recorded test

In action 1 you can notice two things:

1. The "Search" parameter was automatically created. This will allow you to use the same test for searching with different texts.

2. The "Enter" key press was added to the action.

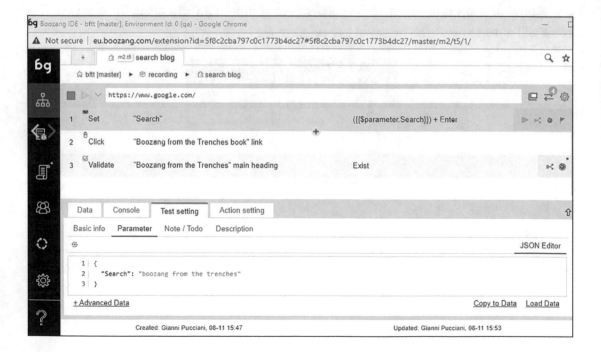

I have added a simple validation on the book title just by clicking the validation button and then selecting the element on the page.

What happened under the hood?

Boozang recorded your actions in the Test using its natural, language-based, element recognition approach. Possible types of actions are

- **Click**: A mouse click event

- **Set**: When entering text in an input box

- **Validate**: When validating a condition on a web element (see section "Validating the Expected Results")

In this simple case, the recorded Test is simple enough to be executed with success without any modifications.

You can notice that, for each action, the Action Setting tab of the Details panel shows the locators that Boozang used to identify the web element on the page on which the action is performed. We will talk about the locators in detail in Chapter 8, "Elements Location Approach."

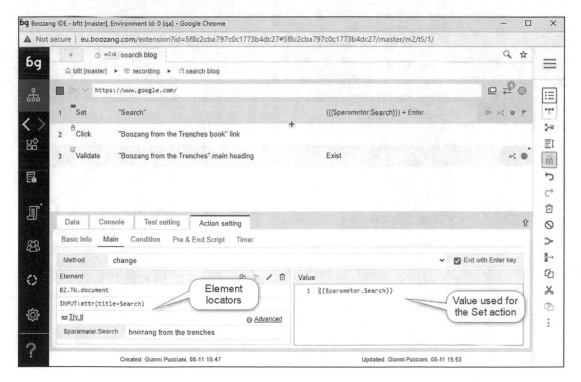

Action setting view

The set of actions recorded within the tests are stored in JSON format, sent over the net to the cloud service, and stored in MongoDB (see section "Boozang Under the Hood"). They will also be propagated immediately to all the other clients currently connected to the same project.

This is possible by having clients connected via web sockets.

Generate and Reference Test

After recording a Test with several actions, you might want to split it and create smaller and reusable parts. You can do this by selecting a set of actions (hold the Shift button and select), and then use the "Generate Test case and reference" button on the right bar.

Let's see the first example of reusable components with our simple Google search example.

Actions 2 and 3 are extracted, stored in a new Test, and the new Test reference is added to the original Test.

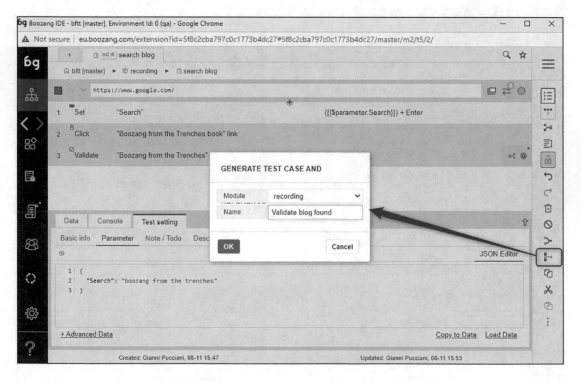

Generate and link new Test

After you select the name and confirm, a new Test will be created and linked to the original Test.

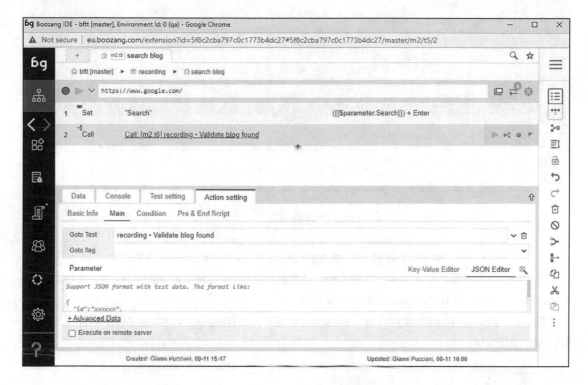

Execution with plugged Test

This was a very basic example. In the following chapters we will see more complex examples with data driven tests (more in this in Chapter 10, "Data Management").

Execution and Reporting

Now that you have the first Test, you will want to execute it locally in the IDE to make sure it works as expected.

Several execution modes are available; in the next section, we see each of them.

Execution Modes

Next to the Record button, you have the Play button, which is the simplest and most common way to run your Test.

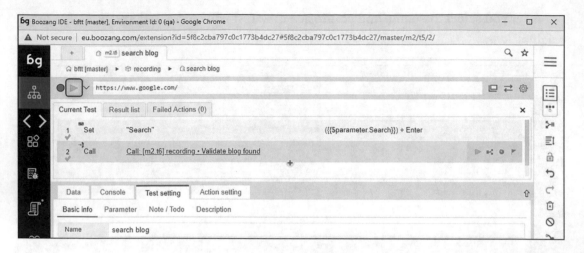

Play in IDE

When you execute your Test, Boozang will open a new window, load the initial URL, and then execute the actions one by one. The green check below the action number shows the successful execution of the action.

Next to the Play button you can access the alternative play modes, as shown in the following figure.

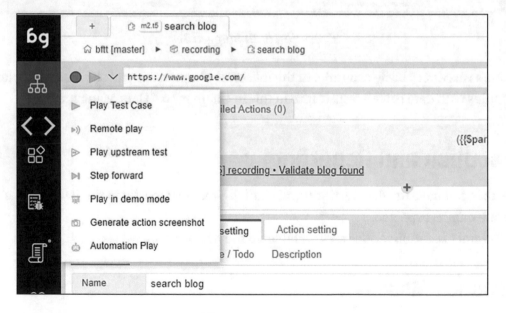

Different play modes

- **Remote play**: It allows you to run the Test on a remote worker. A remote worker can be run on Jenkins and have it listen for client requests. This will be discussed in detail in Chapter 15, "Jenkins and the Boozang Runner."

- **Play upstream Test**: It will play the Test that calls the current test. In case multiple upstream tests exist, the user will be given the choice to select one.

- **Step forward**: It allows you to execute the actions in the test one by one. This is especially useful when troubleshooting issues.

- **Play in demo mode**: It is similar to the Step forward, but it is useful when demoing some executions since the executed action is described in the application GUI.

- **Generate API**: We will talk about this more in Chapter 12, "APIs and Mixed API/GUI Testing." For now, we can just say that this play mode helps to build API tests from existing GUI tests.

- **Automation play**: This play mode will run the Test in a lightweight mode, that is, without the GUI part. You will see the Test running on the application window, and at the end of it, you will have a report. This play mode can be considered an intermediate mode between a local execution and a CI one. Sometimes, failures on the CI tool cannot be reproduced locally: in these cases, the automation mode is a step further in troubleshooting.

Execution Reports

Reporting execution results is a large topic. In this section, we see what Boozang offers as standard reports. Chapter 15, "Jenkins and the Boozang Runner," covers more advanced reporting possibilities using the CI tool.

Let's have a look at the standard reporting capabilities in the Boozang IDE. When you run tests within the IDE, three types of reports are generated:

- **Function Details Log**: It shows the execution of each called test and their actions.

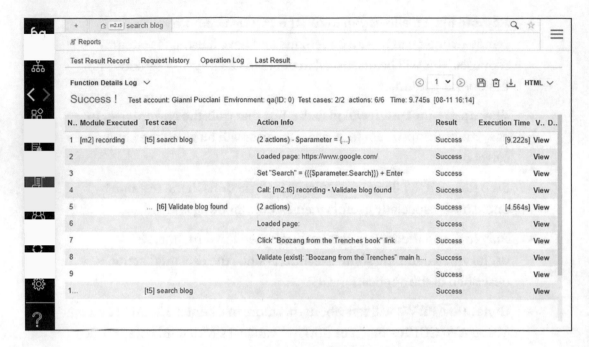

Functions details log

- **Function Summary Log**: It shows a higher level view, without action details.

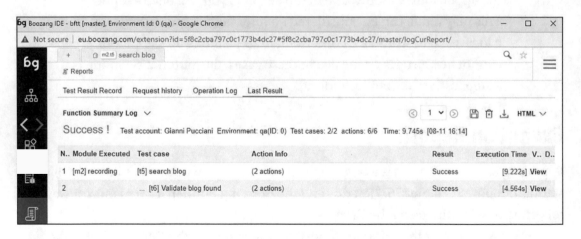

Function Summary log

- **Summary report**: It shows a complete report with more details, including who runs the test, when, and in which environment.

+   ⌂ m2.t5 search blog

🗐 Reports

Test Result Record   Request history   Operation Log   Last Result

Summary Report ⌄

bftt test report

Test account: Gianni Pucciani
Test time: 2021-08-11 16:13:54
Tested APP: qa

1. Test Scope

The test scope includes： Functional Automation Test and Performance Test.

The test content details：

Index	Test type	Test Content
1	Functional Automation Test	search blog
2		Validate blog found
3	Performance Test	Loaded page: https://www.google.com/
4		Set "Search" = ({{{$parameter.Search}}}) + Enter
5		Loaded page:
6		Click "Boozang from the Trenches book" link

Functional Automation Tests, 2. All passed. Reference the details on attachment-1.

Performance Tests, 4. All passed. Reference the details on attachment-2.

Test conclusion

After the Functional Automation Test and Performance Test of bftt, the test result is:

1, The functions were implements as the same as the requirement.

2, The performances are all less than 2s. All the response are in normal.

Attachment-1: Functional Automation Test

Execute functional automation test results:

Summary report

Projects Settings and UI Customization

Boozang offers many configuration options. In this section, we cover the main ones. For a complete list, you can refer to the official Boozang documentation.

The project Settings page has four main sections:

1. **Environments**: To define applications and environments categories as explained in the section "Application Environments"

2. **Content Policy**: To set some advanced options to customize the behavior of actions and locators

3. **Element Definition**: Mainly used to customize the location strategy

4. **Integration**: To set up the integration with external tools

Content Policy

The Content Policy section has quite advanced settings to customize Boozang. The ones you might want to use are

- **APP Dictionary**: It allows you to define your own dictionary for multi-language testing. We have not used this option yet.

- **Ignore Request (URL)**: Here, you can define a set of URLs whose requests will be ignored by Boozang. We used this option to speed up some tests in Salesforce.

- **Priority item for element select**: This might be useful when you have control over your application to be tested and you want to prioritize certain HTML attributes for element location.[3]

The rest of the options usually are good to go with their default value. Some of them allow you to tune the elements location strategy to match specific applications.[4]

---

[3] In Cypress, the equivalent capability is done via its data-cy attribute.

[4] Notice that this, when needed, is a one time operation.

Settings Content Policy section

Integration

In the Integration section you find the option to link Boozang to external tools.

You can, for example, define the integration with JIRA and Xray to import Cucumber features and scenarios. More on this in Chapter 13, "JIRA with Boozang via Xray."

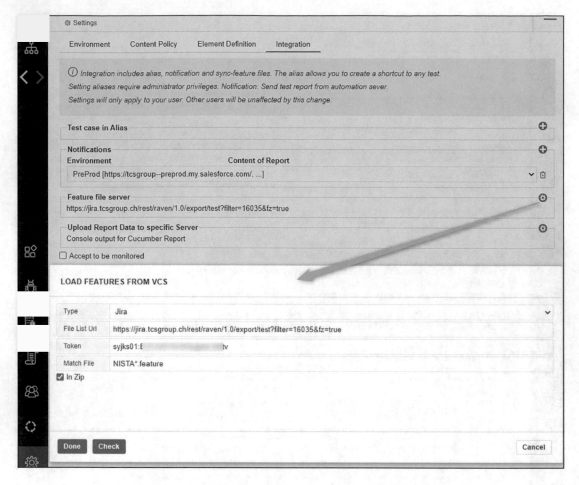

Example of Project Settings Integration section

In terms of Integration capabilities, Boozang has a separate page you can reach from the left side bar which is dedicated to CI integration:

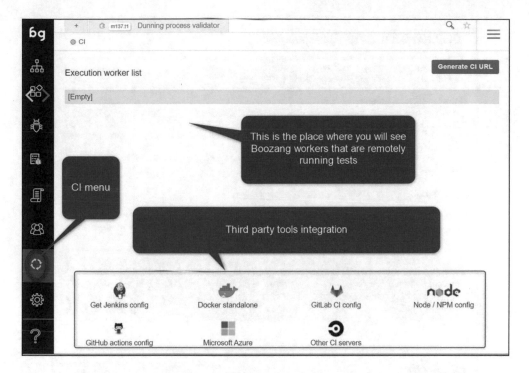

CI page and third-party tools integration

In the following figure we see an example of the Jenkins configuration. After entering your password, Boozang generates detailed information that you can copy paste into a Jenkins job.

GENERATE CI URL - GET JENKINS CONFIG

Project ID	5e60f3e3deb43b53367fb106
Branch	master
Environment	PreProd
Test case	[m74.t1] Full regression

☐ Private

◉ Single worker   ○ Multiple workers (parallel tests)

Fill password to retrieve token

Token	

A cooperator server remote commands to execute test cases. User can through this feature command multiple servers to complete a complex test job (like: Validate realtime socket synchronized data), or command different servers to complete test jobs from different modules at the same time.

Generate   Cancel

Jenkins configuration setup input

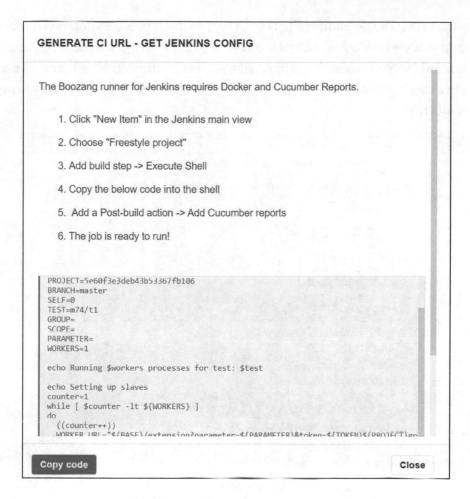

GENERATE CI URL - GET JENKINS CONFIG

The Boozang runner for Jenkins requires Docker and Cucumber Reports.

1. Click "New Item" in the Jenkins main view

2. Choose "Freestyle project"

3. Add build step -> Execute Shell

4. Copy the below code into the shell

5. Add a Post-build action -> Add Cucumber reports

6. The job is ready to run!

```
PROJECT=5e60f3e3deb43b53367fb106
BRANCH=master
SELF=0
TEST=m74/t1
GROUP=
SCOPE=
PARAMETER=
WORKERS=1

echo Running $workers processes for test: $test

echo Setting up slaves
counter=1
while [ $counter -lt ${WORKERS} ]
do
    ((counter++))
    WORKER_URL="${BASE}/extension?parameter=${PARAMETER}&token=${TOKEN}${PROJECT}&gr
```

Copy code   Close

Jenkins configuration setup output

The Jenkins integration is described in detail in Chapter 14, "Jenkins and the Boozang Runner," where we will also show how to run tests in parallel with multiple workers.

UI Customizations

Boozang offers a number of customization options on the GUI client; let's see the main ones.

The first one is the position of the Details panel which provides detailed information on the item you are displaying, like parameters if you are on a test item. This panel can be positioned above or below the actions, like you see in the following figures. I prefer to have them at the bottom because I first look at the action, and if needed I go below, but it is very subjective.

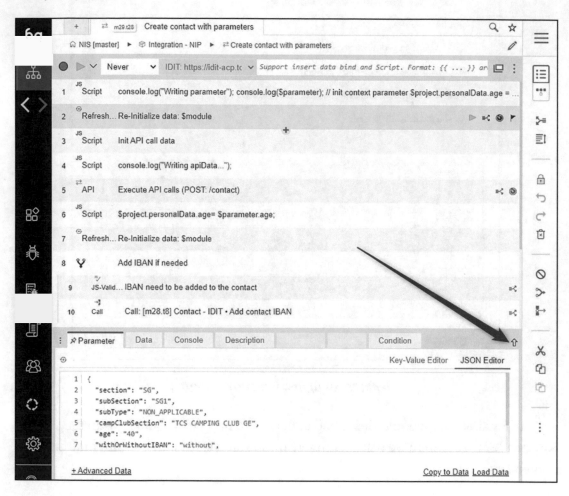

Details panel at the bottom

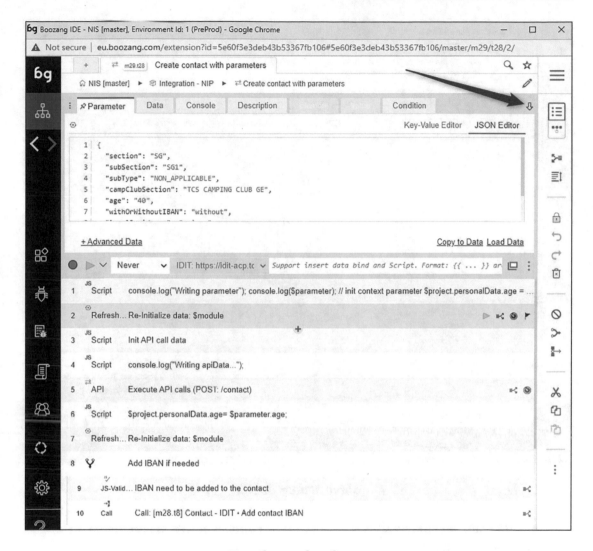

Details panel at the top

In the Test actions panel, it is sometimes useful to have a complete view of each action, including the overridden exit conditions (see section "Exit Conditions") or script details.

You can toggle on or off this view with the button in the right bar, as shown in the following figure.

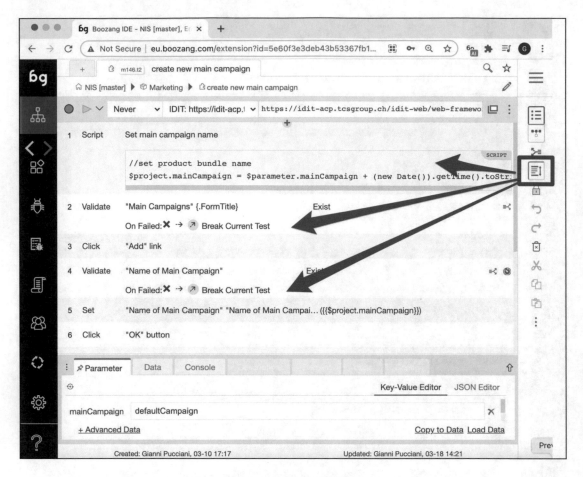

Show actions details

Another useful customization is in the Details panel, where you can toggle on and off the display of certain tabs:

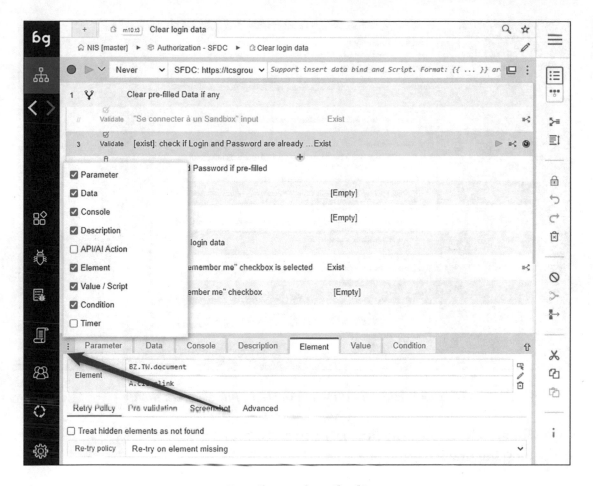

Details panels and tabs

UI customization options are available also in the right bar kebab menu "Advanced operations," where you can change the table style, that is the main window area where actions are shown, to have it more or less compressed.

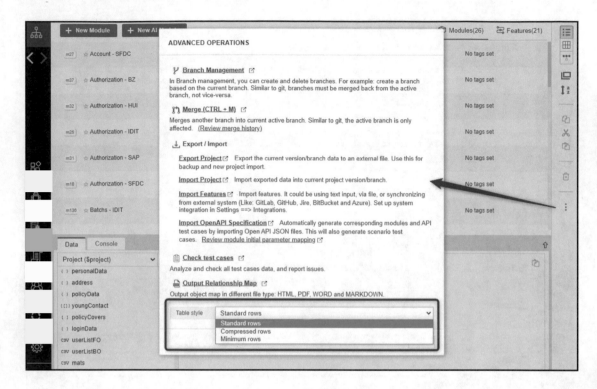

UI customization options in the right panel kebab menu

In the second kebab menu (top bar), you find other advanced options. Let's see some of the most important ones.

Updates from the Trenches

Half-way through the project (Sprint 12), time to share some learnings.

First of all, COVID impact. Like most of the world, we were obliged to work from home for several months, nearly every day of the week. Daily standups, Sprint demos, and retrospective sessions, all via Skype or Zoom. Hard to imagine, but we got used to the new way of working quite soon.

Tools like JIRA, Confluence, Slack, and of course Boozang allowed us to carry on our work with minimal disruption.

The project planning was also adapted: 6 Sprints were added and the initially planned 3 months UAT phase was replaced with 2 "UAT Sprints." Besides COVID, the project extension was mainly due to the complexity of delivering the interfaces to internal and external applications.

Around the end of Sprint 10, we decided to move to the acceptance (ACP, AKA Pre-Production) environment[5] for building our scenarios and reporting nightly executions. On the QA environment deliveries were frequent, once and sometimes twice a day. Remember we are not doing TDD nor BDD. In this environment the features were not yet validated by manual testers; hence we often ran into failures that were preventing us from completing some scenarios.

We wanted a more stable environment, hence the choice to work on the ACP one.

In the ACP environment builds are delivered once at the end of the 3 weeks Sprints. Therefore 3 weeks with an environment stable with features already manually tested.[6] This allowed us to keep an average success rate between 80% and 90%. The 10%–20% of failures were most of the time equally split among system and automation issues.

Let's see some figures half-way through our journey:

- 200 Gherkin scenarios grouped among 19 Features.

- 190 Tests grouped into 26 Modules.

- Maximum depth of a Scenario is 8, meaning that a scenario's step is implemented via Tests that call other Tests until a nested level of 8.

- The most used Test has more than 50 upstream Tests: this means that there are more than 50 Tests that are relying on this critical piece.

- 2 Test Suites (smoke plus full regression). A full regression run, executed nightly via Jenkins takes nearly 2 hours to complete, thanks to a dedicated 8 core Jenkins slave on which we execute jobs with 1 master and 8 workers (more on parallel runs in Chapter 15, "Jenkins and the Boozang Runner").

---

[5] Refer to section "How We Manage Test Environments" where we described our environment categories.

[6] Actually, on the editor side, automated tests are also developed with Selenium and run on their private environment before deployment to QA.

In order to reduce the execution time, we used a lot of API tests (covered in Chapter 12, "APIs and Mixed API/GUI Testing") in the Given part of a scenario. We sometimes created, for a specific Test, both a GUI and an API version. The API version is used when we need to set preconditions, while the GUI version is used in the actual steps (the "When" and "Then" parts in Gherkin).

In the first 10 Sprints we had four major versions of our Jenkins pipeline. We used the most recent feature in Boozang that allows for parallel runs at the Gherkin iteration level (more details on this in Chapter 15, "Jenkins and the Boozang Runner").

We heavily rely on Boozang's branching system, which evolved and improved a lot up until now.

Every automation implementation activity is tracked with JIRA tasks and implemented in a separate Boozang branch. We use a rather classic feature-branch approach, which we will describe in more detail in Chapter 16, "Boozang for Teams."

Finally, around Sprint 8, we started discussing with the Boozang team about a new feature, implemented in Sprint 9, the Root Cause Analysis with the Known Issues repository.

To speed up the analysis of automation failures, we can now record Known Issues in Boozang, and have them automatically recognized and mapped on future executions (more on this in section "Root Cause Analysis" of Chapter 11, "Reporting and Troubleshooting").

CHAPTER 8

Elements Location Approach

Hold on tightly to your web elements!

This chapter describes Boozang's unique approach for locating WEB GUI elements, one of the features that set it apart from other tools. Boozang, with its set of locators based on natural language, allows you to focus on the scenario flow rather than the web page DOM. Most of the time, the locators Boozang selected while recording your scenario are all you need. For some exceptions, especially while working with dynamic data, you can easily tune the location strategy.

© Gianni Pucciani 2023
G. Pucciani, *Boozang from the Trenches*, https://doi.org/10.1007/978-1-4842-9010-1_8

Boozang Location Strategy

Boozang's location strategy is based on natural language. Instead of using hidden HTML elements attributes, it uses what real users see when working on the application.

Using natural language makes it easier to repair the automation scripts when the application changes.

After you have recorded the scenario, for each action, you can find the element used and the locators' details in the *Action config* tab of the Details panel. The following screenshot shows a straightforward case to locate the "Home" text on my book site. The stylo icon will open up the pop-up with the Dom Picker, where you can adjust the locator.

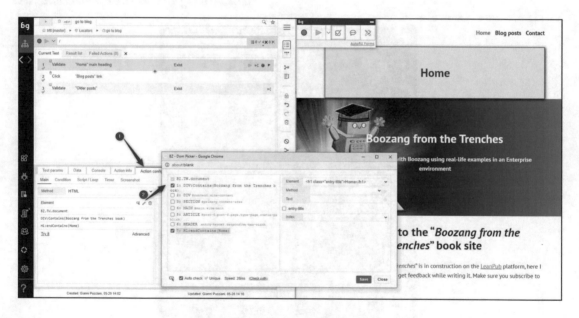

Action config and Dom Picker

Let's zoom in the Test and the Dom Picker to understand better.

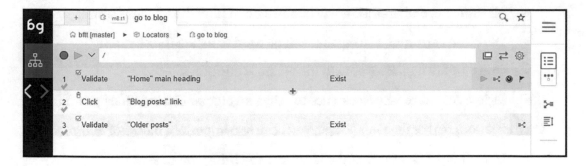

Test "go to blog"

Dom Picker action 1

The Dom Picker is divided into two sections.

On the left section, you have the selected element and all the parents in the DOM tree. You can select any of these parents as selector to uniquely locate the element.

On the right side, you have a section that holds

- **Element**: The element used. The dropdown allows you to select siblings or child elements.

- **Method**: Several methods[1] will enable you to tune the location strategy.

- **Text**: You can enter a string that will be used to locate the element.

- One or more checkboxes with the element attributes.

- **Index:** An index list you can use to select an element based on its position.

On the bottom part of the Dom Picker, you have two important pieces of information:

- **Uniqueness**: Checks that the locators used bring you to a unique element

- **Autocheck**: A checkbox (on by default) to give you real time feedback

- **Speed**: The time needed by Boozang to locate this element

In this basic example the locators selected by Boozang while recording did not need any further work.

In the second action, we see another fairly simple example, where we look for the "Blog posts" link.

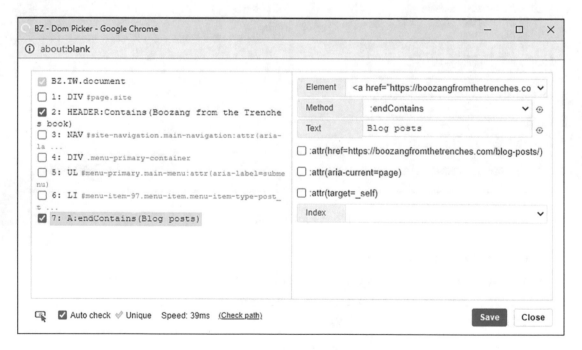

Dom Picker action 2

---

[1] The most common methods are ":text," ":input," ":before," ":after," and ":near."

By removing the check from the HEADER section, the time can be reduced from 39ms to 7ms.

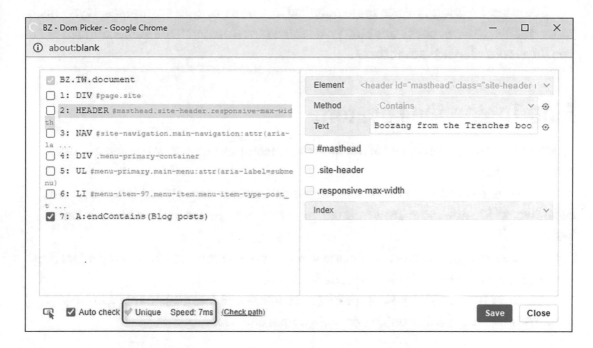

Dom Picker with increased speed

As we mentioned before, most of the time the locators selected by Boozang work just fine.

For each element, you have some methods that allow you to find the text you want, and deal with complex cases:

Methods available to locate text in an Element

It takes a bit of practice to play around with all the options, but as I mentioned before, tuning the locators will happen only occasionally.

In the next sections, we see some practical and more complex examples. If you need more details, you can check this blog post which covers in detail the subject: `https://boozang.com/element-selectors/`.

Fine Tuning the Locators

As we mentioned before, most of the time the selector used by Boozang will not need any adaptation.

However, the stability of a test suite depends on many steps: if only a few of them have "weak" locators, your Tests may fail, or even worse give you non-deterministic results.

In the following sections we selected some complex scenarios from our project that you might encounter, in similar ways, in different applications.

The most interesting cases happen when you need to locate elements within a dynamic table, with either unique or non-unique entries.

Locators with Dynamic Tables and Non-unique Elements

Locating elements in dynamic tables can quickly become a nightmare for automation.

Let's see some examples and how they can be addressed with the Dom Picker.

Use Case 1

In the following figure we want to locate a dropdown list which is related to a text in a line.

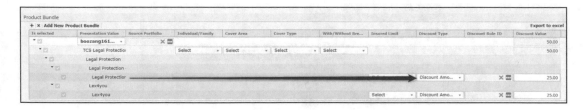

Table with non-unique elements

Let's see how this element is located in the following figure.

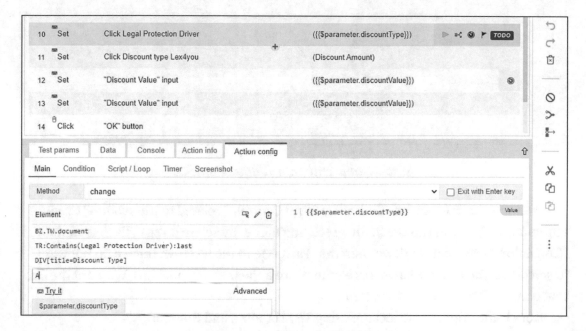

Locating the dropdown list

- *TR:Contains(Legal Protection Driver):last* goes to the last occurrence of a table row that contains the text "Legal Protection Driver."

- *DIV[title=Discount Type]* moves to the column with text "Discount Type."

- A: locate the first link in the section.

Use Case 2

In this example we want to locate a price in the table. We are now using the TR and TD locators.

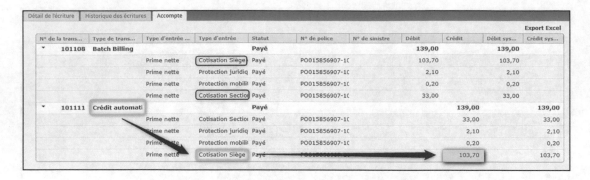

Second table with non-unique elements

We want the price of the "Cotisation Siège Centrale" related to the section "Crédit automatique." As you can see in the preceding figure, there are three cells that contain "Cotisation Siège Centrale": we want the green one in the last row. But we do not want to select just the last line since this element can appear at any position. We want the one that comes after "Crédit automatique."

Here is the appropriate locator, using TR, TD, after, and RowCol.

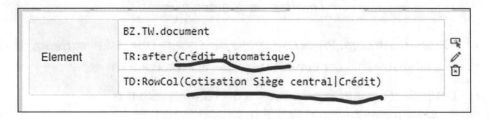

Locator for Use Case 2

The locator is quite self-explanatory. Select a linc after "Crédit Automatique" and go to the cell where the line has "Cotisation Siège Centrale" and column "Crédit."

Use Case 3

In this use case we look for an element where the column index is fixed.

Table with an element at a fixed column

The locator for this use case uses again TR and TD to go to a specific line, but the column index is fixed (5th column).

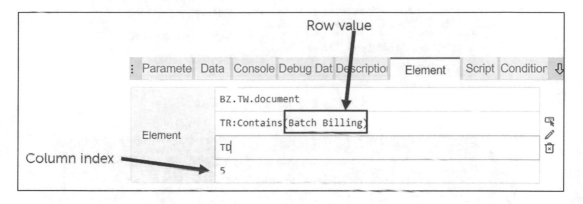

Locator for use case 3

Validating the Expected Results

Validations play a key role in your scenarios, directing your scenarios to look for a specific condition in your application.

A validation can be added as any other action via the plus icon or in the recording support window.

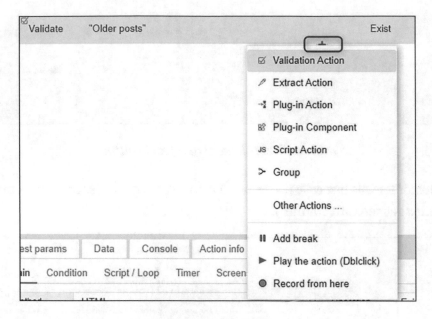

Add validation action, first way

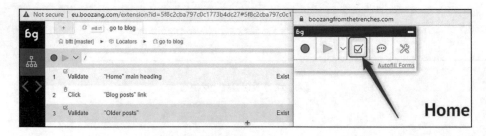

Add validation, second way

The list of all the available actions is shown in the following figure, and a detailed description is available on the Boozang documentation site: `http://docs.boozang.com/#validations`.

Script
Data
innerText
Input Value
Exist
Valid not exist
Dynamic Exist
Screenshot
Is Checked
Is Disabled
Is Enabled

Validations

Let's see some practical examples of the most common ones.

Exist

This validation is used to check if a specific element exists on a page. It will fail if the element is not located.

Example: locate a popup error message.

In this example we used the locator Exist to validate the presence of a blocking alert for a negative test. We used the error code "GD503877" to locate the element.

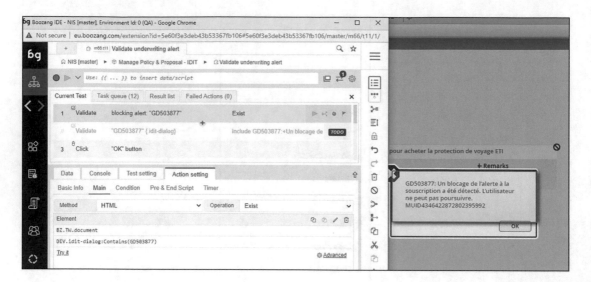

Validate not exist

This validation is the opposite of the previous one. It generates a failure if the element exists.

> **Example: validate that you are at the correct page to continue execution.**
>
> It is sometimes useful, when re-using some tests, to validate that your test is at a correct page. If, for example, you want to make sure to be at the home page, you can insert a if group and use the not exist validation as the group condition.

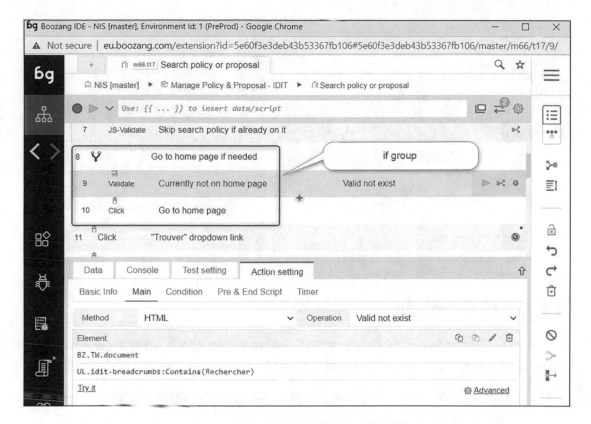

Not exist validation inside IF group

innerText

This validation is used to compare the content of an element with a predefined string. It will fail if the strings don't match, and generate an error if the element is not located.

Example: verify the creation of a contact and its address in the CRM.

After the creation of a contact in the CRM, we check the contact page and validate that the correct street name is displayed. In this case the string that contains the street name comes from a parameter passed to the test ($parameter.streetName; see Chapter 10, "Data Management," for more information on parameters).

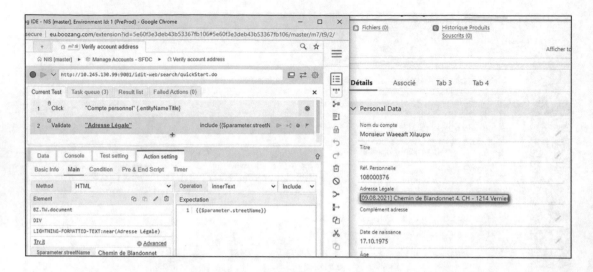

Script: JS-Validate

The script validation is useful whenever you need to validate some logical conditions. It will return failure if the condition is evaluated to false.

Example: validate the price of a product against requirements.

For checking that the price calculation rules are correctly applied, we use the script validation and check the expected price (passed as parameter) against a value extracted from the GUI and stored in a variable at project level.

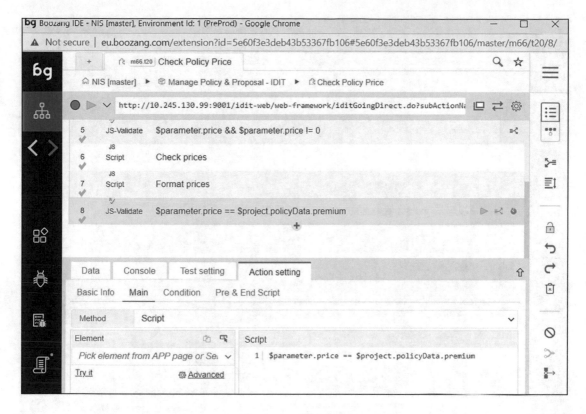

Script validation

Is Checked

Another useful validation is the one for dealing with checkboxes. The operation "Is Checked" supports the expectations "Yes" and "No."

Example: validate product configuration parameters.

In the PCAS application certain operations on a policy are possible only when the product configuration has specific preconditions. In this example we validated that a special product option is not active.

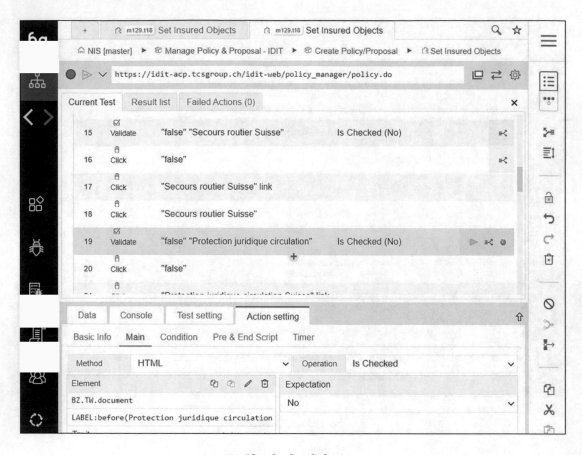

Is Checked validation

CHAPTER 9

Exit Conditions, Conditional Flows, and Timers

Strong entry, but safe exit.

The first test you will try with Boozang will be a simple sequential list of actions. But, as soon as you start implementing real scenarios, you will have to use exit conditions, loops, and conditional flows. In combination with this, you may need to adjust the timing of some locators, as some applications may have slow background processes, heavy loading pages, and/or javascripts.

In this chapter, we see how to apply these concepts to build solid and reusable building blocks.

© Gianni Pucciani 2023
G. Pucciani, *Boozang from the Trenches*, https://doi.org/10.1007/978-1-4842-9010-1_9

Exit Conditions

Exit conditions are essential to design the flow of actions in your Tests, so that they take into account specific events.

Let's see the basics and then some practical examples.

In the following figure, you see the exit conditions icon placed in the action line, next to the play icon. The Action settings tab in the Details panel shows the exit options.

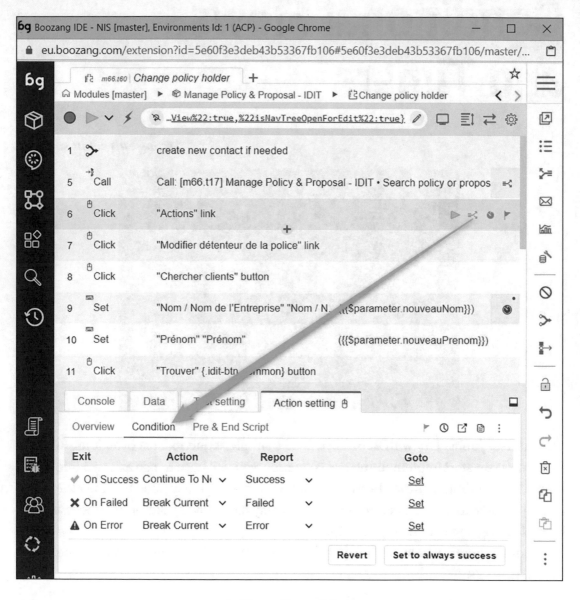

Action exit conditions

A Test action can exit in three ways:

- **Success**: The action was correctly executed.

- **Failed**: In case of validations, the expected condition was not met.

- **Error**: The element on which the action was supposed to run was not found. The only exception is with validations of type "Exists." In this type of action, an element not found still returns Failed.

The difference between Failed and Error can be subtle, but most of the time you can set both in the same way.

Let's now see what you can tell your Test to do for each exit condition.

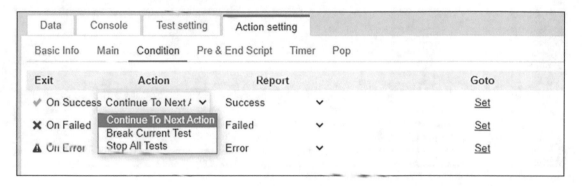

Exit actions

- **Continue to next action**: The Test will simply continue with the next action.

- **Break current test**: The Test will quit. If the Test was called by an upstream Test, the control will pass to it; otherwise the execution will stop.

- **Stop all tests**: Not only the Test will quit, but also all the Tests up until the current one. For example, when using Gherkin Scenarios, you might have a step implemented with several nested Tests. When using this option in a Test, the whole Scenario will fail.

In addition, for each exit option, you can select a specific Goto point, be it a Test or specific action in the same Test flagged with a Goto tag:

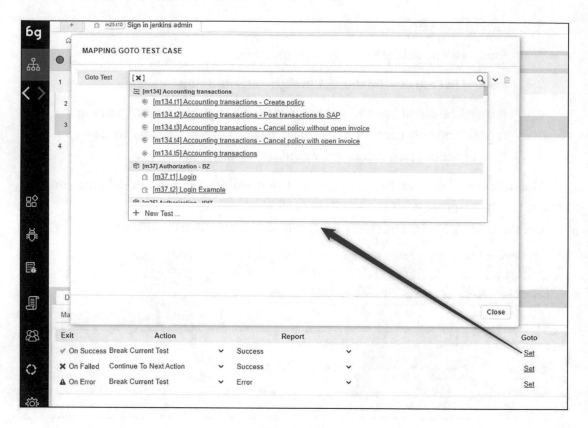

Goto setting

When the exit condition is met, the test flow will then be redirected to the Goto point set. The Goto point is useful for handling some edge cases. In our project we used it only rarely. My suggestion here would be not to rely on it too much in order to keep your tests more readable.

Now that we know how to handle the possible outcomes of an action, we just need to tell Boozang how to report the action: Success, Warning, Failed, Error, and Critical.

When you override the default behavior, Boozang will clearly show it. For example, in the figure below we added a validation and overridden the exit condition in case of Fail. Let's assume we consider that validation not critical enough to stop the Test, we can tell Boozang to raise a warning and continue the execution. Here is what it looks like in the GUI.

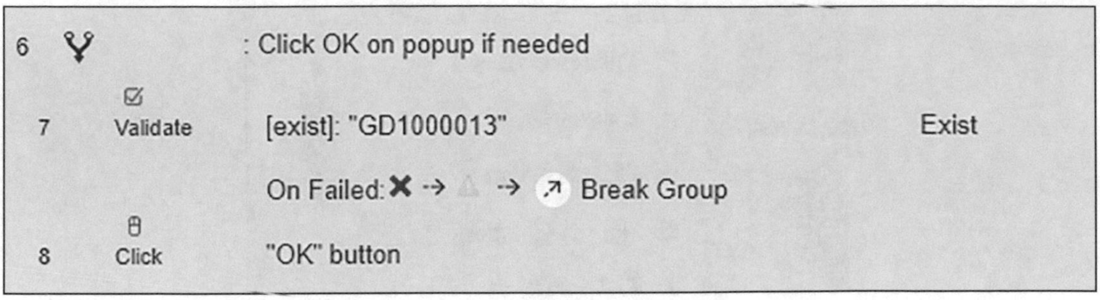

6	Y	: Click OK on popup if needed	
7	☑ Validate	[exist]: "GD1000013"	Exist
		On Failed: ✖ ·→ △ ·→ ⬿ Break Group	
8	⍬ Click	"OK" button	

Overridden exist condition in case of failed validation

In that case we have an informative popup appearing based on some business rules, and we want to click the OK button to continue the flow.

Mastering the exit conditions is fundamental. We will see several examples in the rest of the book where default exit conditions have been overridden.

Conditional Flows

Conditional flows allow you to deal with more complicated scenarios. As all programming languages, Boozang allows you to build *If/Then/Else* or *Switch* groups, and *For* and *While* loop groups.

In the following figure, you see how you can add a group at a given point in your Test, with the + sign that appears when you select an action. That will open a list of action types that you can use, and among them you have the Group.

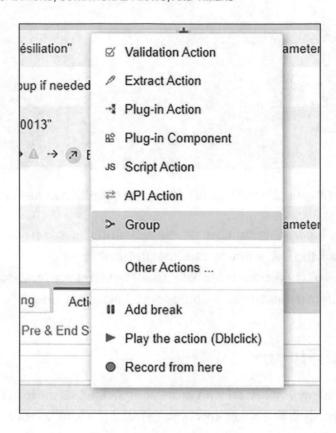

Group action

After you select the Group action, you have access to a range of choices:

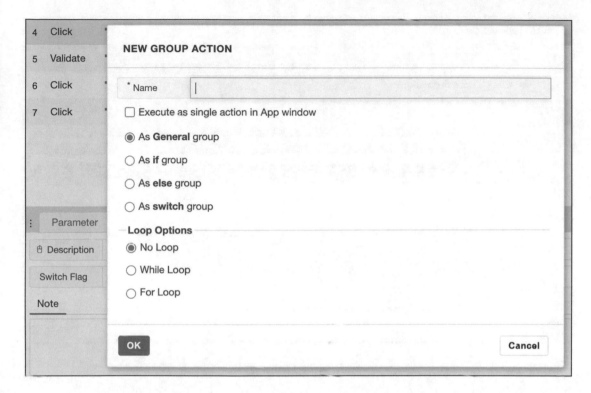

Type of Group actions

All the groups can be named: this is very handy to keep your Tests easy to read.

The default group type is "General." This is useful when grouping some actions together for the sake of readability, and in some cases it can be an alternative to having a plugged Test. However, in terms of modularity, if you expect that part of a Test can be reused by other Tests, you should definitely extract those actions into a separate Test (see section "Generate and Reference Test").

When you select the IF group, you will have the options for

- **Giving a name to the group**: Once more, assigning good names increases the readability of your tests, and you should take this task seriously.

- **Selecting the type of condition**:

  - **HTML**: For example, the existence of a certain web element

  - **Script**: Where you can validate some data (more on Data Management in the next chapter)

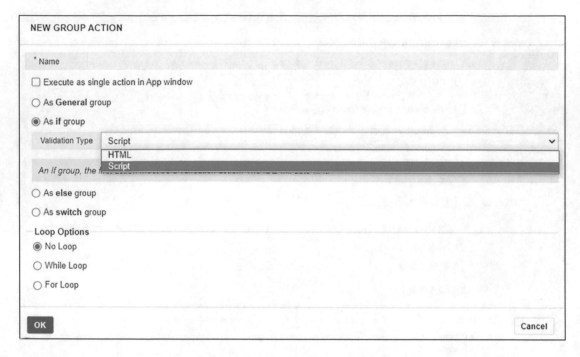

IF group setting

IF group: generated actions

The other group types like *FOR* and *WHILE* are very similar, with the only difference that you need to specify the loop data and add the action to be repeated.

PCAS Logic Part 1

Time to go back to the trenches now, and see some real application of groups. But in order to do that we need a few key concepts of our PCAS (Policy and Claims Administration System; see Chapter 4, "The TCS Project").

We are going to explain more of the PCAS logic, but only what is needed throughout each chapter to understand the examples.

A front-office user of the PCAS can create policies for a particular product when the customer has already paid the premium. Alternatively, he can create a Proposal (i.e., an offer) that the customer can use to pay later on and activate his policy.

Certain operations, like creating back-dated policies (start date in the past), are only possible if the user has a specific profile, like back-office.

A policy has a start and an end date. During this period, the customer is covered against certain risks.

Products and Dependent Products

The "TCS Membership" is the main TCS product. Other products like "TCS Societariat Camping" or "TCS Livret ETI" are called "dependent" products: it means that a customer has access to these products only if they already have an active policy of the TCS Membership.

Other products that we don't need to mention at this point are not dependent products. Therefore, they can be acquired without a TCS membership, but they can have a special discount if the client already has an active TCS Membership.

The workflow to acquire a product is relatively standard, no matter the product. However, each product has specific options that need to be set either in a dropdown list or checkbox.

In the following figure, we see two examples of the PCAS page where product information are entered.

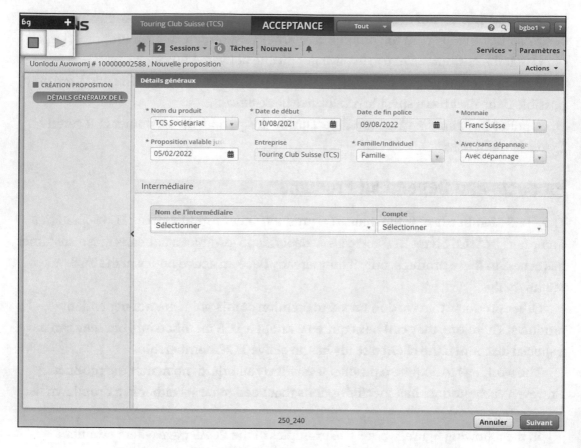

Product configuration for the "TCS Membership" product

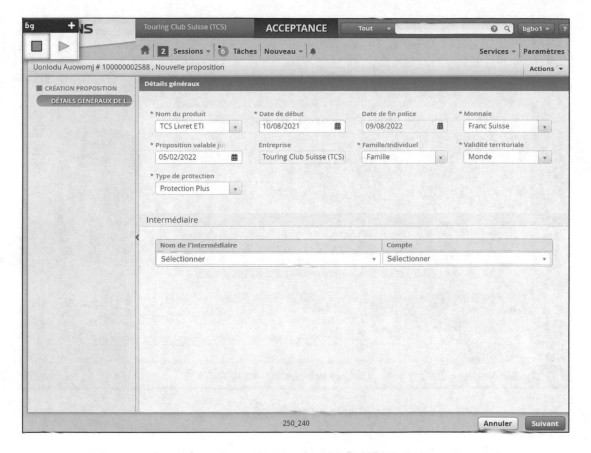

Product configuration for the "ETI" product

While implementing tests, early on, we need to keep an eye on reusable parts, so that we avoid costly refactoring in the future.

If-Then-Else Groups

One of the most used Tests in our project is called "*Create Policy/Proposal Handler*," shown in the following figure.

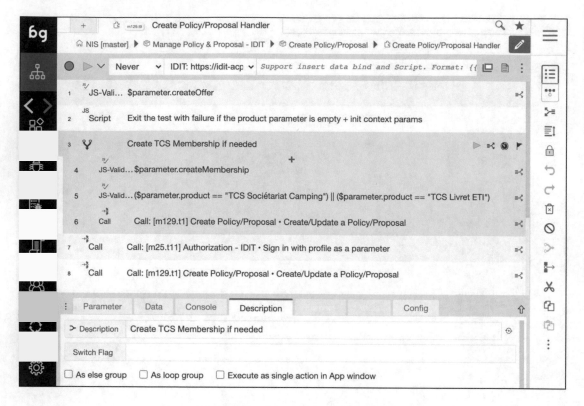

Example of a Test with If Group

This Test is called by many Scenarios who need to execute a product acquisition process.

If the product we want to acquire is a dependent product, the Test will go through the acquisition process for the product "TCS Membership" and then, once more, for the dependent product. If no TCS Membership is needed, the first part is skipped. Here is where the Group comes in: go through the TCS Membership acquisition process, but only when needed.

With the knowledge acquired up until now, we can understand some important bits of this Test.

- Action 2 does what it says in the description: If we do not pass any product as parameter, it makes the Test quit with failure; otherwise it initializes some data (hold on until Chapter 10, "Data Management," to have a full understanding).

- In Action 3, we see how important is the Group description: We can quickly understand that this group is used to create a TCS Membership policy, if needed. This happens in the following cases:

  - We explicitly set the parameter createMembership to true (validation in Action 4) in the parent test.

  - In case of dependent products (validation in Action 5).

If either one of the validations in Action 4 and 5 fails, the test will quit the group, and no TCS Membership policy is created.

- Action 6 has the real logic to create a policy. This logic is enclosed in a separate Test, which accepts a product as parameter.

- Action 7 will take care of logging in with a different profile if needed.

- Action 8 will create a policy for the product we initially wanted to create a policy for.

- Action 6 and Action 8 use the same Test, m129.t1, but they call it with different parameters.

When the data management part will be covered, you can come back to this Test to understand it better. This Test is a good example of modularity.

Loop Groups

Loops (for and while) are very useful when an action or a set of actions must be repeated several times, based on a fixed number of iterations, or until a certain condition is met.

We use the group loops especially when dealing with tables in the PCAS applications.

PCAS Logic Part 2

To introduce the context for the following examples, let's see some bits of the financial domain in the PCAS application and its integration with SAP.

The scenario defined for this domain is the one shown in the following picture.

```
Given a contact is created with the API
And I sell a <product> product with <paymentMethod> options
When the bill is paid using the <paymentMethod>
Then the transactions created are <transactionsType>
When run the job GL Export
Then the transactions sent to SAP are correct

Examples:
| product | paymentMethod | transactionsType |
| TCS Sociétariat | QR-Bill | Batch Billing:Paiement |
| TCS Sociétariat | Cash | Batch Billing:Crédit automatique |
```

Example of Scenario for the PCAS financial domain[1]

Let's see what is behind each step:

- **Given a contact is created with the API:** This step creates a contact in the PCAS application. Normally the CRM is the master for contact management, but in this case we wanted to speed up the scenario; hence we create the contact directly via the REST API of the PCAS. Since the integration with the CRM is tested in another Feature, this shortcut is acceptable.

- **And I sell a <product> product with payment method <paymentMethod>:** This step performs the action of selling a product with a specific payment method. This is a typical action performed by a front-office sales agent. Since the product and the payment method are impacting the transactions sent to SAP, two parameters are used to test several combinations. At the end of this action a bill will be created for the customer to pay and activate the policy.

- **When the bill is paid using the <paymentMethod>:** Here we perform the payment action, which can be done in different ways depending on the payment method. The act of performing a payment generates the financial transactions in the PCAS application.

---

[1] Two "When" in the same scenario is not a good practice when writing Gherkin; we might review this scenario in the future.

- **Then the transactions created are <transactionsType>**: Here we perform the first validation of the scenario. We want to validate that the correct type of transactions are created, which depend on the product and payment method.

- **When I run the job GL Export**: The action of preparing transaction data to be sent to SAP is performed by a batch job in the PCAS, called "General Ledger" (GL) Export batch job. This job in a production environment would be scheduled to run with a given frequency, but for our tests we want to launch it directly to be able to validate the data produced.

- **Then the transactions sent to SAP are correct**: Finally we validate the transactions data that are shown in the PCAS application: these are the data that will be sent to SAP. In this case we intentionally kept some of the business rules complexity out of the Gherkin scenario; in Boozang we have a table to store, for each combination of products and payment methods, the expected transactions. To perform this last step, the entries of the table shown in the next picture have to be parsed. We have highlighted the columns that hold values to be validated.

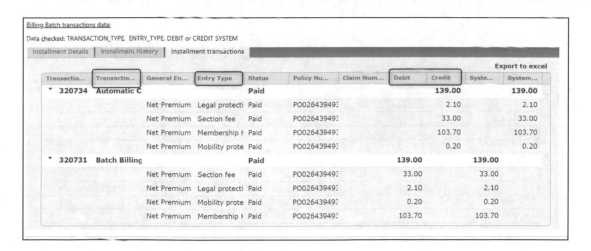

Transactional data table to be validated

_key	transactions
ACQUIRE_TCS_SOCIETARIAT_QR_BILL_BATCH_BILLING	[30000;103,70;Crédit];[10200;103,70;Débit];[30000;33,00;Crédit];[10200;33,00;Débit];[30000;2,10;Crédit];
ACQUIRE_TCS_SOCIETARIAT_QR_BILL_PAIEMENT	[10200;0,20;Crédit];[10200;2,10;Crédit];[10200;33,00;Crédit];[10200;103,70;Crédit]
ACQUIRE_TCS_SOCIETARIAT_CASH_BATCH_BILLING	[10200;103.70;Débit];[30000;103.70;Crédit];[10200;0.20;Débit];[30000;0.20;Crédit];[10200;2.10;Débit];[30
ACQUIRE_TCS_SOCIETARIAT_CASH_AUTOMATIC_CREDIT_TRANSACTION	[10200;0.20;Crédit];[10200;2.10;Crédit];[10200;33.00;Crédit];[10200;103.70;Crédit];[20017P;139.00;Débit]
ACQUIRE_TCS_SOCIETARIAT_CASH_CREDIT_AUTOMATIQUE	[10200;33,00;Crédit];[10200;2,10;Crédit];[10200;0,20;Crédit];[10200;103,70;Crédit];[20017P;139,00;Débit];
RENEWAL_TCS_SOCIETARIAT_QR_BILL_BATCH_BILLING	[30000;112,70;Crédit];[10200;112,70;Débit];[30000;33,00;Crédit];[10200;33,00;Débit];[30000;2,10;Crédit];
RENEWAL_TCS_SOCIETARIAT_QR_BILL_PAIEMENT	[10200;0,20;Crédit];[10200;2,10;Crédit];[10200;33,00;Crédit];[10200;112,70;Crédit]
RENEWAL_TCS_SOCIETARIAT_CASH_BATCH_BILLING	[10200;112.70;Débit];[30000;112.70;Crédit];[10200;0.20;Débit];[30000;0.20;Crédit];[10200;2.10;Débit];[30
RENEWAL_TCS_SOCIETARIAT_CASH_AUTOMATIC_CREDIT_TRANSACTION	[10200;0.20;Crédit];[10200;2.10;Crédit];[10200;33.00;Crédit];[10200;112.70;Crédit];[20017P;148.00;Débit]
RENEWAL_TCS_SOCIETARIAT_CASH_CREDIT_AUTOMATIQUE	[10200;33,00;Crédit];[10200;2,10;Crédit];[10200;0,20;Crédit];[10200;112,70;Crédit];[20017P;148,00;Débit]
UPGRADEINDFAM_TCS_SOCIETARIAT_QR_BILL_BATCH_BILLING	[10200;0.20;Débit];[30000;0.20;Crédit];[10200;2.10;Débit];[30000;2.10;Crédit];[10200;10.00;Débit];[30000
UPGRADEINDFAM_TCS_SOCIETARIAT_QR_BILL_INTERCO_BILLING	[40800;0,20;Débit];[20080;0,20;Crédit];[10280;0,20;Débit];[30100;0,20;Crédit];[40800;2,10;Débit];[20080;
UPGRADEINDFAM_TCS_SOCIETARIAT_QR_BILL_PAIEMENT	[10200;0,20;Crédit];[10200;2,10;Crédit];[10200;10,00;Crédit];[10200;26,70;Crédit]
UPGRADEABREAKOWNASSISTANCE_TCS_SOCIETARIAT_QR_BILL_BATCH_BILLING	[10200;0,20;Débit];[30000;0,20;Crédit];[10200;1,52;Débit];[30000;1,52;Crédit];[10200;23,00;Débit];[30000
UPGRADEBREAKOWNASSISTANCE_TCS_SOCIETARIAT_QR_BILL_INTERCO_BILLING	[40800;0,20;Débit];[20080;0,20;Crédit];[10280;0,20;Débit];[30100;0,20;Crédit];[40800;1,52;Débit];[20080;
UPGRADEBREAKOWNASSISTANCE_TCS_SOCIETARIAT_QR_BILL_PAIEMENT	[10200;0,20;Crédit];[10200;1,52;Crédit];[10200;23,00;Crédit];[10200;68,28;Crédit]
UPGRADEALL_TCS_SOCIETARIAT_QR_BILL_BATCH_BILLING	[10200;0,20;Débit];[30000;0,20;Crédit];[10200;2,10;Débit];[30000;2,10;Crédit];[10200;33,00;Débit];[30000
UPGRADEALL_TCS_SOCIETARIAT_QR_BILL_INTERCO_BILLING	[40800;0,20;Débit];[20080;0,20;Crédit];[10280;0,20;Débit];[30100;0,20;Crédit];[40800;2,10;Débit];[20080;

Data table (matrix) stored in Boozang

A deep understanding of this scenario is out of the scope for this book. The goal is to give a general understanding that is enough to understand the following examples.

In the examples that follow, some data management concepts are used. You can come back here after reading the next chapter if needed.

Let's see what is behind the final validation. The Gherkin step calls the "Open inquire GL Share File" with a set of parameters (more on parameter in the next chapter).

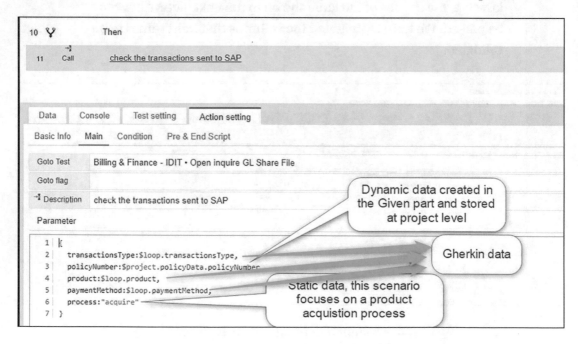

Step implementation: calling a Test with a mixed set of parameters

The parameters passed from the Step definition to the Test include a mix of

- Gherkin examples data

- Dynamic data created during the scenario execution

- Static data to drive a specific behavior

Checking Financial Data Tables with Loops

In the following example, we use a for loop to execute a validation over a set of data passed as an array to the Test via the $parameter variable (the following chapter will clarify what's in $parameter and how to use it). We want to validate that, in the PCAS application, the financial data produced for each policy are correctly produced.

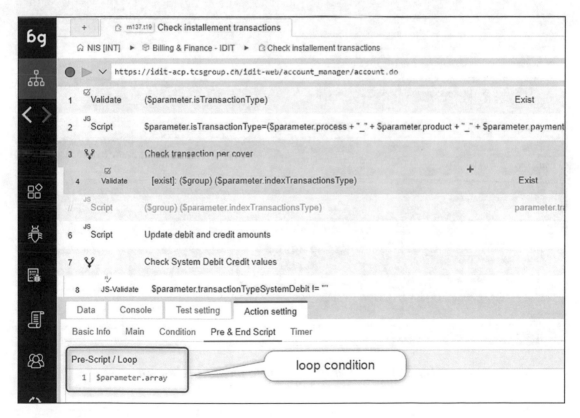

Example of loop condition

This case is especially interesting because the action 4 uses the array value of the current iteration, stored in the variable $group, to locate the element used in the Exist validation.

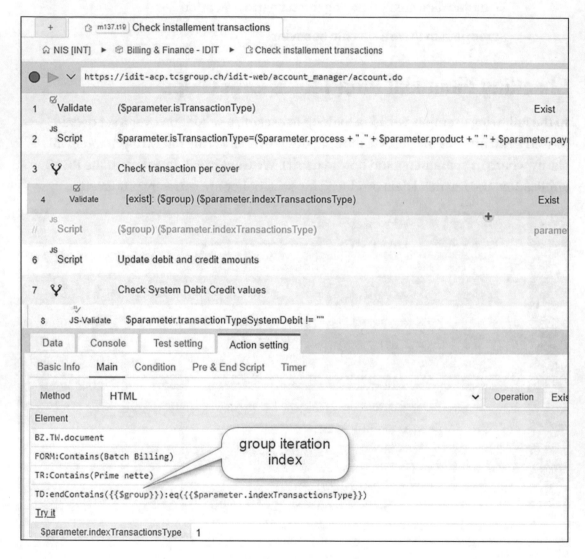

Using the loop iteration value to locate an element

Another example of looping within a group is shown in the following picture.

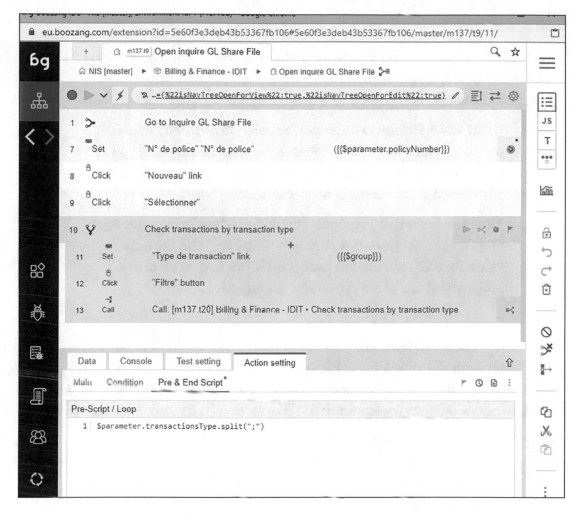

Loop group to parse the content of an array passed as parameter

The preceding test parses a table in the application window to validate that it contains the values passed by the upstream Test.

A while loop can be implemented in a similar way, with the only addition of an action that takes care of evaluating a certain condition and quitting the group when the condition is met.

We did not implement this type of loop until now, but a good example can be found here: `https://boozang.com/logic-and-loops-using-groups/`.

Timers

We already discussed Timers in section "Timing and Waits" when mentioning the pain points of the Selenium approach.

Boozang handles timing constraints on each action with two options:

- **Delay Time**: Default to 0 seconds. You should be careful when using this option since it will slow down all the executions. When you add a delay, the action will start only after the delay you specified. This corresponds to the concept of implicit wait.

- **Timeout**: Default to 2 seconds. This option is used to set a timeout; most of the time you will do this on validations. With the default value, Boozang will execute the action with a frequency of one second until one of the two conditions are met:

  - Action executes successfully.

  - Timeout is reached.

This corresponds to the concept of explicit wait.

It is worth noting that, while you are recording a scenario, Boozang will automatically add a timeout when some background calls take more than 2 seconds to return a value.

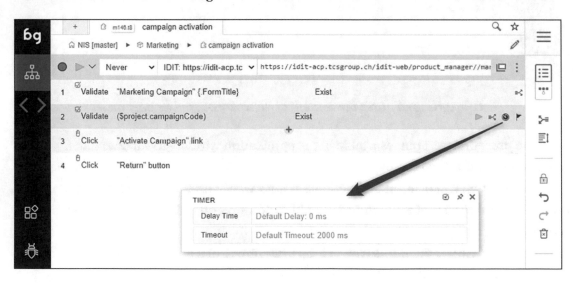

Delay Time and Timeout

In our project delays are used only rarely, but Timeouts quite often. In the PCAS application, for example, while finishing the creation of a policy, several objects are stored in the DB and the confirmation popup with the OK button can take a few seconds to appear.

In the following example the timeout was set to 20 seconds on the action used to extract the proposal number from the confirmation popup window.

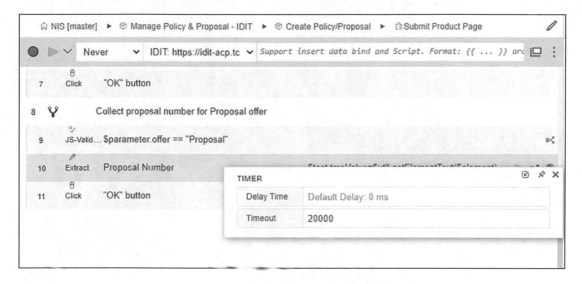

Example use of Timeout

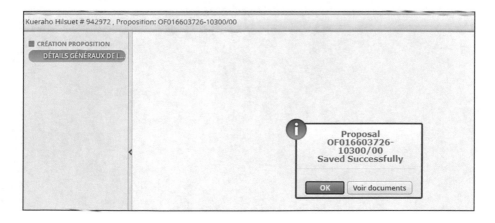

PCAS Application window

CHAPTER 10

Data Management

Keep your tests healthy and feed them properly with good data.

This is probably one of the most important chapters, as data management is one of the main keys to build reusable components. Boozang is extremely powerful and flexible when it comes to managing test data. But power and flexibility can hide a complexity cost if you don't use it properly.

© Gianni Pucciani 2023
G. Pucciani, *Boozang from the Trenches*, https://doi.org/10.1007/978-1-4842-9010-1_10

Data Management Concepts

What does it mean "data management" within a Test Automation project? Automated tests need some input while running. The simplest test, an application login, will need username and password.

A Test that creates a contact (e.g., in a CRM application) may need some information about the contact like first name, last name, email address, etc.

A Test that runs a product acquisition may need, besides contact information, product information like the name of the product and some mandatory or optional information.

A Test validating that the correct pricing is applied, besides user and product information, will also need the expected price.

Tests need data not only to feed the SUT or validate outcomes, but also to evaluate what to do in special situations, like we saw in the section "If-Then-Else Groups," hence to drive the flow of the scenario.

Different Tests may need the same data. For example, when running a scenario for a product acquisition process, the client information may be needed initially to create the contact into the system, and then later on to find this contact and go through the acquisition process.

We therefore need a way to store test data and have them available for different tests.

We also need a way to extract data from the system at a certain point in our Scenario, and use these data later on in the same Scenario.[1]

In Test Automation we often hear the term "Data-driven" tests. This means that their execution depends on the data input they receive.

In standard software development data have properties:

- **Name or Key**: A way to reference the data

- **Type**: The type of information you can enter, like a number or string.

- **Default value**: The value that should be used when the data value is not explicitly set.

- **Scope or visibility**: It defines who can have access to the data.

---

[1] Scenarios, in a Gherkin context, are meant to run independently of one another. Hence, no need to share data across scenarios. Exceptions to this rule are environment settings like the application URL.

Boozang supports different types of data, from plain key-value pairs, to array and csv tables.

All data are stored in JSON format,[2] with a default value, and support different scopes, that we are going to see in the next sections.

In Boozang we have two main types of data: parameters and data.

Test Parameters

Each Test can have a set of parameters. These parameters can be used by upstream tests to pass certain data. For example, a login test can be called with two parameters, login and password. For developers this concept will be very familiar since it is commonly used in standard software development, where functions or methods can be called with parameters or arguments.

It is important to remember that parameters always belong to Tests. Therefore they are visible only within the Test. The following figure shows the parameters tab in the Details panel, their name, and default value.

---

[2] JavaScript Object Notation, https://en.wikipedia.org/wiki/JSON

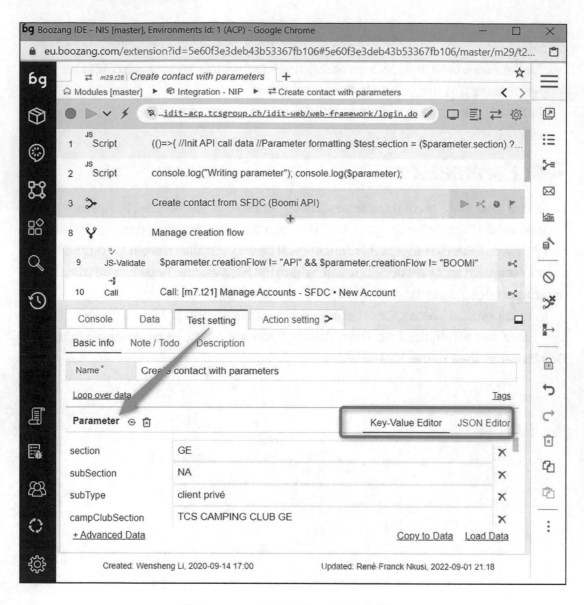

Test parameters in Key-Value Editor

You can define parameters either with a simple form (Key-Value Editor) or with a JSON editor.

In the following figure we see how the same parameters are shown with the JSON editor.

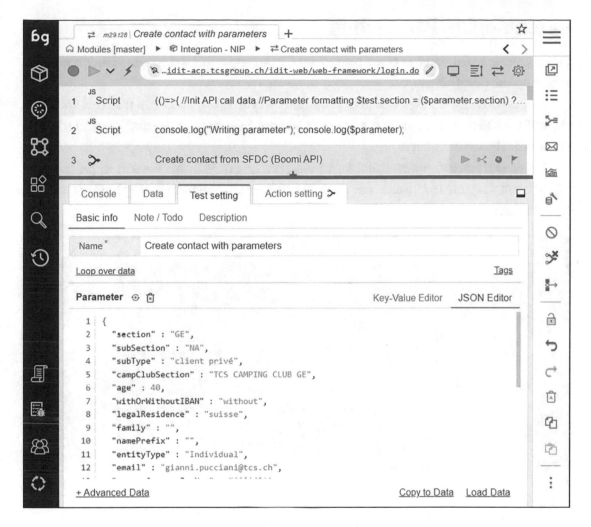

Test parameters in JSON Editor

The JSON editor is necessary when you want to set up complex objects (lists and arrays); otherwise the Key-Value Editor saves you some typing and is less error prone since Boozang takes care of adding brackets and commas to make it a good JSON object.

Within the Test, each action can refer to the parameters via their name added to the $parameter scope. In the preceding Test, the "section" parameter value can be accessed via *$parameter.section*. *$parameter* is the scope, which has its own JSON object.

We will see later on how, in the Console tab, at any point in the test you can type *$parameter* to have the full list of parameters with their current value. Or you can also type *$parameter.<key>*, for example, *$parameter.section*, to check the current value of a specific parameter.

Automapping Parameters

When calling a test that has some parameters, Boozang offers the magic wand icon to automap the parameters.

When you have defined a data or parameter in your Test, and from this Test you call another Test that supports the same parameter, you can use the magic wand to automatically do the match.

This has been extremely useful for us when calling tests from Gherkin steps. You might need to come back here after reading Chapter 13, "Gherkin and Behavior Driven Development."

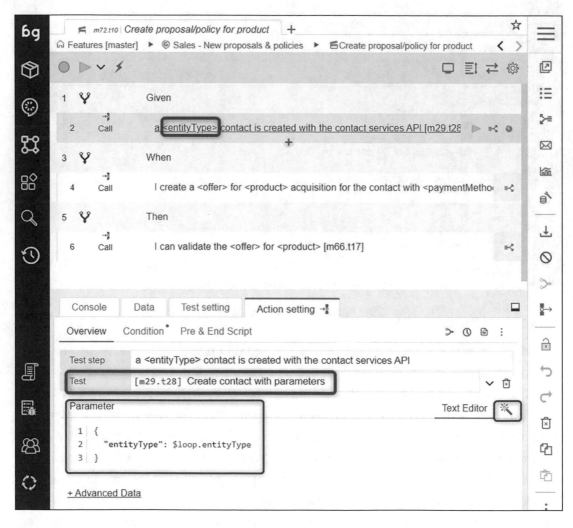

Auto mapping Gherkin data

In the preceding figure you can see a Gherkin scenario with a Given step that has a parameter "entityType."

In the *Goto Test* section you see that the step will call a Test "Integration - Nip - Create contact with parameters." This Test supports a parameter called "entityType."

By pressing on the magic wand, the part highlighted in green will be automatically generated.

For this operation to work smoothly, you need to make sure to use the same name to identify the same data and adopt a naming convention (we use the camelCase for data and parameters).

In the preceding example, the $loop means that this mapping will be done for each data of the Gherkin examples. We will see more about the $loop context later on in this chapter.

Project Data ($project)

The top most data scope in Boozang is project, accessible via the object *$project*.

All data in Boozang can be created in the Details panel, Data tab, as shown in the following figure.

By default the data scope is Test, but you can change the scope before creating the data.

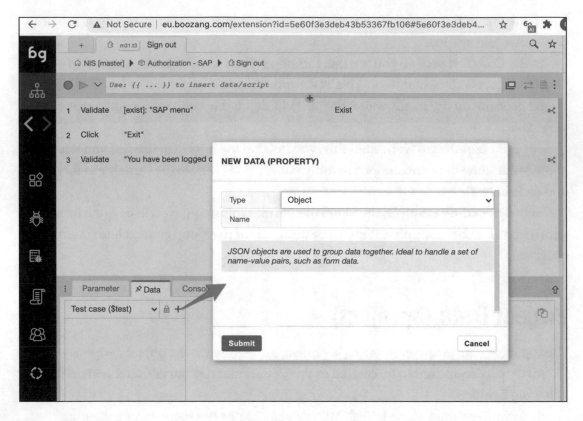

Create new data form

In that form you can change the object type and assign the name.

Several object types are available. The ones we use the most are

- **Object**: A simple JSON object made of multiple key-value pairs

- **Mixed**: A complex JSON object where you can have arrays besides simple key-value pairs

- **CSV**: A tab delimited table[3]

Other data types are available; for this you can check the Boozang documentation at docs.boozang.com.

Data defined in the project scope are available to all tests, and are accessible via *$project.<name>*.

---

[3] It is called CSV (Comma Separated Values) but uses TAB as delimiter.

When using Cucumber Scenarios, we will see that the project scope is separate for each Scenario. Therefore, when running scenarios in parallel, each scenario runs with its own set of data, and it is completely independent from the other scenarios.

In our project we rely on $project data whenever we have information that can be used by many tests and scenarios, across several modules.

Some examples are login account information (usernames and passwords for several test profiles), client information (first name, last name, email, addresses, etc.), as well as products and policies information.

It definitely depends on your setup, but in general the rule is to start with the smallest possible scope, and increase it if needed. If only one Test or a subset of Tests in a specific Module need some data, do not pollute your *$project*, but rather use *$test* or *$module*.

Module Data ($module)

The module data scope, with its related object $module, contains data that can be shared among Tests belonging to the same Module.

An "authentication" module, for example, can hold data related to users login.

The grouping of Tests into Modules highly depends on the application context. As we already mentioned in section Modules, Boozang Modules should reflect more or less the grouping of functionalities in your application.

In our project we followed this approach, and used the *$module* scope to hold some reference data in a specific application context.

Test Data ($test)

If you are sure that some data will be relevant only to a specific Test, then the *$test* object is a good choice. As a guideline, you should aim at the smaller possible scope for each data set.

Note the difference between *$parameter* and *$test*. They have a similar scope, but their usage is totally different. Use *$parameter* to allow a Test to receive data from an upstream Test. Use *$test* for data used only by a single Test.

The difference can be initially a bit subtle, but it will make more sense once you get more comfortable with the tool.

Loops ($loop, $group, $action)

Loops can be done at different levels. You can execute a test in a loop ($loop), a set of actions within a group ($group), or a specific action ($action).

The $loop variable is very important when working with Gherkin scenarios including several examples (Scenario Outline).

We already saw an example of $loop usage when mapping the Gherkin data from the examples table and passing these values to the Test linked to a Step definition (see section "Automapping Parameters").

Another example was the one seen in the section "Loop Groups."

Wrapping Up

At this point we saw all the main elements you have at your disposal to effectively build reusable tests and deal with complex scenarios. Boozang offers a lot, and it might take some time to fully digest all these topics. In the next section we will apply all these concepts to real tests developed in our project.

Examples from the Trenches

Time to challenge our understanding of topics covered until now.

Let's go back to our key Test "*Create Policy/Proposal Handler*" and see how the different data objects are used.

We introduced the Test "Create Policy/Proposals Handler" in Chapter 9, "Exit Conditions, Conditional Flows, and Timers," when talking about If-Then-Else groups. Let's review it now more in depth.

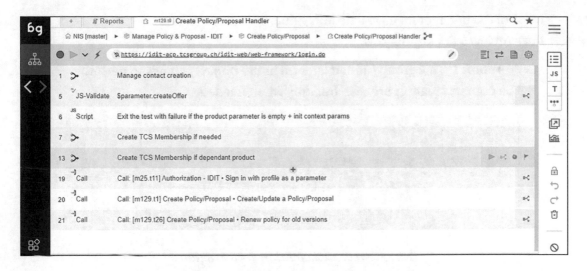

Test definition (groups collapsed view)

This Test is the key test for all the scenarios which need to go through the acquisition process.

The Test has a number of parameters that allow to manage the execution flow of the actions:

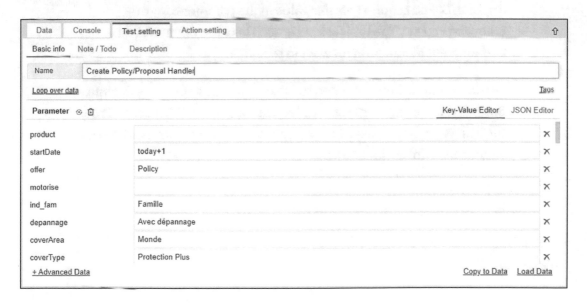

Test parameters (truncated view)

Most of the parameters have a default value.

Let's review a few key actions:

- **Action 1**: This group (added later on in the project) allows to perform a contact creation process, but only when needed.

1	⅄		Manage contact creation	
2		JS-Validate	!$parameter.contactExternalID || $parameter.contactExternalID == " "	+
3		Call	Call: [m29.t28] Integration - NIP • Create contact with parameters	
4		JS Script	$parameter.contactExternalID = $project.personalData.externalID;	

Manage contact creation group actions

If the test is called without any "contactExternalID" value (validation in Action 2), that means without any contact reference, then the Test creates a contact via an API call in the Test "Integration - NIP - Create contact with parameters" in Action 3. This called Test, when used, will set a data value at project level, in *$project.personalData. externalID*, and action 4 sets this value in the parameter for the following actions. The project level is used because different Tests and different Modules might want to refer to it.

- **Action 5**: This action is needed to make Gherkin steps more flexible. Basically, if the handler Test is called without CreateOffer set to True, the Test will quit its execution (without reporting any errors, since it's wanted and not accidental).

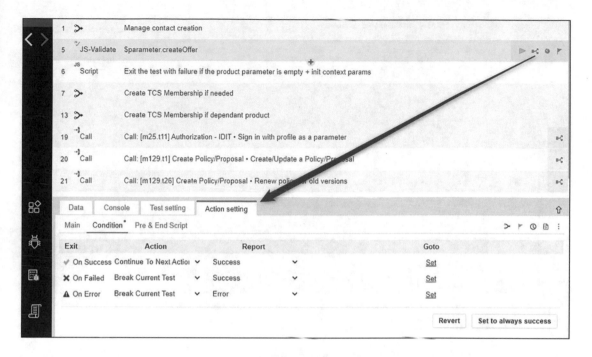

Action 5 exit rules

- **Action 6**: More business logic is inside this action, whose purpose
  is similar to the previous one; quit the test in some special cases. In
  addition, some extra data are set from project level to parameter to
  drive the following actions. Full understanding of this logic is not
  important; this part is meant to show how Boozang can be extended
  with some simple javascript to deal with more complex situations.

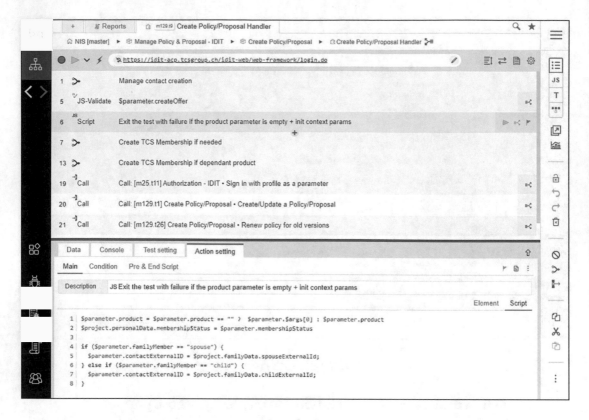

Exit logic

- **Action 7 and Action 13**: As already mentioned in Chapter 9, "Exit Conditions, Conditional Flows, and Timers," these actions are meant to drive the acquisition of a Membership product only when needed, that is,

    - When the parameter "membershipStatus" is passed as True value (group Action 7).

    - Or when the product being acquired is a dependent product which needs an active acquisition (group Action 13)

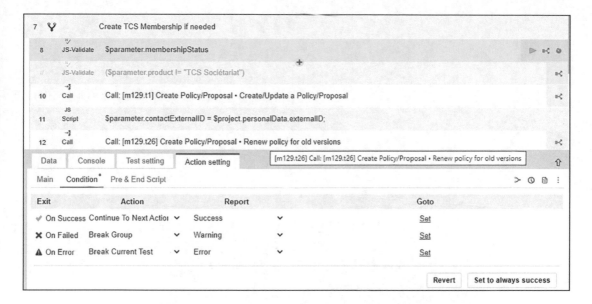

Drive a required product acquisition if needed

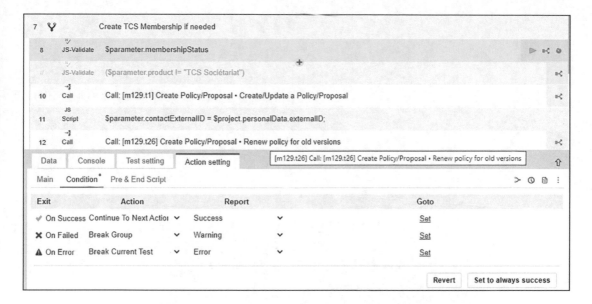

Drive the acquisition of Membership in case of depended product

Action 18, the last of the block 13, takes care of performing a renewal operation if needed. Some scenarios in fact are meant to be executed in a situation where the client has an open invoice, that is, an invoice that is not yet paid. For this, the handler test is called to execute an acquisition in the past, and then a renewal.

CHAPTER 11

Reporting and Troubleshooting

Your test failed, elementary, my dear Watson!

This chapter covers some standard and more advanced reporting features available in Boozang as well as the best way you can analyze failures with minimal effort.

© Gianni Pucciani 2023

G. Pucciani, *Boozang from the Trenches*, https://doi.org/10.1007/978-1-4842-9010-1_11

Test Reports

When running a Test, a Scenario, or a Test Suite, you want to know the outcome (pass or fail) and all the necessary details in case of failure.

Boozang offers several possibilities in terms of test reports; let's see all of them starting with the standard reports integrated in the IDE.

IDE Real-Time Reports

In the section "Execution and Reporting," we saw how to run a Test or Scenario from the IDE.

When you run a Test in the IDE, Boozang switches the actions panel into an execution mode, as you can see in the following picture.

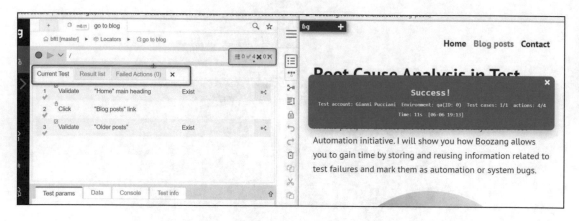

Execution screen

The execution screen has three tabs:

- **Current Test**: It shows the actions with the green check or red cross in case of failure.

- **Result list**: It shows a real-time view of the execution of all the actions and tests.

- **Failed Actions**: It reports the action failed and all the Tests called until that.

- **Tasks queue**: It shows the list of Tests and Actions that should be executed as part of a Test or Scenarios. This tab is only visible during the execution.

The Results list is very useful when running Gherkin scenarios that include several linked Tests. In the previous example, this view is very basic like you see in the following figure: only one test. If you open the view with the plus icon, you see more details.

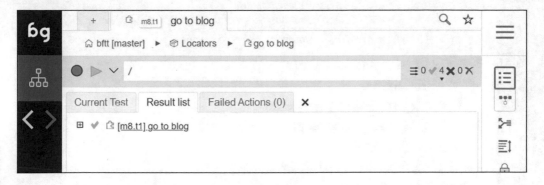

Result list view

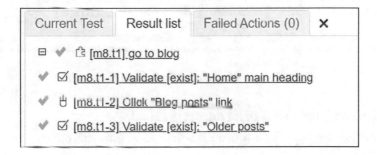

Details Result list

If, instead of a single Test, we run a Scenario, this tab becomes much more interesting. Let's see an example of a Gherkin scenario that creates a new Salesforce account.

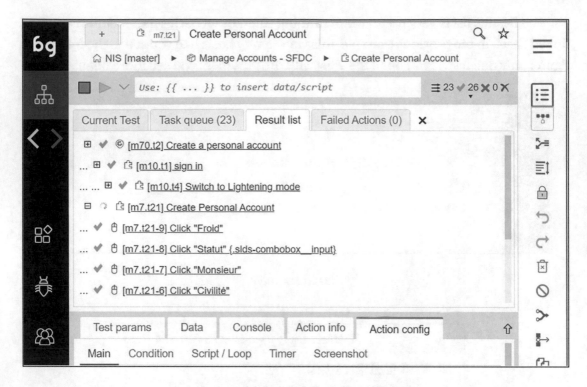

Result list with several Tests in a Scenario

You now see a real-time view of all the Tests called.

Let's see another example of a more End-to-End Scenario that creates an account in Salesforce (including an address) and then checks that this same account is visible in the PCAS application. The failure (artificially provoked by removing the connection to PCAS application) gives me the opportunity to show an example of the Failed Actions tab.

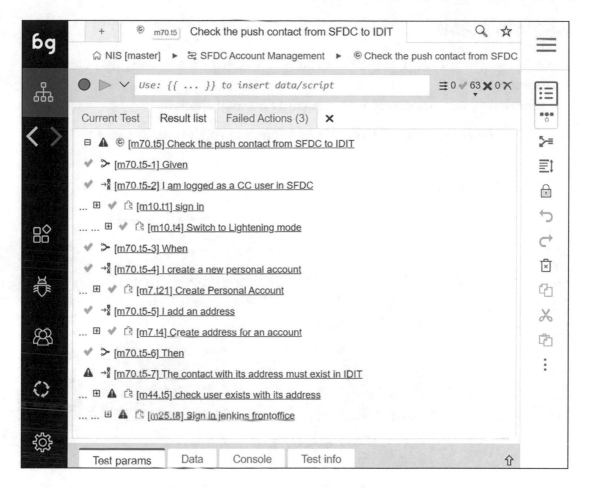

Result list view for an End-to-End Gherkin scenario

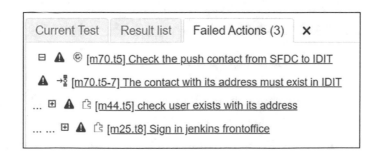

Failed Actions view

The Failed Actions tab shows, from top to bottom, the Scenario executed, the Step, and the Tests called. It relies on the indentation to show Tests called within other Tests.

Reports Menu

In the left side menu bar, you have the Reports icon which leads you to a list of reports for recent executions.

From here you can access the two standard Boozang reports:

- **Summary report**: With high level information of the tests run and the outcome

- **Function details log**: A detailed report with action level information

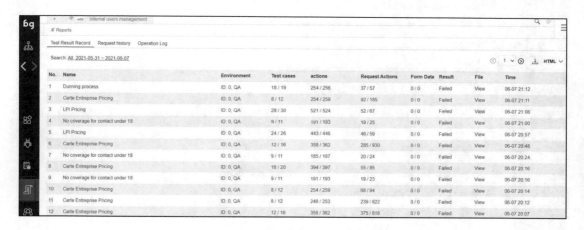

Reports page

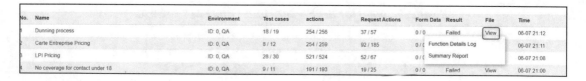

Reports for a specific execution

The execution reports integrated in the IDE are useful when initially implementing Tests and Scenarios, but once they run as expected you will soon want to switch to remote executions scheduled via Jenkins or any other Continuous Integration (CI) tool.

The Jenkins and Cucumber integrations will be covered in details in Part 3. For now, I just want to give you an idea of how reports will look like when running Cucumber scenarios via Jenkins, so that you can better understand the Root Cause Analysis (RCA) in the next section.

When running Cucumber Scenarios via Jenkins, you can use the Cucumber Report Jenkins plugin.[1] Boozang can produce a report that complies with the Cucumber specifications so that it can be used by the plugin. Via the Cucumber reports, you can analyze the execution of your Test Suite and have a view by Feature, Scenario, Step all down to the last Test called by Boozang.

Let's see a quick example, and refer to Part 3 for a more in-depth presentation.

Feature	Steps						Scenarios			Features	
	Passed	Failed	Skipped	Pending	Undefined	Total	Passed	Failed	Total	Duration	Status
[m142] FNOL and Claim	16	0	0	0	0	16	4	0	4	19:38.338	Passed
[m125] Endorsements management	112	0	0	0	0	112	26	0	26	4:21:8.507	Passed
[m133] Billing	23	7	2	0	0	32	1	7	8	45:58.672	Failed
[m70] SFDC Account Management	11	0	0	0	0	11	3	0	3	9:5.481	Passed
[m117] Policy cancellation	322	0	0	0	0	322	54	0	54	5:24:6.129	Passed
[m118] Sales - negative checks	162	0	0	0	0	162	29	0	29	2:11:25.088	Passed
[m72] Sales - New proposals & policies	60	0	0	0	0	60	19	0	19	1:44:48.057	Passed
[m42] IDIT - Contact Management	23	0	0	0	0	23	5	0	5	6:5.997	Passed
[m116] Product pricing	243	29	18	0	0	290	43	29	72	17:43:41.017	Failed
[m127] Policy numbering	32	0	0	0	0	32	7	0	7	25:13.019	Passed
[m68] SFDC Family links	18	0	0	0	0	18	4	0	4	17:22.553	Passed
	1022	36	20	0	0	1078	195	36	231	1 9:28:32.858	11
	94.81%	3.34%	1.86%	0.00%	0.00%		84.42%	15.58%			81.82%

Cucumber reports example

We can drill down and look at the third feature ("Billing") which has some failures.

---

[1] https://plugins.jenkins.io/cucumber-reports/

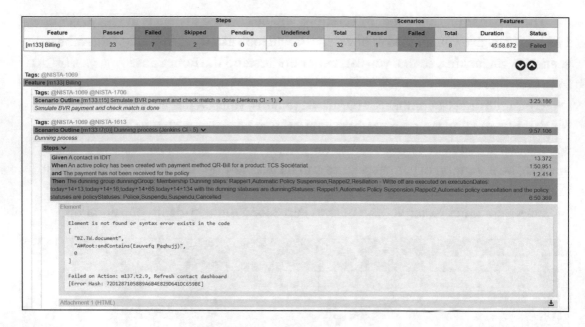

| Feature | Steps | | | | | | Scenarios | | | Features | |
	Passed	Failed	Skipped	Pending	Undefined	Total	Passed	Failed	Total	Duration	Status
[m133] Billing	23	7	2	0	0	32	1	7	8	45:58.672	Failed

Tags: @NISTA-1069
Feature [m133] Billing

Tags: @NISTA-1069 @NISTA-1706
Scenario Outline [m133.t15] Simulate BVR payment and check match is done (Jenkins CI - 1) ❯   3:25.186
Simulate BVR payment and check match is done

Tags: @NISTA-1069 @NISTA-1613
Scenario Outline [m133.t7(0)] Dunning process (Jenkins CI - 5) ⌄   9:57.106
Dunning process

Steps ⌄

Given A contact in IDIT	13.372
When An active policy has been created with payment method QR-Bill for a product: TCS Sociétariat	1:50.951
and The payment has not been received for the policy	1:2.414
Then The dunning group dunningGroup: Membership Dunning steps: Rappel1,Automatic Policy Suspension,Rappel2,Resiliation - Write off are executed on executionDates: today+14+13,today+14+16,today+14+65,today+14+134 with the dunning statuses are dunningStatuses: Rappel1,Automatic Policy Suspension,Rappel2,Automatic policy cancellation and the policy statuses are policyStatuses: Police,Suspendu,Suspendu,Cancelled	6:50.369

Element

```
Element is not found or syntax error exists in the code
[
  "BZ.TW.document",
  "A#Root:endContains(Eauvefq Peqhujj)",
  0
]

Failed on Action: m137.t2.9, Refresh contact dashboard
[Error Hash: 72D1287105889A6B4E829D641DC659BE]
```

Attachment 1 (HTML)   ⬇

Feature view of Cucumber reports

In the preceding picture we can see that the first Scenario passed, but the second one failed in the "Then" step. Boozang injects additional information in these reports, so that for each failure we can see the failed test (with the *module.test.action* id), the error message, and the Error Hash that will be used for Root Cause Analysis.

If you open up the "Attachment (HTML)" link, you find more "goodies."

```
     0
  ]
  Failed on Action: m137.t2.9, Refresh contact dashboard
  [Error Hash: 72D1287105889A6B4E829D641DC659BE]

Attachment 1 (HTML)                                                                    ⬇

  Time: 2021-06-04 06:10:21    Log Details   Screenshot

  Data:

  {
     "$module.billingData.policyAccount": "Police PO522779224-10100",
     "$parameter.dunningGroup": "Membership Dunning",
     "$project.personalData.Nom": "Peqhujj",
     "$project.personalData.Prenom": "Eauvefq",
     "$test.dunningData.dunningExecutionDate": "01/07/2021",
     "$test.dunningData.dunningStatus": "Rappel1",
     "$test.dunningData.policyStatus": "Police"
  }

  Stack trace:

  [m133.t7.6] Dunning process • The dunning group dunningGroup: Membership Dunning steps: Rappel1,Automatic Policy Suspension,Rappel2,Resiliation - Write off are
     [m137.t1.9] Dunning process validator • Call: [m137.t2] Billing & Finance - IDIT • Validate dunning steps
        [m137.t2.7] Validate dunning steps • Validate dunning step
           [m137.t2.9] Validate dunning steps • Refresh contact dashboard

  Log Details:

  BZ-LOG: Start time: 2021-06-04 06:03:28
  BZ-LOG: vvvvv New Data vvvvv
  BZ-LOG: $project.$groupType = then
  BZ-LOG: ^^^^^ New Data ^^^^^
  BZ-LOG: Action[6, Group: "Then"]
  BZ-LOG: timeout in ms:0
```

Failure details in Cucumber reports

Besides the timestamp of the failure, you find

- A snapshot of the data used by the failed test with the different scope (project, module, test, and parameter)

- A stack trace of the failed test, from the failed Step down to the Test that caused the failure

- Full log details of that execution

To summarize, the execution reports integrated in the IDE gives you a detailed and real-time view of the execution, and it allows you to quickly identify the issues even with complex End-to-End scenarios including multiple applications. When using Cucumber Scenarios, Boozang is compatible with the Cucumber reports Jenkins plugin and can enrich these reports by adding precious information to quickly find the root cause of the failures.

Trend Reports

With version 7.0 Boozang introduced the trend reports, a very useful feature to allow you to see trend results of your scenarios and tests.

There are two ways to access the trend reports.

From the main report page, you can see a trend submenu:

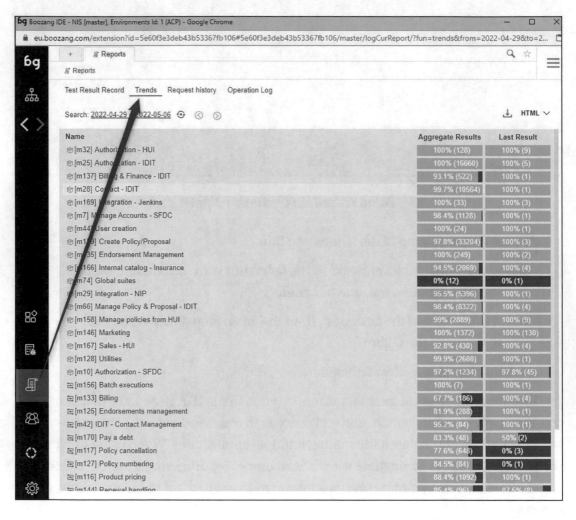

Trend reports menu

Here you have an overview with a default filter, but when you click on the search link you can customize the search criteria:

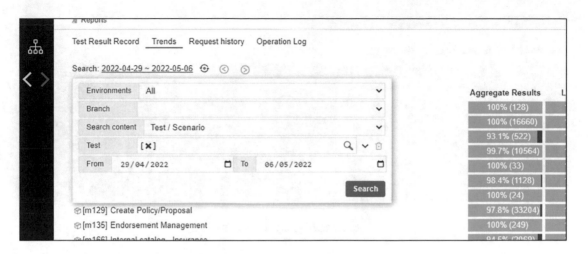

Search criteria

In here you can select the environments, the branch, the module/feature, or scenario/test on which you want to analyze the trend on. All selection will show you the items available.

Let see an example to analyze a feature, on the master branch, for the ACP environment in the last week:

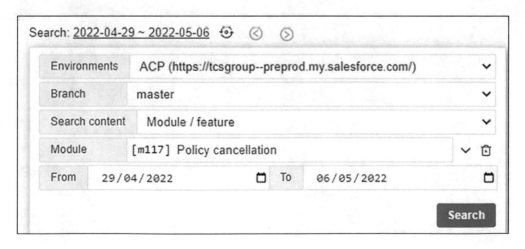

Example search

Test Result Record	Trends	Request history	Operation Log		

Search: 2022-04-29 ~ 2022-05-06 ⊕ ⊗ ⊙   ⬇ HTML ⌄

Name	Aggregate Results	Last Result
⊚ [m117.t5] Policy cancellation - Cancellation notice period	78.4% (88)	0% (8)
⊚ [m117.t4] Policy cancellation - Default settings	85.6% (187)	0% (17)
⊚ [m117.t1] Policy cancellation - Immediate cancellation	81.8% (33)	0% (3)
⊚ [m117.t7] Policy cancellation - Product Dependencies	81.8% (33)	0% (3)
⊚ [m117.t8] Policy cancellation - Reception date	79.5% (44)	0% (4)
⊚ [m117.t6] Policy cancellation - Reopen policy	87.5% (88)	62.5% (8)
⊚ [m117.t45] Policy cancellation - Revive policy	92% (88)	62.5% (8)
⊚ [m117.t31] Policy cancellation - with or without IBAN	81.8% (33)	0% (3)

Example search results

The results show the scenario's outcome within the feature.

This view can be drilled down: if you click on one scenario, the report is refreshed to show the results of the scenario.

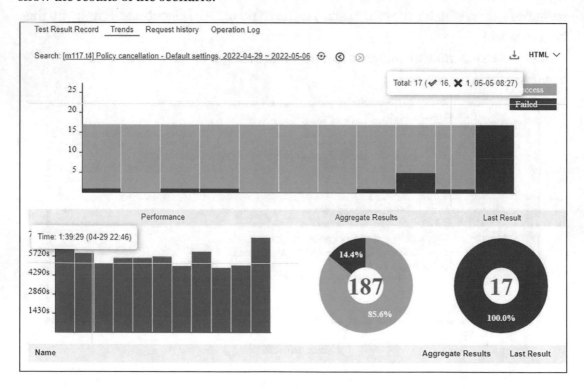

Trend results on a scenario

On the x-axis you have all the runs with the predefined week. On the y-axis you have the iterations results: this scenario is a scenario outline, and it shows all the results within the examples table.

The blue diagram offers an interesting view on the performance. Each bar shows the time needed to execute the scenario (all the iterations). Next to the performance you have two pie charts with the aggregate and latest results.

If you re-open the search, you can now select a specific iteration, for example, the first one:

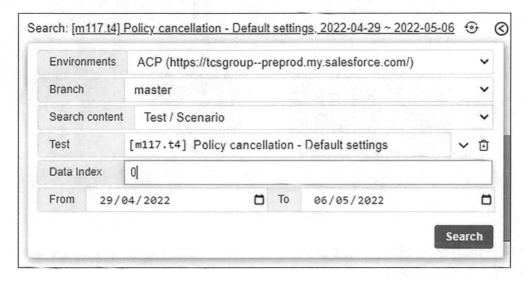

Search filter to target the first iteration of a scenario outline

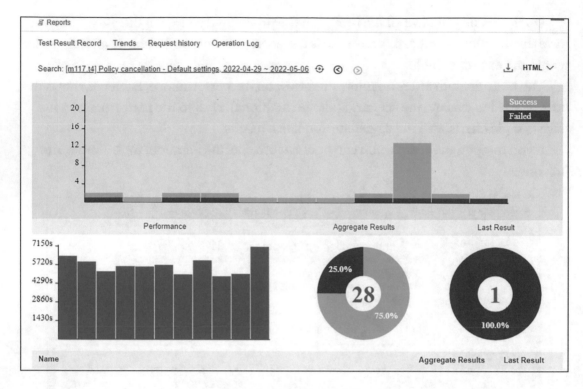

Single iteration trend

Note that the iteration trend can show more results in a single day when the iteration ran multiple times that day.

The alternative way to access the trend reports is within a scenario or test page using the trend reports button:

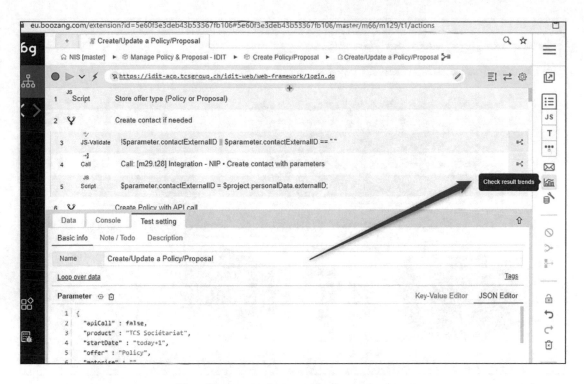

Trend reports shortcut from a test page

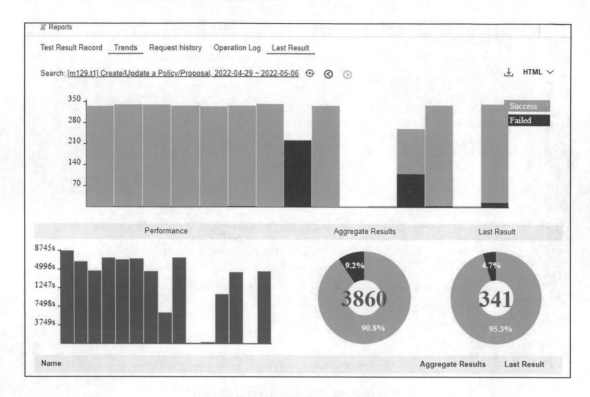

Trend results of the selected test

Trend results are extremely useful when analyzing results. These views give you an idea of the overall health at different levels: feature, module, scenario, and test. The possibility to select a time interval allows you to relate some failure with events like the deployment of a certain feature, or an architecture change that might have impacted the test results.

Troubleshooting Failures

Cucumber reports are great to give you a quick view of the automation runs. You can see the overall health at Feature, Scenarios, and Steps level.

You might get, for example, a 95% success rate at scenarios level. Should you be happy? It depends.

If the 5% of the failures are linked to existing application bugs, already known, and with low impact, yes, you can be happy.

But if among the 5% of the failures there is one new bug, maybe critical, potentially blocking your release, then the 95% success rate is not at all a good result.

Execution reports are only meaningful when complemented by the nature and impact of the failing tests.

Like many others, I have struggled keeping up with failure analysis many times in the past. I was keeping a known issues database first in Excel, then in Confluence. Everytime the daily analysis of the failure was a recurrent, boring, and error-prone activity, like manual regression testing ;).

At some point we installed and tested Report Portal,[2] but we needed something simpler and easier to use. Not an AI machine, but a simple and efficient repository of known issues.

Root Cause Analysis

One of the most recent features developed by the Boozang team focuses on the analysis of the execution results.

While developing automated tests, the automation team usually spends a significant amount of time analyzing automation failures and finding the root cause of them.

Some failures may be due to real application bugs, others to bugs in the automation code.

Once the root cause is identified, it is important to store it and re-use it for the following runs, so that, in case the same failure happens, the root cause can be directly associated.

This is even more important when different team members share the analysis effort.

Let's see how to work with this feature.

Once the Test Suite has been run from Jenkins, Cucumber reports are available. Here each failure is tagged with a hash code of the failure detail and the scope (*module.test. action*).

In the following figure we see an example of it.

---

[2] `https://reportportal.io/`

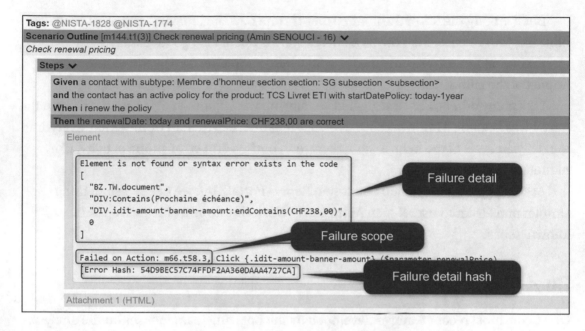

Failure details, hash, and scope in Cucumber reports

This failure can be due to a system bug, an automation bug, or it could require further analysis.

This is exactly the information we can enter in Boozang.

In the following screenshot we see how to create a Known Issue from the Boozang IDE. The Known Issues icon is available on the left panel.

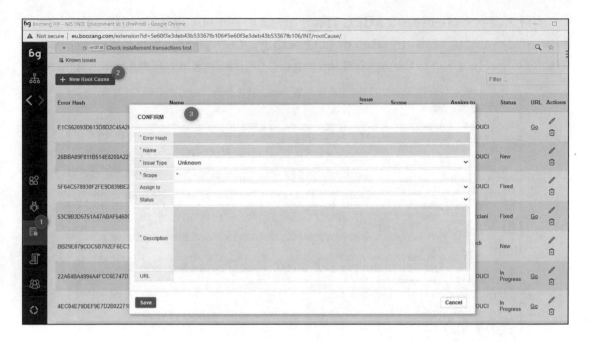

Root Cause window

Creating a Known Issue consists in taking the hash code from the failure in the Cucumber reports and adding it here. You can then select the Issue Type:

- Application bug

- Automation issue

- Not sure

- Unknown (still to be analyzed)

Then you can define its scope, that is, the impact in the automation project. This is done in terms of module.test.action id. A scope m2.t3, for example, will state that this Known Issue impacts a single Test, t3, in the module m2. If you remove the t3 and leave m2, it means that this issue impacts all the m2 module.

It's a best practice to never include the action in the scope. Why? Because the test can be modified, actions can be added, and the original action ID can change. If this happens, your scope will not match anymore, and you will have to adapt the Known Issue.

In the description you can enter the reason for this issue, once you found it.

And finally, you can enter a URL. This is useful to link your known issue to JIRA issues, for example, or to any other defect tracking system you are using. We use this link to refer either to a Bug in the Application project, or to a Task in our Automation project.

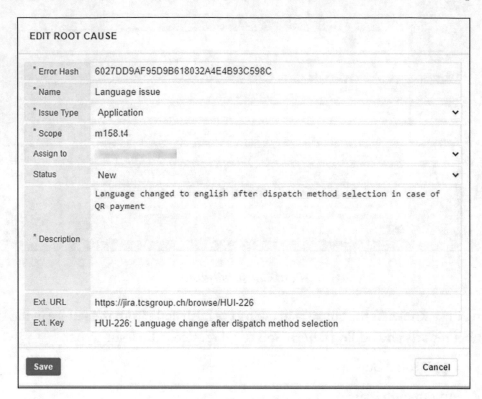

Root cause example

Once you have created the Known Issue in the Boozang database, Boozang will use it in future runs: in case it finds the same failure within the same scope, the match will be done and the failure will be associated with the Known Issue in the Root Cause Analysis report.

RCA Report

When you run Cucumber tests via Jenkins, you can use a script[3] provided by the Boozang team to create the RCA report page. In Part 3 we will go over the setup of Jenkins including how to integrate this script into your pipeline execution.

---

[3] https://github.com/ljunggren/bz-utils/blob/main/scripts/generate_summary.sh

An example of the RCA report is shown in the following figure.

RCA Report integrated in Jenkins

In the red box you have the summary with the number of Scenarios, how many failed, and how many workers were used (more on parallel runs in Chapter 15, "Jenkins and the Boozang Runner"). In the pink box you have the number of Steps with their status. The violet "Total Issues" box gives a summary on how many issues were found and their category: application issues, automation issues, unknown, and to be defined. Finally, in the green "Failed Scenario Breakdown" gives a view of how many tests failed in each category.

In the Issue Overview table you have the details that you have previously entered in Boozang for all the matched failures. And from there, via the URL, you can easily check the status of the related issue in JIRA. The example shown in the preceding screenshot was taken right after a new version was deployed in our test environment, with a new issue still to be analyzed impacting 24 test cases.

The second and third lines in the table instead refer to known issues already linked to Application bugs.

This is a very powerful tool, especially when working in a team. An issue already analyzed by one person will be available for all the future runs to all the other team members. Moreover, reporting execution results with failures is not an issue anymore, as long as you can explain that the failures are related to real application Bugs.

Another example from a later stage of the project is shown in the following picture. In there only one issue is present and it is a known one: it refers to an application Bug, about the language, with an associated JIRA ticket.

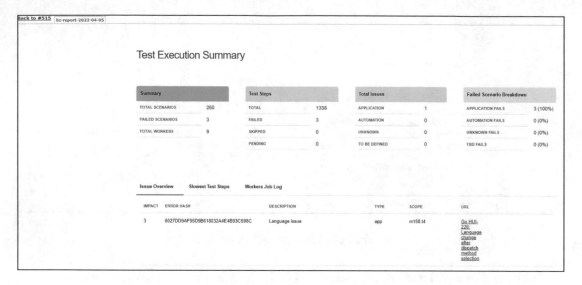

Another RCA report example

PART III

Integrations and Advanced Topics

Bring it all to the next level.

After seeing all the main elements in Part 2, it's now time to dive into more advanced topics that will bring your Boozang project to the next level.

In Chapter 12, "APIs and Mixed API/GUI Testing," we will see how to extend our GUI tests with API calls and how you can speed up your tests by transforming GUI tests into API tests.

In Chapter 13, "Gherkin and Behavior Driven Development," we introduce Gherkin and the BDD approach, which allows you to make your scenario business readable and improve your development process.

In Chapter 14, "JIRA with Boozang via XRay," we cover the integration with JIRA and XRay, a powerful toolset to manage Releases and Test management all in one place, including the automated tests with Boozang.

In Chapter 15, "Jenkins and the Boozang Runner," we explain how to integrate Boozang with Jenkins for Continuous Integration and Continuous Delivery. We also show how to parallelize your tests to reduce the execution time.

Finally, in Chapter 16, "Boozang for Teams," we see how Boozang supports a collaborative approach to Test Automation and allows you to manage the automation project as for a typical software development process, via branching and merging.

CHAPTER 12

APIs and Mixed API/GUI Testing

We come from the earth, we return to the earth, and in between we garden.

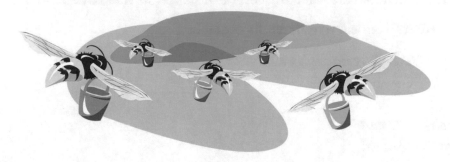

In today's world applications are highly interconnected, both with internal and external systems. Restful APIs are becoming the de-facto standard to allow this communication. This chapter explains how to test Restful APIs and create scenarios with both GUI and API actions. Boozang allows you to do API testing as well as mix API calls within your GUI tests.

© Gianni Pucciani 2023
G. Pucciani, *Boozang from the Trenches*, https://doi.org/10.1007/978-1-4842-9010-1_12

Restful APIs

REST (Representational State Transfer) is an architectural style for designing and implementing APIs. It defines a set of rules to make optimal use of an HTTP-based infrastructure and the HTTP protocol. In this chapter, we provide the main concepts to be able to implement API tests in Boozang. If you are new to REST APIs, the book from Mathias Biehl[1] is an excellent resource.

In REST APIs the "resource" is at the core. A resource is identified by a unique URI and has a representation, normally in JSON format.

REST APIs are stateless in that the server component does not store any session information among calls, allowing for high scalability.

The HTTP methods are used to access the resource provided by an API:

- **GET**: To retrieve a resource, for example:

```
GET https://domain.com/customers/1234
-> 200 Ok
{
"firstname": "John",
"lastname": "Smith"
}
```

- **POST**: To create a new resource:

```
POST https://domain.com/customers
Content-Type: application/x-www-form-encoded
firstname=John&lastname=Smith
-> 201 Created
Location: https://domain.com/customers/1234
```

- **PUT**: To create a new resource at a specific URI or updating an existing one:

```
PUT https://domain.com/customers/1234
{
"firstname": "John",
```

---

[1] Biehl, Matthias. RESTful API Design: Best Practices in API Design with REST (API-University Series Book 3). API-University Press

```
"lastname": "Smith"
}
-> 201 Created

PUT https://domain.com/customers/1234
Content-Type: application/json
{
"firstname": "John",
"lastname": "Smith-Kline"
}
-> 200 Ok
```

- **DELETE**: To delete an existing resource:

```
DELETE https://domain.com/customers/1234
-> 200 OK
```

These are by far the most used methods, but others are possible like PATCH, HEAD, and OPTIONS.

A call to a REST API returns a status code, like "200 OK" and "201 created." Status codes are standardized in IETF RFC 7231 and IETF RFC 6585, but the general rule is

- 2xx means that the request was processed successfully

- 3xx is used to redirect to another resource

- 4xx means client-side error

- 5xx means server-side error

An API can receive input via path or query parameters.

Path parameters are passed with the following format: *https://domain.com/api/resource/{parameter-value}*

E.g. *GET https://domain.com/api/person/address/*

Query parameters have the format:

https://domain.com/api/resource?parameter1=value1&parameter2=value2

E.g. GET *https://domain.com/api/person?firstName=Gianni&lastName=Pucciani*

In a REST API call, some parameters can also be passed via the HTTP Headers.

HTTP Headers are mostly used for

- Request and Response Body metadata

- Request Authorization

- Response Caching

- Response Cookies

REST APIs are designed and documented via JSON or YAML files.

The Open API Specification (now at version 3) is used and supported by many tools like swagger.[2]

With these concepts in mind, let's now dive into how to test REST APIs and how to do it with Boozang.

Why Boozang for Testing APIs?

Testing APIs can be done with several tools. The most commonly used ones are Postman[3] and SoapUI,[4] both available with free and commercial licenses. Top of the market commercial tools for Test Automation also support API testing.

For developers, there are also a lot of frameworks available for testing REST APIs, like Citrus[5] and PACT,[6] each with its own peculiarities.

No matter the tool you use, API Testing should be an integral part of any Test Automation Strategy. API tests are normally easier to implement and faster to execute compared to GUI tests, but their scope is more limited.

When testing REST APIs, it is important to have access to the API documentation, which is commonly provided by the API provider with tools like swagger.

Depending on the API, some tests might need to manage data on the server-side.

---

[2] https://swagger.io/

[3] www.postman.com/

[4] www.soapui.org/

[5] https://citrusframework.org/

[6] https://docs.pact.io/

In our project API testing was critical given the number of interconnected systems (see section "NIS Project Introduction"). All REST APIs were designed in YAML: the PAS provider documented their API with a swagger instance available online while on our side we used Stoplight[7] and the IBM API Connect platform.[8]

A lot of developers are testing their API using Postman. The problem is that reusability is compromised: these tests are sitting on each developer's workstation, and are launched manually. It is not possible to share them, reuse, and execute them frequently via Jenkins.

This is why for regression testing, we decided to switch to Boozang.[9] With Boozang, not only do we get some additional features for free (Jenkins integration, parallel execution, and root cause analysis among the main ones), but we also allow several people to collaborate on their maintenance. Another additional advantage is that these API tests can be reused in our E2E scenarios: in many cases, we decided to speed up the Given part of the Gherkin scenarios using API tests. Finally, on data management, there is a clear plus in the possibility of sharing the data among GUI and API tests.

API Tests in Boozang

In Boozang, API Tests are a specific type of Test whose action types are limited to API actions, scripted actions, and validations. GUI actions cannot be added to an API Test.

API Tests can be created inside Modules like GUI Tests.

In the following figure, we see the button for creating APIs, and in the following an existing module with API Tests from our project.

---

[7] https://stoplight.io/
[8] www.ibm.com/cloud/api-connect
[9] Since August 2021, Boozang API testing module is free of charge.

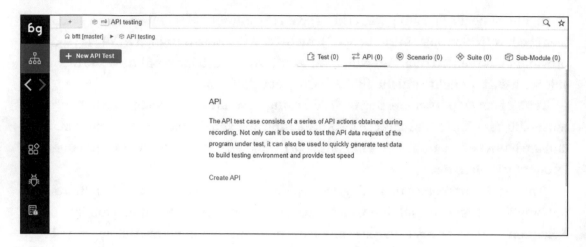

Empty module with API view

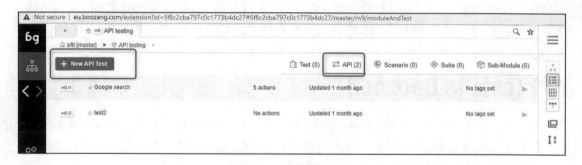

NISTA module view with existing API tests

When you create an API Test, you first have to enter its name and the API Host. The host must be defined in the Environments list in Boozang (see section "Application Environments" in Chapter 7, "Main Concepts and Entities").

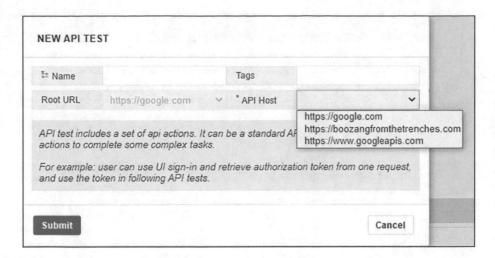

API Test creation window

For a quick demonstration we use the Google APIs. We will then see more complex applications within our project.

After you create a new API test, a default API action is present, and you can quickly start by customizing it to suit your needs.

Setting Up a Simple Test with the Google APIs

To execute a simple test with the Google books APIs, I first created an API key on the Google Cloud platform[10] and enabled the Google Books API.[11] I then entered this key in the Authentication tab of the Action setting.

---

[10] https://developers.google.com/books/docs/v1/using

[11] If you don't do this step, you will get a 403 error.

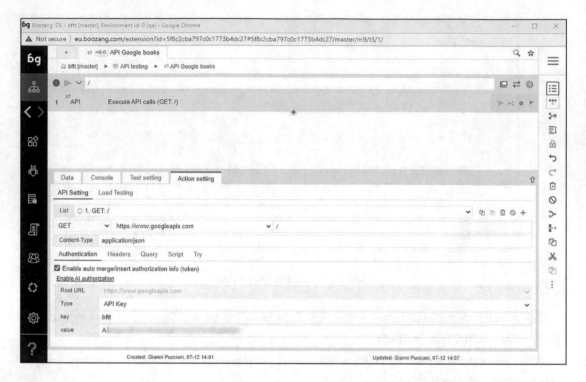

Setting the API Key

Other authentication methods are available; the most used ones are Basic Auth and Oauth2.

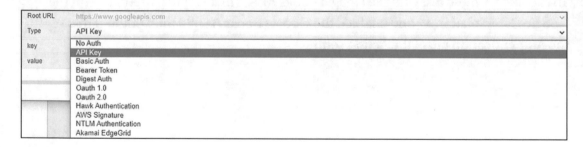

Authentication methods

To test the API call you can use, you can run the request, and check the status code returned.

The request used here searches for volumes and takes as query parameters the query terms and the API key as explained in Google Books API: working with volumes.

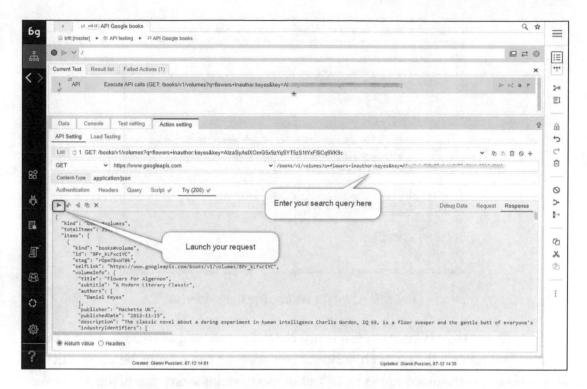

Example of a GET request to the Google Books API

The same call in curl would be

```
curl --location --request GET 'https://www.googleapis.com/books/v1/volumes?
q=flowers+inauthor:keyes&key=Axxxxxxxxx' \
--header 'Content-Type: application/json'
```

Parsing and Validating the Response

An essential part of an API Test is the script, where you can parse the response object and validate its content.

The default script is fairly simple:

```
Authentication    Headers    Query    Script    Try

 1 | (function(){
 2 |    let v = $result.responseText;
 3 |    try{
 4 |      v=JSON.parse(v);
 5 |    }catch(e){}
 6 |    //To get validation result
 7 |    let vr = $result.status > 0 && $result.status < 400;
 8 |    //Insert other validation code. Like
 9 |    //vr=vr&&v.name==' .... ';
10 |
11 |    //Insert assign variable code. Like
12 |    //$test.tmpData=v.name;
13 |
14 |    return vr;
15 | })()
```

Default script for validating the response

If we do not want to limit our test to just check for a 200 response code, but we want to parse and validate the JSON object in the response, we can modify the script. The *$result* object, with autocompletion, will allow you to validate any part of the response. In the following example, we validate that the query returns a number of results greater than 0.

```
Authentication    Headers    Query    Script ✔    Try (200) ✔

 1 | (()=>{
 2 |    if($result.status>=400){
 3 |      return false;
 4 |    }
 5 |    if($result.responseJSON.totalItems>0) {
 6 |      console.log("BZ-LOG: found items:" + $result.responseJSON.totalItems);
 7 |      return true;
 8 |    }
 9 |    else {
10 |       console.log("BZ-LOG: no items found")
11 |       return false;
12 |    }
13 | })()
```

Script that parses the result object

To close this introduction, let's take a step back and see the main items you can use in an API action.

- **Authentication**: You can set the authentication method as we saw before.

- **Headers**: Here you can set additional headers. You can use either a Key-Value Editor or the JSON Editor.

- **Body**: To define the body of the request (for POST, PUT, and PATCH). You can use the Key-Value Editor or the JSON Editor. You can refer to any data defined in your project by using the *$project*, *$module*, *$test*, and *$parameters* scopes.

- **Query**: Used to map a JSON key-value property to a query parameter. This allows you to easily work with URLs containing lots of query parameters.

- **Script**: This section is where you can define your javascript code to parse and validate the response. A predefined script is available to start your response validation.

Server Side Mock with JSON Server

The JSON Server[12] is a handy tool that allows you to set up a mock server and test your APIs in a few seconds.

You can install the JSON Server with npm (Node Package Manager): "*npm install -g json-server.*"

Once installed, you can insert some data into the server by adding JSON objects into the db.json file.

You can then start the server with "*json-server --watch db.json.*" The server listens on the default port 3000 at localhost.

More information on the JSON Server is available here: `www.npmjs.com/package/json-server`.

---

[12]`www.npmjs.com/package/json-server`

JSON Server ○ Node.js CI `passing`

Get a full fake REST API with **zero coding** in **less than 30 seconds** (seriously)

Created with <3 for front-end developers who need a quick back-end for prototyping and mocking.

- Egghead.io free video tutorial - Creating demo APIs with json-server
- JSONPlaceholder - Live running version
- **My JSON Server** - no installation required, use your own data

See also:

- 🐶 husky - Git hooks made easy
- 🦉 lowdb - local JSON database
- ✅ xv - a beautifully simple and capable test runner

JSON Server Readme on GitHub

API Tests from the Trenches

In our project, we used API Test with two main use cases:

- Testing APIs during the Sprint deliveries
- Using APIs to create the context for a scenario with GUI validations

  Let's see these use cases with some practical examples and tips.

API Test Examples

The example in the picture below is an API call used during an E2E Scenario for generating a payment slip. The PCAS application provides the endpoint, which accepts a proposal number passed to the test via a parameter.

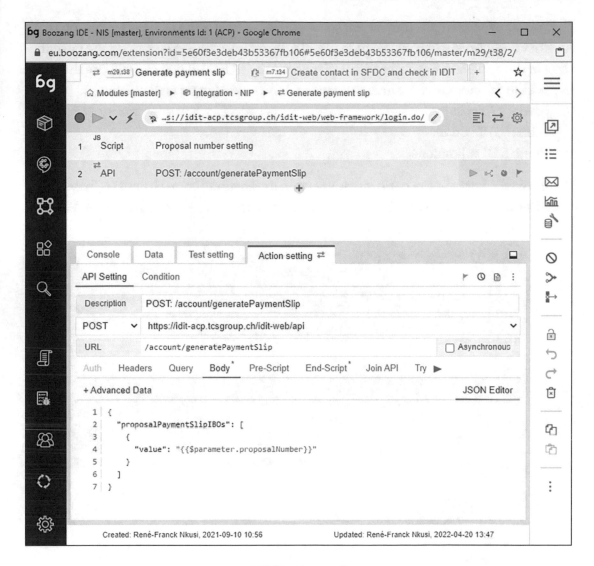

API Test example

Mixed API/GUI Scenarios

The possibility of mixing API and GUI actions is a real plus.

You can, for example, implement some scenarios before the GUI part is complete. Another use case is when you want to speed up your Scenarios. You can set the current state in the application quicker with API than via the GUI. And you can still use the GUI to perform the steps and the final validations. In Gherkin language it means:

Given: API calls

When: GUI actions

Then: GUI validations

If we take back the Scenario already seen in the section "Loop Groups" (Chapter 9, "Exit Conditions, Conditional Flows, and Timers"), we can see two examples of API calls within a mixed API-GUI Scenario.

1	Y		Given
2	Call		a contact is created with the API
3	Call		I acquire a <product> <offer> product with <paymentMethod> options
4	Y		When
5	Call		the bill is paid using the <paymentMethod>
6	Y		Then
7	Call		the transactions created are <transactionsType>
8	Y		When
9	Call		run the job GL Export
10	Y		Then
11	Call		check the transactions sent to SAP

Example of Scenario with API and GUI actions

The first step is using an API Test to create a contact in the PCAS application directly via the API.

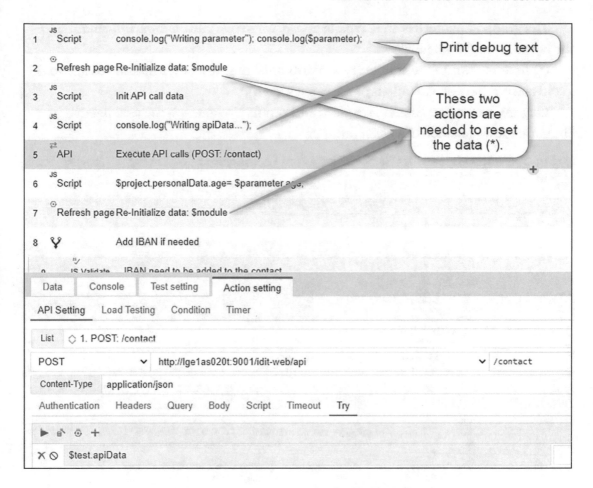

API Test to create a contact in the PAS application

Besides some actions to print debug data and refresh data, the two main actions are

- **Action 3**: Initialize the JSON body to send via the POST call. This is a
  scripted action where we prepare the JSON payload starting from a
  template stored in the $test scope and modified with parameters passed
  at runtime to this Test. In this action, we also do some necessary data
  manipulation to make sure the JSON payload is well-formatted.[13]

- **Action 5**: Execute the POST call.

---

[13] It is often necessary to transform the data coming from Gherkin, which are human readable, to
a format suitable for the API call that is optimized for system to system communication. For this
you can use all the Javascript String methods: www.w3schools.com/js/js_string_methods.asp

The group at Action 8 is an IF type of group, where we add banking information to the contact only when needed.

(*) Actions 2 and 7 are temporary workarounds: they reset the $module data and avoid clashes between iterations of the same scenario.

Let's go back to our Gherkin scenario and zoom into Action 3, the step needed to simulate the acquisition of a given product.

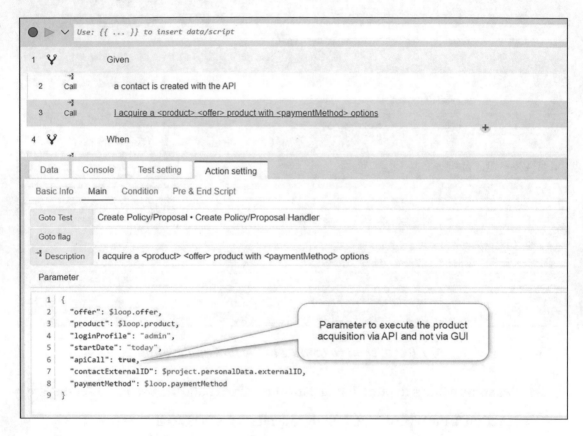

Product acquisition step

There are a few things to note here:

- The called test "Create Policy/Proposal Handler" is called passing parameters in three ways:

  1. Passing Gherkin examples data via the *$loop* object.

  2. Passing data stored at *$project* level; these are information collected from the previous step where the contact was created.

3. Passing data directly as "*apiCall = true*," to influence how the next Test will be executed.

- The called test "Create Policy/Proposal Handler" is built in such a way that it can execute product acquisition action either via the GUI (apiCall = false) or via the API ("apiCall = true"). This is necessary because the same Test is used in "Given" steps, but also in "When" steps. We use the APIs with "Given" steps, and the GUI with "When" steps.

Finally, Boozang is also able to trace API calls while manipulating the GUI. This can be an interesting use case when you do not know the APIs of the application under test in advance.

CHAPTER 13

Gherkin and Behavior Driven Development

Given a current state, When I execute an action, Then the current state will change...hopefully for the better.

This chapter introduces the reader to the Gherkin language and the practice of Behavior Driven Development (BDD), also known as Acceptance Test Driven Development (ATDD).

© Gianni Pucciani 2023
G. Pucciani, *Boozang from the Trenches*, https://doi.org/10.1007/978-1-4842-9010-1_13

Behavior Driven Development

Behavior Driven Development can be quickly and superficially defined as the evolution of TDD, Test Driven Design.

In reality it pushes the concept of TDD further including different roles of an agile team into the construction of a software solution via the definition of examples early on. These examples define how the solution should behave and are the starting point for the implementation of a new feature.

This chapter is not meant to be a thorough explanation of the BDD approach; for this the best pace to look for are the two BDD books from Seb Rose and Gáspár Nagy.[1]

The first one, Discovery, goes through the practice of collaboratively defining the features to implement with examples. Examples are key to creating the shared understanding and avoid the typical communication gaps.

The second one, Formulation, explains how to pass from the shared understanding to proper Gherkin features and scenarios. Building good Gherkin scenarios is not an exact science, but certainly something that can be learned and improved with practical experience.

Although the application of BDD by the books can be challenging to apply for certain contexts, the ideas and principles are always good to keep in mind to increase the quality and efficiency of your development process.

A key success factor for succeeding with BDD is a proper split of your scope. The more vertical is this split, the easier it will be to apply BDD. A vertical split is an organization of User Stories done to achieve an independent feature that brings value. A horizontal split instead is done according to architectural layers (GUI, backend, DB).

Another great resource for learning BDD is the book from John Ferguson Smart *BDD in Action*.[2]

Applying BDD for COTS Integration Projects

All the BDD books and online resources I came across offer examples of BDD applications for pure software development projects, or better, for a new product built from scratch.

However, many IT professionals, like me, work in enterprises where the IT department is a service for other business units (the ones who make cash-in for the company).

---

[1] https://bddbooks.com/

[2] www.manning.com/books/bdd-in-action

In this context, developing software from scratch is rare, and the common use case is the integration of Commercial Off-The-Shelf (COTS) software into an existing IT landscape. This IT landscape may include a CRM (Customer Relationship Management) system, an ERP (Enterprise Resource Planning) system to manage the Finance and HR departments, a website with possibly an e-commerce solution, and a mobile application.[3] Connecting all these applications you will probably find an API management platform.

When integrating a COTS solution in an IT landscape like that, the project scope will include some custom development and a lot of configuration and integration work. You do not build features from scratch, but mostly adapt and integrate existing features.

Another peculiarity for this context is about the organizational boundaries. Responsibilities for development, configuration, and integration might be split across and outside your organization. Hence, you will not work with a small and colocated group of people but rather several remotely distributed teams.

The project team most of the time is made of specialists, with special technological skills rather than generalists split by functional domain.

Finally, the project scope will be hard to split vertically, and small and frequent deliveries quite hard to achieve. This is true especially when the COTS solution replaces a legacy system, and maintaining two applications live might have an unacceptable price for the business.

All these elements will make the BDD adoption not impossible, but certainly more challenging compared to a small software development company that builds a product from scratch.

Gherkin Without BDD: Pros and Cons

"We are only human after all, don't put the blame on me." Indeed, using Gherkin for your automated test does not mean you are doing BDD. And many say that just using Gherkin for defining your regression tests only adds an extra complexity layer.

In my experience using Gherkin in a post-implementation phase does have some benefits.

First of all, when you include the business stakeholders in the definition process, you can better target the scenarios that have value.

---

[3] This is exactly our case, most quite common for medium and large enterprises.

Moreover, the fact of having your automated regression suite in a business readable language allows you to better share and report your automation results and onboard other stakeholders.

Certainly, the benefits of the discovery process applied before implementation has great benefits. But depending on your context, starting up with just using Gherkin could be a first step toward a more BDD-oriented approach.

Gherkin Language: Readability Above All, If Possible

Gherkin is a business readable language created as part of the Cucumber tool.[4] Besides the Formulation book, if you want to learn how to use Gherkin, you can head to Cucumber website[5] which contains the reference for all the keywords and a lot of examples.

Another good source of best practices for defining Gherkin scenarios is the blog post "BDD 101: Writing Good Gherkin" from automationpanda.com.

Here is short and good set of practices:

- One scenario, one behavior: Keep your scenarios focused on a single behavior, to validate a single rule.

- Remove any GUI noise that might keep the user's focus away from the behavior described.

- Keep a consistent language across scenarios and do not hesitate to refactor when needed.

- Always question the need to have many columns in the data tables; less is better.

- Use the comments to add description of features and scenarios.

- Don't overrate re-usability; focus on readability.

Scenario Readability

When working with Gherkin scenarios, one of the basic principles is to favor readability above all. The steps used in the scenarios must reflect your business language, and be easy to read. The objective of each scenario should be crystal clear.

---

[4] https://cucumber.io/docs/bdd/history/

[5] https://cucumber.io/docs/gherkin/

The first approach is therefore to focus on the readability of the test definition in the outline. Reading the outline one should immediately understand the objective of the scenario. This comes with a cost though, which is a less optimized steps implementation (less reusability) and more "code" to maintain.

An alternative approach is to focus on automation suite maintenance and re-usability. For this, one sacrifices a bit the readability to allow for an easier implementation and maintenance of the scenarios.

Between these two approaches, there are trade-offs to do, especially when resources and timelines are strict.

In our case we made some exceptions to the readability principles, but we consider this as a project debt. We discuss some real examples in the next section.

Some Good and Bad Examples

Let's see a few examples from our project.

Example 1

The first example comes from the "Policy numbering" feature. When policies are created, based on the product, the policy ID will change. In these scenarios we want to validate the business rules that govern the policy ID.

Scenario Outline: Proposal and policy numbering

Given A contact is created with the contact services API
And I am logged in as frontoffice in IDIT
When I create a \<offer\> for \<product\> acquisition
Then The \<offer\> number is correctly formatted
And Contains the \<productIdentifier\> of the \<product\>

Examples:

product	offer	productIdentifier
TCS Sociétariat	Proposal	101
TCS Sociétariat Camping	Proposal	102
TCS Sociétariat	Policy	101
TCS Sociétariat Camping	Policy	102

These scenarios can pose several questions:

- The Given step is used to create a contact needed as a precondition; does it really need to appear? Probably not, we decided to keep it for simplifying the steps implementation, but we went against the readability principle.

- Is the login role specification really needed? Probably not.

- The two last steps are OK, the Then does some validations on the format, and the And makes it explicit the link product-productIdentifier.

We could rewrite this scenario as follows:

Scenario Outline: Proposal and policy numbering

    Given *A new client*
    When *I create a <offer> for <product> acquisition*
    Then *The <offer> number is correctly formatted*
    And *Contains the <productIdentifier> of the <product>*
    Examples: *[...]*

Example 2

This example is part of the "Policy cancellation feature." The use case is that of a client wanting to cancel an active policy. The system should allow the cancellation based on the user profile dealing with the request, and the status of the policy should be updated.

Scenario Outline: *Policy cancellation - Immediate cancellation*

    Given *A <entityType> contact is created with the contact services API*
    And *I am logged in as backoffice*
    And *I create a retroactive policy for <product> acquisition for the contact*
    When *I cancel the policy for <product> with effective date at <effectiveDate>*
    Then *the policy is canceled successfully with effective date at <effectiveDate> and status <policyStatus>*
    And *I sign out*
    Examples:

entityType	product	effectiveDate	policyStatus
Individual	TCS Sociétariat	today	Police annulée
Individual	TCS Sociétariat Camping	today	Police annulée
Individual	TCS Livret ETI	today	Police annulée

Some issues with this scenario:

- In the first step the entity type does not change in the examples, does it need to be specified? We kept it like this to allow for different cases in the future, but it does make the scenarios harder to read. Also, the details about contact creation can be omitted.

- The second step is about the role: the backoffice role is needed to create a retro-active policy, that is, a policy with a start date in the past. One could argue that this step might be implicit in the one that follows.

- The effectiveDate and the policyStatus are constant in the examples; they should not appear as parameters.

- The final step is needed to make sure we are properly logged out from the application: it does not really add any value in terms of readability; on the contrary it creates unwanted noise.

We could then rewrite this scenario as follows:

Scenario Outline: *Policy cancellation - Immediate cancellation*
      Given *An existing contact with entityType <entityType>*
      And *A retroactive policy for <product>*
      When *I cancel the policy with immediate effect*
      Then *The policy is canceled successfully*
      And *The policy status is "annulèe"*
      Examples:

```
| entityType    | product                 |
| Individual    | TCS Sociétariat         |
| Individual    | TCS Sociétariat Camping |
| Individual    | TCS Livret ETI          |
```

Example 3

This example is part of the "Endorsement management" feature. An endorsement is a modification of the policy with an impact on the premium. In some cases a refund should be performed, also based on the user's profile. In this example we see the type of endorsement that is done on the policy when the policy holder changes.

Scenario Outline: *Change policy holder*

 Given *A contact of age <oldContactAge>*

 And *The contact has an active TCS Membership policy*

 When *I change the policy holder with a contact of age <newContactAge>*

 Then *I am <allowedOrNot> to perform a refund*

 Examples:

oldContactAge	newContactAge	profile	allowedOrNot
20	40	frontoffice	not allowed
40	20	frontoffice	allowed
20	40	backoffice	not allowed
40	20	backoffice	true

This last example is definitely more readable, and each parameter contributes to validate the business rule.

CHAPTER 14

JIRA with Boozang via XRay

Great time ahead for those three guys.

This chapter shows how to effectively manage releases via JIRA, XRAy, and Boozang to have a complete quality view on releases when using both manual and automated tests.

G. Pucciani, *Boozang from the Trenches*, https://doi.org/10.1007/978-1-4842-9010-1_14

Using JIRA with XRay

JIRA is probably the most used platform for software development and release management. Originated as an issue tracker, today with its ecosystem of add-ons offers IT companies a complete solution to manage the delivery process, from requirements definition to implementation and test. It can integrate with a lot of other tools, from the same vendor (Atlassian) and not (GitLab, Jenkins).

XRay[1] is the number one JIRA add-on for Test Management. I was lucky enough to be among their first users, and I saw the tool growing and improving at a constant rate.

Today XRay offers a complete solution to manage your test activity in JIRA, both via manual and automated tests.

When you install XRay in JIRA, you get some additional issue types:

- **Test**: To hold your test definition. Tests can be linked to other issue types like Stories and Bugs. This link is named "tests" or "tested-by" in the opposite direction.

- **Test Set**: To logically group a set of Tests, they are basically containers for tests.

- **Test Execution**: To track the execution of a set of Tests. When a Test is added to a Test Execution, a Test Run is created to track the execution status of a Test within a Test Execution. A Test Run however is not an issue type in JIRA, but rather an internal XRay object.

- **Test Plan**: A higher level issue type that you can link to several Test Executions and follow up on their overall status.

- **Pre-Condition**: When you need to explicitly separate a pre-condition from one or more Tests.

A typical process flow for manual testing using these items would be something like this:

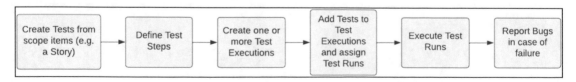

A typical test process with XRay objects

---

[1] `www.getxray.app/test-management?hsLang=en`

In our case, within the context of a project or release, wc follow these steps:

- Test Cases are defined and linked to the Stories.

- When we start a test phase, we create n Test Executions, based on the processes or functional domains to be tested. Test Executions have a start and end date.

- A Test Plan is created, and Test Executions linked to it. Each test phase or campaign has one Test Plan.

- Test Runs are dispatched to users.

- Users execute the Test Runs and report Bugs if needed.

- When Bugs are fixed, Test Runs are re-executed and their status updated.[2]

- During the whole process, a JIRA Dashboard is used to track the progress and align all the stakeholders.

A typical testing dashboard will look like this:

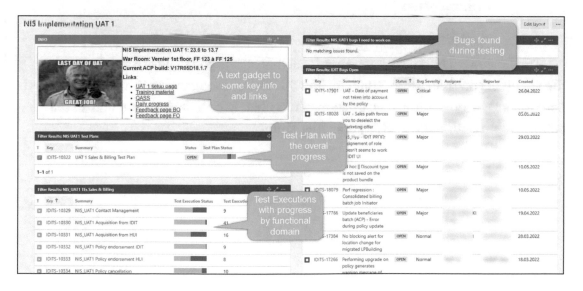

Example of a UAT dashboard we used during the project

---

[2] This is our practice. One can also create a new Test Execution whenever a Test needs to be re-run. By doing this you have clearer history of all the Test Runs.

This gives a good overview of the progress and allows us to see all the details of the test activity, who tested what, which bugs were found when, by who, what part of the scope has been tested, and what are the issues open and their priority/impact.

To set this up some key JQL functions need to be used:

- *testPlanTestExecutions()*: returns a list of Test Execution attached to a Test Plan

- *defectsCreatedDuringTestExecution()*: returns the list of defects created and linked to the Test Executions

All this and more can be found in the Xray official documentation.[3]

One of the cool features of XRay is the coverage chart. Tests can, and should be, linked to scope items like Stories. In the XRay administration screens, you can define what are the "scope" issue types, like Features, Requirements, Stories, and Bugs. These are called requirement issue types, and they allow you to:

- Create Tests from these issues

- Have an automated link set up between Bugs raised during testing, and those issues

- Create the coverage chart

The Coverage chart is a handy visual tool that allows you to have a quick view on the health of your release. In XRay you find this chart among the gadgets that you can place on a Dashboard. The construction of this chart is very flexible; you find all the configuration option on the XRay documentation.[4]

---

[3] https://docs.getxray.app/display/XRAY/About+Xray
[4] https://docs.getxray.app/display/XRAY620/Overall+Requirement+Coverage+Report

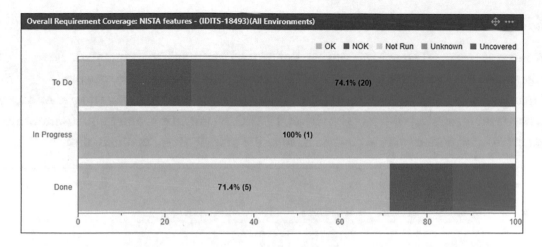

Example of a coverage chart

The above chart shows the results with the following configuration:

Coverage gadget configuration

Xray for Test Automation

When you create a Test in Xray, you can define it as "manual" or "automated." For automated tests you have two options, "Cucumber" and "Generic." We use the Cucumber way, which allows us to use Gherkin to define the test steps. The Generic type is used when working with tools like JUnit, TestNG, NUnit, xUnit, and Robot framework; for more information on this, you can head to the official XRay documentation.[5]

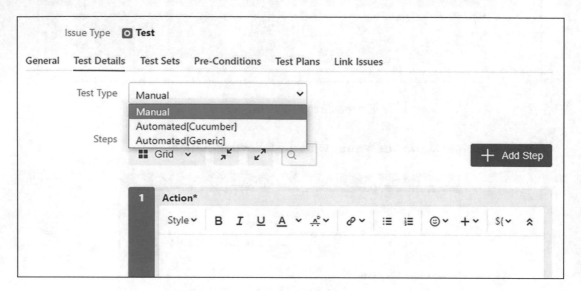

Creation of an automated test definition in XRay

---

[5] https://docs.getxray.app/display/XRAY/Using+Generic+Tests+for+Automation

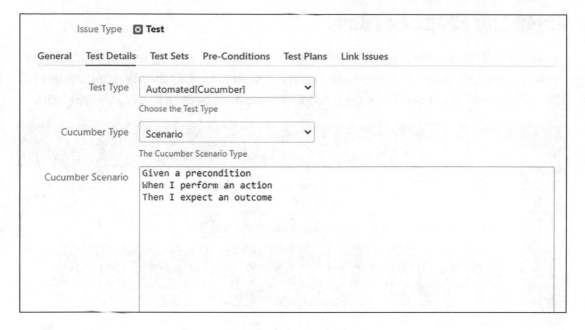

Gherkin definition

The difference between manual and automated tests is that for executing an automated test, you will use an external tool, like Boozang. This is the topic of the next section.

Once automated Tests are defined in XRay, they can be run with an external tool, and via the XRay API we can import test results.

Boozang Integration with XRay

In Boozang the connection to Xray is used to import the definition of the automated Tests. Therefore, in this approach, JIRA (XRay) will be the master for Test definition.

After automated Tests are executed via Boozang, you can also report back the results to XRay, and you will normally do this in your automation pipeline, which will be discussed in the next chapter.

Importing Features Files

Let's see the first step to set up the import process. From the Setting menu, you can go to the Integrations tab, and there you will find the option to specify the "Feature file server." This is the server that hosts the scenario definitions, in our case a JIRA-XRay endpoint.

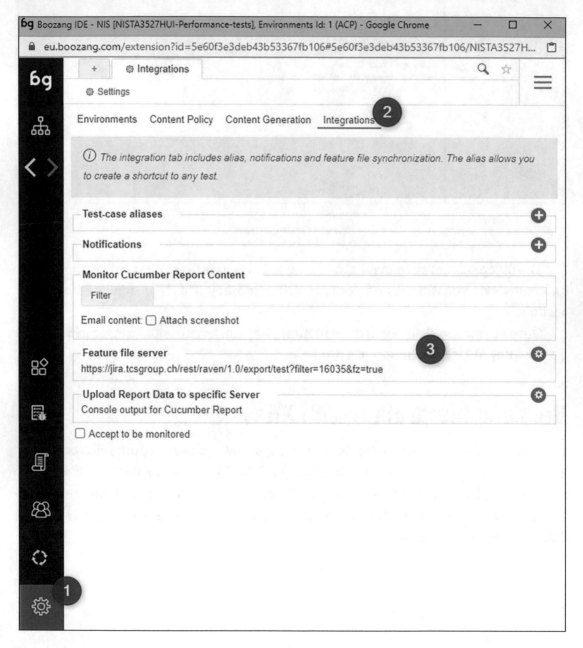

XRay integration for importing feature files into Boozang

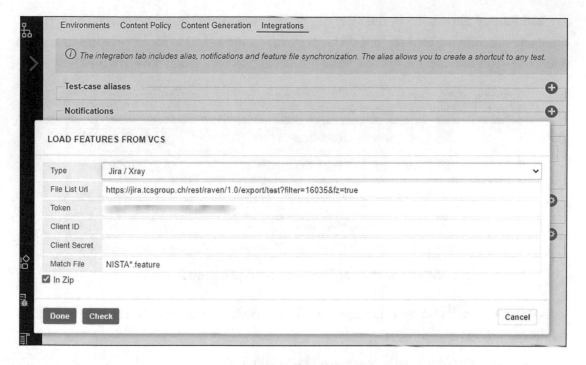

Integration setup details

In the setup dialog shown above, the token corresponds to a username-password for a system user who has the necessary access to the JIRA project.

In this integration we pass the XRay endpoint a filter that retrieves all the Tests issue type from our JIRA project whose status is not "Canceled":

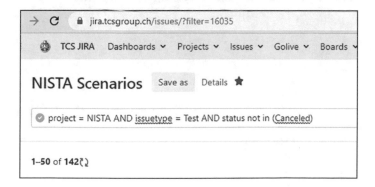

JIRA filter to export Tests

The feature file created by the XRay API will be constructed based on the results of this filter, and considering the link "tests." Our Tests in fact are linked to Features issues; therefore XRay will generate a zip file with a feature file for each feature found linked to the Tests.

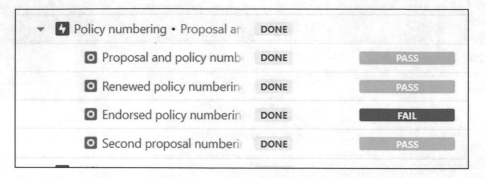

Structure view of Tests linked to a Feature in JIRA

For more details on how the export works on the XRay side, you can check the official documentation:

- `https://docs.getxray.app/display/XRAY/`
  `Export+Cucumber+Features`

- `https://docs.getxray.app/display/XRAY/Exporting+Cucumber+T`
  `ests+-+REST`

Once you setup the connection details on Boozang, the import of features can be done in the Advanced Operations button of the right side panel:

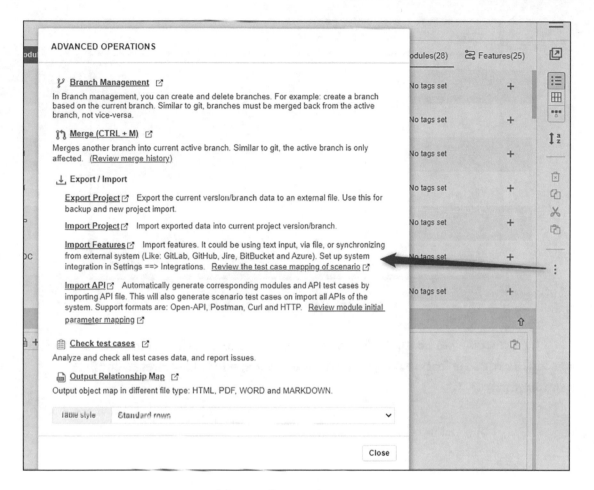

Advanced operations screen

Or you can use the shortcut "CTRL+i" (i stands for import).

In both cases you will reach the Confirmation window to select the import method: if you setup the JIRA connection, the default option is to Synch from server:

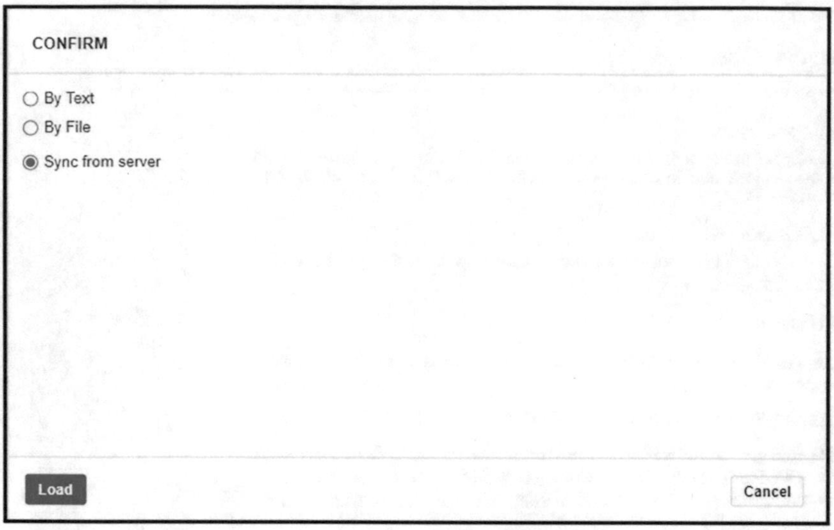

CONFIRM

○ By Text
○ By File
◉ Sync from server

Load   Cancel

Import method confirmation

Once you click on Load, the Boozang IDE will connect to JIRA, retrieve and unpack the zip file with the feature files, and then present you a list of features to confirm your import:

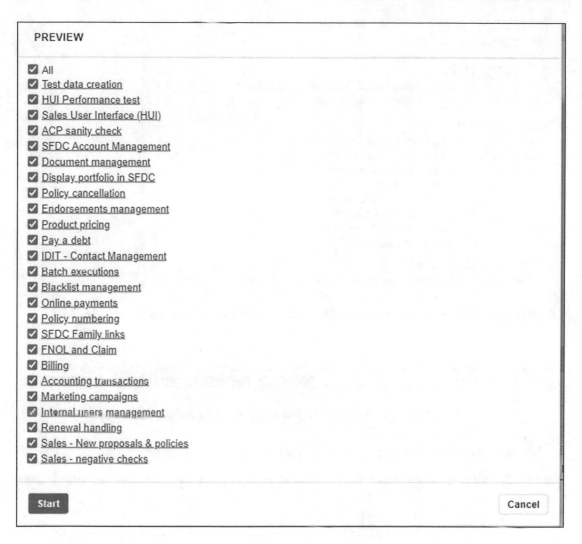

List of features ready to import

Depending on the number of features and scenarios to import, this may take a while. In our case, with 35 features and 140 scenarios, it lasts around 90 seconds for a full synchronization, and only a few seconds for minor updates. The progress view will also tell you which scenarios have been added and/or updated:

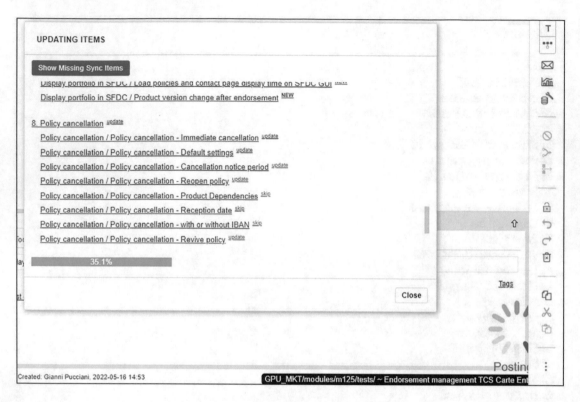

Progress window while importing features and scenarios

For new scenarios, the steps will be shown as "not implemented":

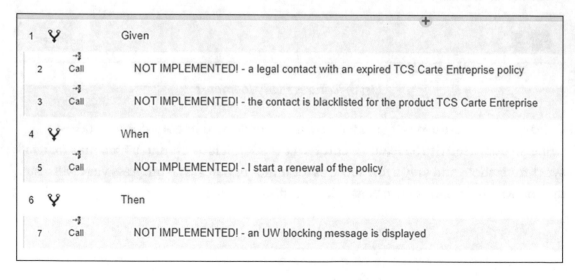

Not implemented steps definitions

Importing features files must be handled with care when working in a team because of the branching and merging process that will be described in Chapter 16, "Boozang for Teams." We decided to never import features from the master branch, but only do this in the features branches and let the merging process take care of updating the master.

Pushing Test Results Back to XRay

Once the automation suite has run, you can use the XRay API to return back results to JIRA.

The XRay team made this step easier by providing a Jenkins plugin.[6]

The plugin has three main features:

- Export Cucumber features files from Xray.

- Import Cucumber features files to Xray.

- Import your test results in any format supported by Xray.

In this section we will consider only the third feature, to import tests results into JIRA-XRay.

The other two scenarios are well documented on the XRay documentation site.[7]

When importing test results into Xray, a new Test Execution will be created, and for each Test a new TestRun will be added with the related result (PASS or FAIL).

If you use a GUI configuration in Jenkins, the plugin offers you a post build action:

---

[6] https://plugins.jenkins.io/xray-connector/

[7] https://docs.getxray.app/display/XRAY/Integration+with+Jenkins

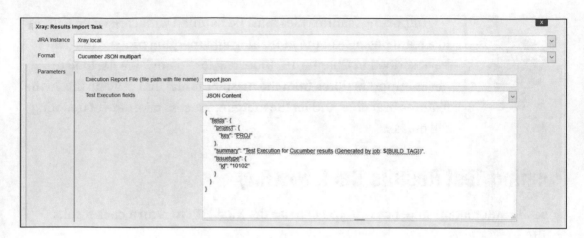

Post build action to import tests results

The JIRA instance is managed in the Jenkins administration, and in there you can select the connection details (server and token).

Concerning the format, several options are available; in case of Boozang the best option is the "Cucumber JSON multipart."

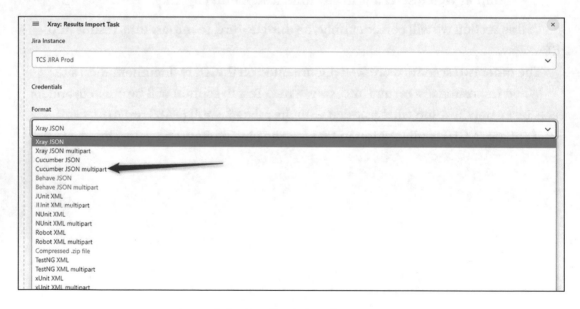

Selecting the input format

After choosing the import format, you need to specify the location of the results file:

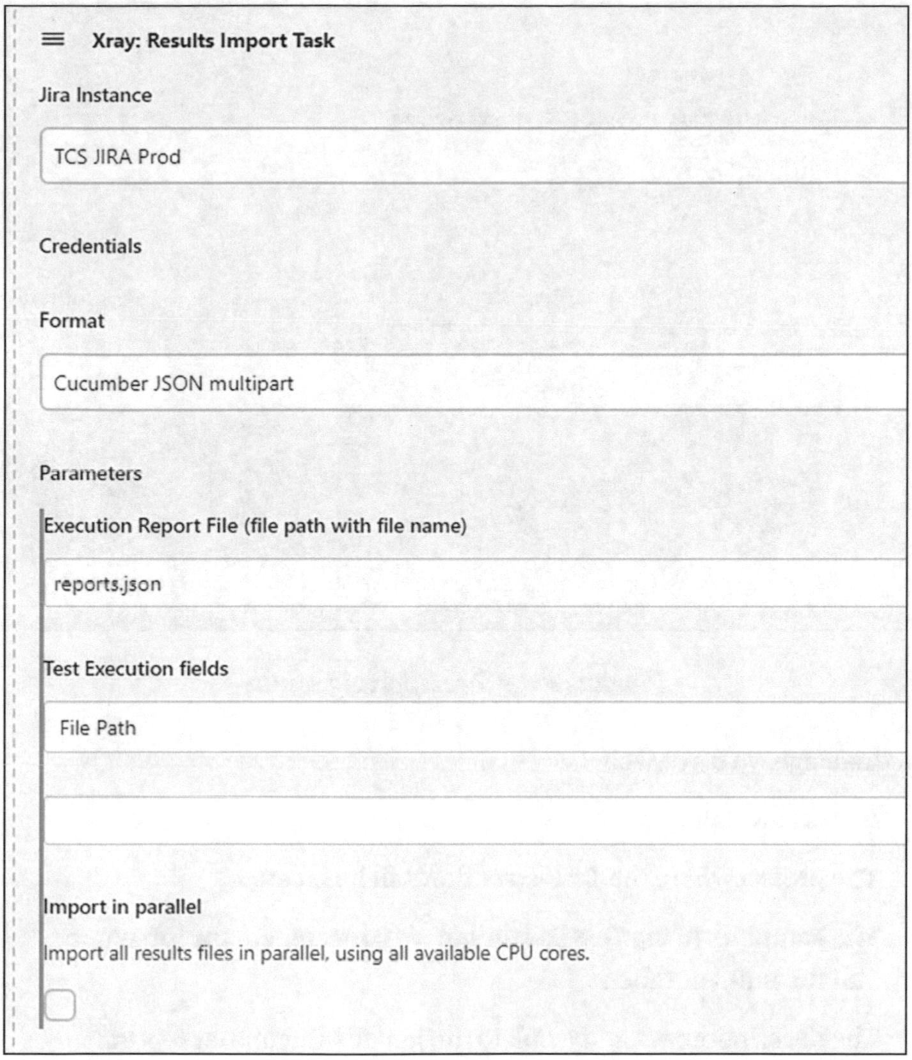

≡   Xray: Results Import Task

Jira Instance

TCS JIRA Prod

Credentials

Format

Cucumber JSON multipart

Parameters

Execution Report File (file path with file name)

reports.json

Test Execution fields

File Path

Import in parallel

Import all results files in parallel, using all available CPU cores.

Results import options

In our case, we use a declarative pipeline instead of the GUI configuration. This offers better versioning and tracking of changes.

The entire pipeline will be discussed more in details in Chapter 15, "Jenkins and the Boozang Runner." For now, we just show the stage related to the results import.

```
/*************************************************************************************************
 *  Upload cucumber results to Jira
 *************************************************************************************************/
stage('Jira: Import execution results') {
    steps {
        step([$class: 'XrayImportBuilder',
                endpointName: '/cucumber/multipart',
                importFilePath: "${reportsDir}/${cucumberReport}",
                //importFilePath: '/tmp/boozang/results.json',
                importInfo: """{
                                "fields": {
                                    "project": {
                                        "key": "IDITS"
                                    },
                                    "summary": "$JOB_NAME build $BUILD_ID",
                                    "description" : "$BUILD_URL/cucumber-html-reports/overview-features.html",
                                    "labels": ["${params.JIRALABEL}"],
                                    "versions":  [{ "name": "$jira_version"}],
                                    "customfield_10516": ["IDIT_ACP"],
                                    "issuetype": {
                                        "id": "10106"
                                    }
                                }
                }""",
                inputInfoSwitcher: 'fileContent',
                serverInstance: 'SERVER-e427f454-1c58-44d0-b99a-196bf141911b'
        ])
    }
}
```

Pipeline stage for importing results

With this stage we can specify:

- Import file path.

- The project where the Test Execution will be created.

- The summary of the Test Execution: we concatenate the job name and the build number.

- The description: we add a link to the Jenkins Cucumber reports (more on this in Chapter 15, "Jenkins and the Boozang Runner").

- A label.

- An environment and a version to specify on which version the tests run: we use the GoLive plugin to retrieve the version currently installed on the System Under Test (more on this in Chapter 15, "Jenkins and the Boozang Runner").

- The issuetype which must correspond to the issuetype ID of the Test Execution in your JIRA instance.

The full process for the XRay-Boozang integration is also described in the XRay documentation site.[8]

---

[8] https://docs.getxray.app/display/XRAY620/Integration+with+Boozang

CHAPTER 15

Jenkins and the Boozang Runner

Fly me to the moon.

This chapter shows how to use Jenkins for scheduling and reporting automated tests results in a CI/CD pipeline. We will see how Boozang can be used with other tools to provide a fully automated pipeline and also how to reduce the execution time through parallel runs.

© Gianni Pucciani 2023
G. Pucciani, *Boozang from the Trenches*, https://doi.org/10.1007/978-1-4842-9010-1_15

Continuous Delivery and the Need for Automating Acceptance Tests

About continuous integration and continuous delivery, a lot has been already said and written. My favorite resource is the book by Jez Humble and David Farley *Continuous Delivery*.[1]

The practice of continuous delivery is all about shortening the feedback loop by automating all the necessary steps to provide quality software to end users. And among these steps, there are of course the tests.

Continuous integration on the other hand is about frequently integrating the developments into a main branch, but not necessarily deploying this into production.

The main pillars of continuous delivery are

- **Configuration management**: Which includes code versioning and dependencies management

- **Continuous integration**: Which includes development practices like Extreme Programming and Test Driven Development

- **Test Strategy and Test Automation**

- **Deployment automation**

In these four domains, several constraints and maturity levels can be present in an organization.

In our project, a COTS integration type of project, some steps were possible and others not, either due to technological or organization constraints or by choice.

For example, until the 1.0 release, it was not possible to deliver frequently some functionalities or part of it. This is mainly to avoid having the business work with two systems.

The development work was done by the editor; therefore the continuous integration and code versioning was not under our control.

In terms of testing, unit testing was not under our control either, and our focus was on Acceptance Testing and automation of the regression tests.

---

[1] www.amazon.com/Continuous-Delivery-Deployment-Automation-Addison-Wesley-ebook/dp/B003YMNVC0

The deployment automation was possible: the Jenkins pipeline was provided by the editor and adapted to our environments.

Acceptance testing can be defined as the last level of testing in most cases. Automating acceptance tests is important to catch issues that other test levels don't catch.[2] Once automated, acceptance tests can be run often and early on, unlike manual tests.

Regression testing must be part of the acceptance test suite. The challenge to cover new features can be addressed by adopting a BDD approach, as explained in Chapter 13, "Gherkin and Behavior Driven Development."

When designing and implementing automated acceptance tests, the INVEST principles normally used for user stories are always handy to keep in mind:

- **I, Independent**: Each scenario should run independently of the others and without any sequential order. This will allow you to fully benefit from the parallel execution (more on this later in this chapter).

- **N, Negotiable**: They must be the result of a discussion and collaboration effort.

- **V, Valuable**: They must provide a real value to the users, that is, they must prove that the released software brings the expected benefits.

- **E, Estimable**: They must be clear enough to be able to estimate and plan, like User Stories.

- **S, Small**: Not always for E2E case, but in general they should focus on a specific goal, not many at the same time.

- **T, Testable**: Speaks for himself. ;)

In the next section we dive into the steps necessary to automate the regression tests.

---

[2] Among this you can find issue related to environment setup and/or architectural design, which will not be found by unit or integration tests.

Puppeteer and the Boozang Runner

Puppeteer[3] is a node.js library used for Web UI automation. Much like Selenium, it provides an API to control the browser, but compared to Selenium has some significant differences. First of all the age; the project was developed in 2017 (Selenium in 2004) by Google, hence focused on Chrome support (Selenium instead supports all the most common browsers). In terms of supported languages, Puppeteer is full JavaScript, while Selenium supports many different languages.

Compared to Selenium, Puppeteer is simpler to install and use. The protocol used is also different (DevTools[4] vs WebDriver[5]), providing important advantages in terms of testing capabilities.

From a goal point of view, Puppeteer's focus is not on testing, but on pure Web UI automation. It therefore lacks all those extra features that are useful for testing, like recording, but this is what Boozang does.

The Boozang runner is a node-js package[6] built on top of Puppeteer that allows you to execute Boozang tests from the command line.

Another (beta) version of the Boozang runner[7] is based on Microsoft Playwright.[8] Both versions of the runner are freely available on GitHub under the MIT license.

When you run tests through Jenkins however, you will not use the CLI runner, but rather a docker container that encapsulates the CLI and makes it easy to run tests. This is the topic of the next section.

How to Use the Docker Runner

Let's see how to run a simple test via the Docker runner.

First of all, make sure to have Docker installed on the machine where you will run the tests.

---

[3] https://github.com/puppeteer/puppeteer

[4] https://chromedevtools.github.io/devtools-protocol/

[5] www.w3.org/TR/webdriver/

[6] https://github.com/ljunggren/bz-puppeteer

[7] https://github.com/ljunggren/bz-playwright

[8] https://playwright.dev/

To execute a test, you need a "tokenized" URL, that is, the URL of the Test with your personal token (linked to your Boozang account). To get this URL, from any Test in the IDE simply open the Advanced Operations menu, select the link "Generate Tokenized URL," and input your Boozang account password. You will then be able to copy the URL.

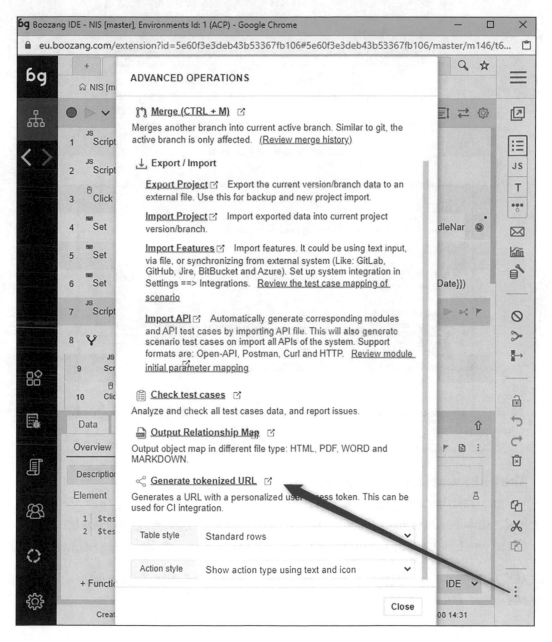

Generate tokenized URL in the Advanced Operations menu

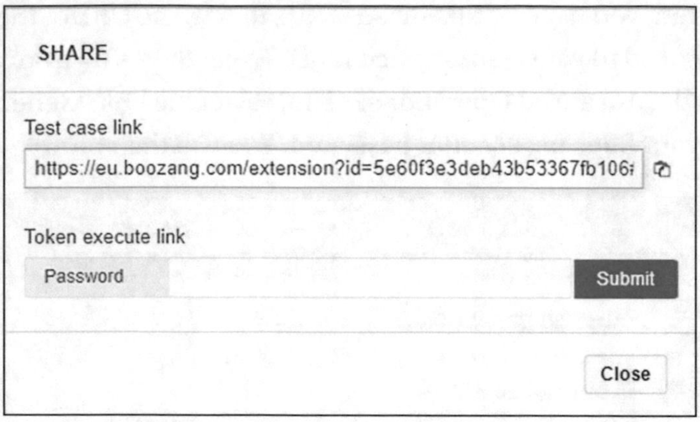

Enter password screen

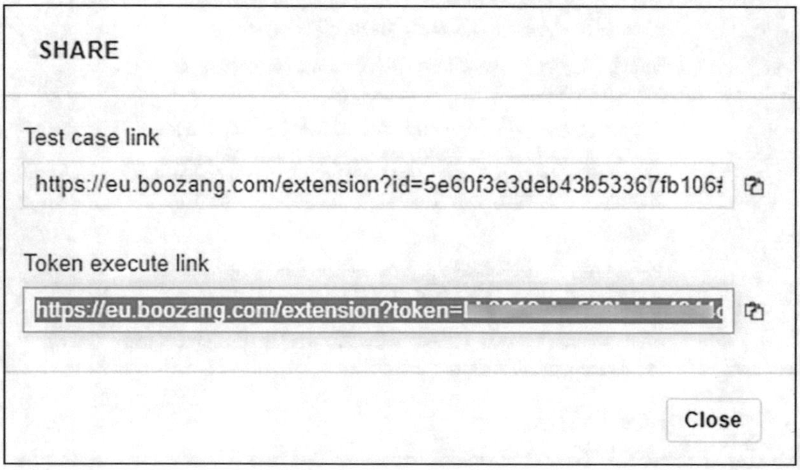

Tokenized URL to copy

The URL format is the following:

https://eu.boozang.com/extension?token=<*your personal token*>&env=<*environment ID*>#<*project ID*>/<*branch*>/<*module ID*>/<*test ID*>/run

Once you have the URL, you need to run the Docker container with a command like:

```
docker run --rm -v "$(pwd):/var/boozang/" styrman/boozang-runner
"<tokenized URL>"
```

- The -rm options are used to remove the container after run.

- The -v is used to specify the volume mapping[9] and be able to locally store the test report that will be generated.

To see all the available options of the Docker runner, you can head to the github repository page.[10]

In the previous example we used a single Test, but of course this process can be followed to execute a Test Suite that contains Tests or Scenarios. It won't be available however on Modules and Features since these two objects are mainly to group Tests and Scenarios.

Keeping Execution Time Low with Parallel Runs

Execution time of your test suite is crucial. You want your full suite, which might include hundreds or even thousands of scenarios to run easily overnight for regression testing. And you want a subset of them, critical, to run in 15 or 30 minutes so that, while implementing new tests, you can check their impact on existing tests.

Executing tests or scenarios in parallel is the main solution, combined with other good practices like using APIs to setup the initial state, and keeping the scenarios focused on a single objective.

Parallel Execution and Workers Setup

When your acceptance test suite starts growing, the execution time might soon become an issue. In this case, executing tests in parallel is your main ally.

In the NIS project we started with parallel runs early on, around the third implementation Sprint.

We initially used GNU Parallel , then used plain Jenkins pipeline, and finally moved to the new feature developed by the Boozang team, the distributed master-slave setup. In the next sections, we will go through these three options. Clearly, the latest option is the best one, and we will spend more time on it.

---

[9] https://docs.docker.com/storage/volumes/
[10] https://github.com/ljunggren/bz-docker-xvfb

Boozang Workers Concepts

The workers approach is similar to an agile team. Each **_worker_** is a team member, and each team is a **_group_**. Each worker can have a **_scope_** that is like a specialization (like BA, Developer, Tester). There is finally a **_master_** that is like a PO or the backlog itself.

The master can dispatch tests to workers, based on their scope. Normally master and workers belong to the same group.

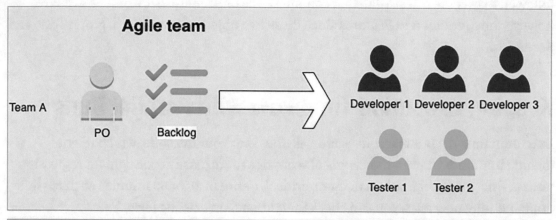

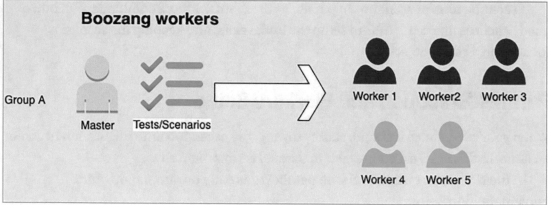

Boozang distributed execution approach

Each worker must have a specific ID, and a worker can be associated with only one group.

This organization offers a lot of flexibility for running your tests in a distributed way. We will focus mainly on parallel runs, which is just one of the possible use cases for distributed runs.

In this case all the workers have the same scope, no specialization. The master dispatches scenarios to the workers as soon as a worker is available.

But it gets even better; the parallelism is at scenario iteration level: this means that when you have Examples with Scenario Outlines, examples can be run in parallel. As far as I know, Boozang is the only Test Automation tool that offers this level of parallelism.

One interesting use case for having several groups is to reserve a group for nightly run, and another for debugging. Another one is in the case of a large organization with several automation teams; each team could have its own group of workers that can run independently of others.

Boozang Workers Setup in the Jenkins Pipeline

When using a declarative pipeline in Jenkins, there are some key steps to follow to run tests in parallel.

1. Launch n workers (the number will be limited by the resources available on your server[11]). Workers will stay idle until they receive some execution tasks.

2. Launch the master with the Test Suite you want to run. The master will dispatch the execution tasks to workers as they are available.

Launching the Workers

In order to launch the worker containers, we have two steps: creation of the worker URL and execution of the docker run command. To define the worker URL, let's see a snapshot taken from our pipeline with variables defined for each URL element.[12]

worker_url = "http://${params.BZBASEURL}/extension?token=${params.BZ TOKEN}&env=${env}&group=${group}&key=$worker_key&self=${self}#${params. BZPROJECT}/${params.BRANCH}"

---

[11] Each worker will run in a different docker container; hence the limit to check is how many containers you can run in parallel on a given server.

[12] Jenkins declarative pipeline syntax available at `www.jenkins.io/doc/book/pipeline/syntax/`

This URL is like the previous tokenized URL already seen, with the following differences:

- There is no Test or Suite ID at the end, which means the docker runner will run and listen for tasks from the master.

- There are three additional fields:

  - **Group**: An identifier to group workers (we currently use the Jenkins build number for this). This can be the counter of the loop mentioned below.

  - **Key**: An identifier unique for each worker.

  - **Self**: It can be either 1 or 0. 1 means that the worker is private to the user linked with the token specified in the URL. 0 means that the worker can be shared among different users.

Create a loop to launch the container in detached mode to allow the pipeline to continue.

```
sh "nohup docker run --name bg-worker$counter -e TZ=Europe/Paris --rm -v
\"$/var/boozang:/var/boozang/\" -v \"/var/common:/var/common/\" styrman/
boozang-runner \"$worker_url\" > ${reportsDir}/boozang-worker_${worker_
key}.log &"
```

Let's see the elements of this command:

- **nohup**: Used to detach the command from the user session.

- **name**: To name each worker container.

- **-e**: Set an environment variable for the timezone, so that timestamps in the logs are aligned with your time.

- **rm**: Already mentioned, it will remove the containers after run.

- **-v**: Set some volumes for logs and reports.

- The output of the command is redirected to a worker log file, that can be useful when debugging.

- Finally the whole command is run in detached mode.

Launching the Master

To launch the master we follow two similar steps: URL creation and docker run command.

master_URL = "http://${params.BZBASEURL}/extension?token=${params.BZTO KEN}&env=${env}&group=${group}&key=$master_key&self=${self}#${params. BZPROJECT}/${params.BRANCH}/${params.TEST_ID}/run"

This is a very similar URL to the one used for the workers, the only differences are

- The key is the one of the master, another unique ID.

- We have the information of the suite to run (TEST_ID parameter) with the "/run" to launch the execution.

sh "docker run --name bg-master -e TZ=Europe/Paris --rm -v \"/var/boozang:/ var/boozang/\" -v \"/var/common:/var/common/\" styrman/boozang-runner \"$master_URL\" > ${reportsDir}/boozang-master.log"

This is a very similar command to the previous one used to run the worker containers. The only difference is that now we do not use the `nohup` nor the `&` so that the pipeline will wait for this command to finish before passing to the following stages.

Reports and Log Files

When the pipeline is executed, you want to make sure to have all the necessary log and report files generated by Boozang. What are those files located and what do they contain?

Execution Reports

Test execution reports are stored, within the container, in /var/boozang. In this folder you will find the Cucumber JSON reports. These reports can be used in two ways:

- With the Jenkins cucumber reports plugin[13]

- By sending these reports to XRay (as mentioned in the previous chapter, section "Pushing Test Results Back to XRay")

---

[13] https://plugins.jenkins.io/cucumber-reports/

It must be noted that if you do not use the Gherkin layer, you still have access to the Boozang standard reports, but these are by default stored on the server side. If you want to download them, you need to specify the "auto-download" option in the Boozang settings.

Log Files and the Log Formatter

Each Boozang container will produce some execution logs, which will be stored as well in /var/boozang.

When running several workers, each worker will produce a log file.

As we will see later, in our Jenkins pipeline, we have a stage to aggregate the worker log files into a single one.

Log files published on Jenkins

Having an aggregated log file allows us to use the log formatter that is available from the add-on icon:

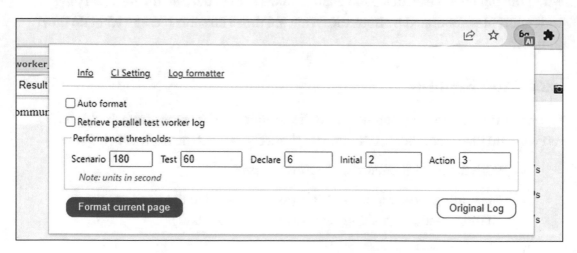

Log formatter

Using the log formatter will give you the possibility to better troubleshoot the scenarios, adding a structure, colors, and useful performance information directly from your Jenkins page:

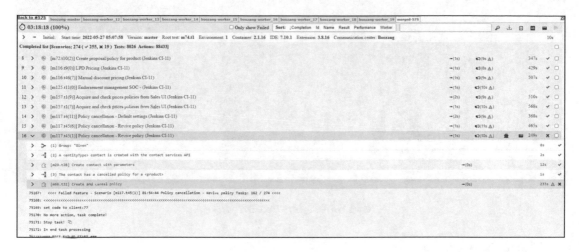

Log files formatted

Root Cause Analysis Report

The Root Cause Analysis report (see Chapter 11, "Reporting and Troubleshooting") is a special type of report that is produced by a script that you can download from GitHub at the URL:

https://raw.githubusercontent.com/ljunggren/bz-utils/main/scripts/ generate_summary.sh".

Here is the pipeline stage used to produce the RCA report:

```
/***************************************************************************************
 *  Root Cause Analysis
 ***************************************************************************************/
stage('Perform RCA') {
    steps {
        echo "Analyse root causes..."
        script {
            try {
                sh "sudo apt-get -yq install jq"
                sh "jq --version"
                sh "sudo apt-get -yq install bc"
                sh "bc --version"
                sh "curl -o ${reportsDir}/generate_summary.sh https://raw.githubusercontent.com/ljunggren/bz-utils/main/scripts/generate_summary.sh"
                echo "RCA script downloaded"
                sh "chmod +x ${reportsDir}/generate_summary.sh"
                echo "Rights adapted"
                sh "${reportsDir}/generate_summary.sh ${reportsDir}/${cucumberReport} > ${reportsDir}/rca.txt | echo 'Script executed'"
                sh "cp bz-report* ${reportsDir}"
            }
            catch (err) {
                echo "Error executing the RCA stage"
                currentBuild.result = "UNSTABLE"
            }
        }
    }
}
```

RCA report generation stage

The main steps are

- Install prerequisites packages: jq and bc

- Download the shell script, adapting the rights if needed

- Run the script giving as input the JSON reports files

- Copy the html reports produced in a report folder of later use
  and display

Publishing Reports on Jenkins and JIRA

To publish reports on Jenkins, we rely on the Cucumber reports plugin[14] and on the
HTML Publisher plugin.[15]

We have four main sections to publish for each Jenkins build:

- Cucumber reports → Cucumber report plugin

- Log files → HTML publisher

- Cucumber reports → HTML publisher

- RCA report → HTML publisher

---

[14] https://plugins.jenkins.io/cucumber-reports/
[15] https://plugins.jenkins.io/htmlpublisher/

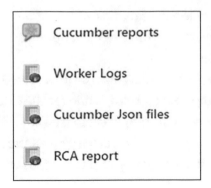

Reports sections

Here are the two stages used to publish these reports.

Cucumber Reports

The following picture shows the pipeline stage for producing the Cucumber reports.

```
/****************************************************************
 *  Collect the results with the cucumber report publisher plugin
 ****************************************************************
stage('Prepare Jenkins Cucumber reports') {
    steps {
        step([$class: 'CucumberReportPublisher',
            buildStatus: 'UNSTABLE',
            failedFeaturesNumber: 0,
            failedScenariosNumber: 0,
            failedStepsNumber: 0,
            fileExcludePattern: "${cucumberReport}",
            fileIncludePattern: "*.json",
            jsonReportDirectory: "${reportsDir}",
            pendingStepsNumber: 0,
            skippedStepsNumber: 0,
            mergeFeaturesById: true,
            mergeFeaturesWithRetest: false,
            undefinedStepsNumber: 0])
    }
}
```

Stage to publish cucumber reports

Boozang when running Gherkin scenarios will produce a JSON result file for each Scenario, and in case of Scenario Outline, for each iteration. You will then have a lot of JSON files in the report folder.

To send the execution reports to XRay, all those files need to be aggregated into a single one (more on this in the next section), while for the Cucumber report plugin we let the plugin take care of it (mergeFeatureById set to true).

The main thing to note in this stage is that we give all the reports to use (*.json) via the fileIncludePattern property, and these files will be looked for in the jsonReportDirectory.

We use the fileExcludePattern to avoid picking up a JSON file that is the aggregation of all the JSON files.

The results will then be shown as in the following picture.

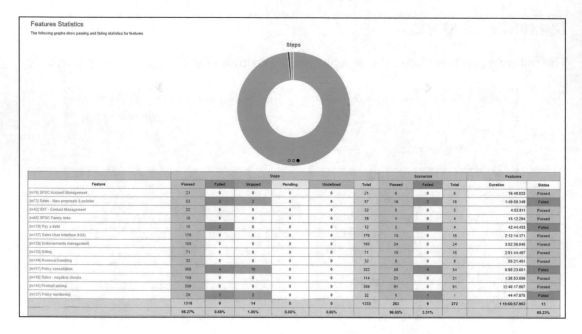

Feature	Steps						Scenarios			Features	
	Passed	Failed	Skipped	Pending	Undefined	Total	Passed	Failed	Total	Duration	Status
[m76] SFDC Account Management	21	0	0	0	0	21	6	0	6	16:48.033	Passed
[m72] Sales - New proposals & policies	53	2	2	0	0	57	16	2	18	1:49:59.349	Failed
[m42] iDIT - Contact Management	22	0	0	0	0	22	5	0	5	4:53.811	Passed
[m68] SFDC Family links	18	0	0	0	0	18	4	0	4	15:12.294	Passed
[m170] Pay a debt	10	2	0	0	0	12	2	2	4	42:44.433	Failed
[m157] Sales User Interface (iIUI)	170	0	0	0	0	170	15	0	15	2:12:14.171	Passed
[m125] Endorsements management	103	0	0	0	0	103	24	0	24	3:52:36.845	Passed
[m133] Billing	71	0	0	0	0	71	15	0	15	2:51:44.497	Passed
[m144] Renewal handling	32	0	0	0	0	32	8	0	8	55:21.451	Passed
[m117] Policy cancellation	308	4	10	0	0	322	50	4	54	6:50:23.681	Failed
[m118] Sales - negative checks	114	0	0	0	0	114	21	0	21	1:38:53.656	Passed
[m116] Product pricing	359	0	0	0	0	359	91	0	91	12:40:17.867	Passed
[m127] Policy numbering	29	1	2	0	0	32	6	1	7	44:47.875	Failed
	1310	9	14	0	0	1333	263	9	272	1:10:56:57.963	13
	98.27%	0.68%	1.05%	0.00%	0.00%		96.69%	3.31%			69.23%

Cucumber reports

These reports are interesting and quite nice for communicating the results. For troubleshooting they allow you to zoom in the failures and see the details.

HTML Reports

The following step for the HTML reports is shown. We execute this step in the post section, so that it will be produced even if some of the previous stage fails.

```
//"Publish logs and conditional Sleep SSH agent for DEBUG during 999999 seconds"
post {
    always {
        //publish worker logs
        publishHTML target : [allowMissing: false,
        alwaysLinkToLastBuild: true,
        keepAll: true,
        reportDir: "${reportsDir}",
        reportFiles: '**/*.log',
        reportName: 'Worker Logs',
        reportTitles: '']

        //publish json reports
        publishHTML target : [allowMissing: false,
        alwaysLinkToLastBuild: true,
        keepAll: true,
        reportDir: "${reportsDir}",
        reportFiles: '**/*.json',
        reportName: 'Cucumber Json files',
        reportTitles: '']

        //publish root cause report
        publishHTML target : [allowMissing: false,
        alwaysLinkToLastBuild: true,
        keepAll: true,
        reportDir: "${reportsDir}",
        reportFiles: '**/*.html',
        reportName: 'RCA report',
        reportTitles: '']

        script {
            if (params.DEBUG == true)
                sh "sleep 999999"
        }
    }
}
```

Each section creates a menu in the left bar of Jenkins with the name mentioned in the "reportName" property. The options are quite self explanatory; you need to specify the files you want to include in the page and the folder containing those files, always relative to the Jenkins workspace.

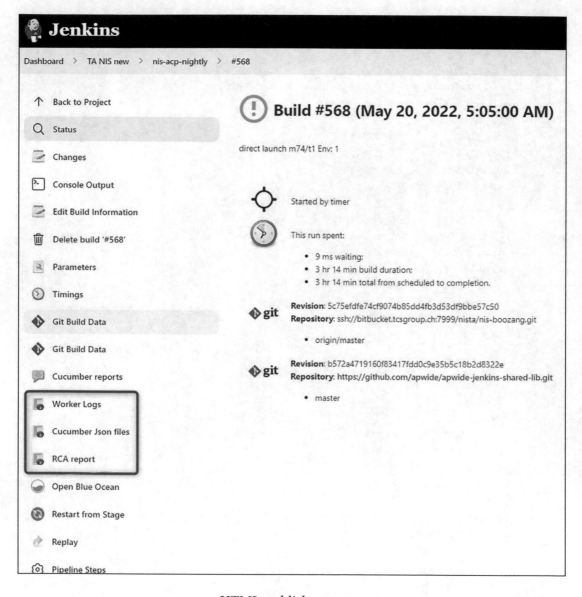

HTML publisher menus

JIRA Reports

The stage to import test results in JIRA has been already covered in Chapter 14, "JIRA with Boozang via XRay."

For simplicity, we report it again here as follows.

```
/*******************************************************************************************
 *  Upload cucumber results to Jira
 ******************************************************************************************/
stage('Jira: Import execution results') {
    steps {
        step([$class: 'XrayImportBuilder',
              endpointName: '/cucumber/multipart',
              importFilePath: "${reportsDir}/${cucumberReport}",
              importInfo: """{
                                "fields": {
                                    "project": {
                                        "key": "IDITS"
                                    },
                                    "summary": "$JOB_NAME build $BUILD_ID",
                                    "description" : "$BUILD_URL/cucumber-html-reports/overview-features.html",
                                    "labels": ["${params.JIRALABEL}"],
                                    "versions":  [{ "name": "$jira_version"}],
                                    "customfield_10516": ["IDIT_ACP"],
                                    "issuetype": {
                                        "id": "10106"
                                    }
                                }
                            }""",
              inputInfoSwitcher: 'fileContent',
              serverInstance: 'SERVER-042?F451 1c5A-44d0-b99a-196bf141911b'
        ])
    }
}
```

Complete Working Pipeline

In this section we review our pipeline which has now reached a good level of maturity and stability.

The following picture shows the main stages, and then the following sections will review the code in each stage.

The exact code was reported to help the reader and see a real working example.[16]

---

[16] This is especially useful for a pipeline code to see how different variables can be used, paying attention to escape characters.

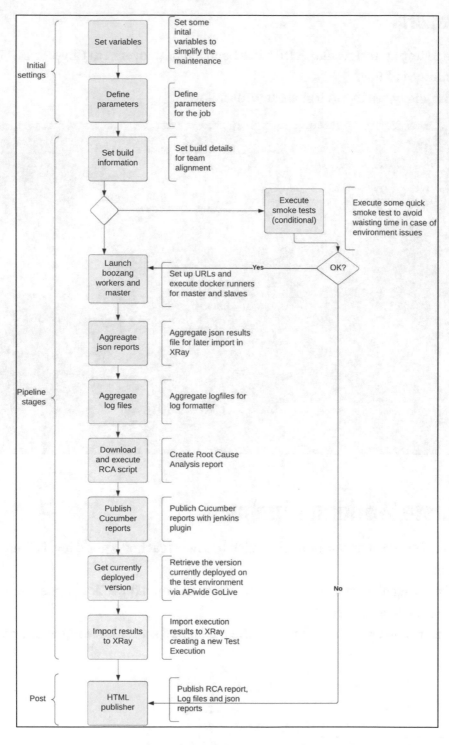

Jenkins pipeline

The first step to prepare for a parallel execution with different credentials is to set up the test users. This is done directly in the application and then aligned in Boozang as explained in the next section.

Test Users Setup

A specific constraint that we needed to consider in our project was about the test users.

To execute scenarios in parallel in our PCAS application, we needed a different user for each worker. This is to avoid conflicts among scenarios execution.

We found that 9 parallel workers were a good target to have an acceptable execution time, and therefore we created 9 test users in the application, one for each of the needed "role." Since we needed 2 roles (front-office and back-office), we created 18 test users.[17]

The credentials of these test users are stored in a data object at project level (*$project. userListFO* and *$project.userListBO*).

In the Login test, we then use function in Boozang called *getRealCoopKey()* which returns the ID of the worker:

```
$test.worker = $project.getRealCoopKey();
$util.addLogData({"worker":$test.worker});
```

Based on the role that is passed as parameter, we then select the correct credentials and make sure that each worker runs with a different user:

```
switch($parameter) {
  case "frontoffice":
    console.log("BZ-LOG: running branch front office")
    $test.username = $project.userListFO[$test.worker].username;
    console.log("BZ-LOG: username" + $test.username)
    $test.password = $project.userListFO[$test.worker].password;
    break;
  case "backoffice":
    console.log("BZ-LOG: running branch back office")
    $test.username = $project.userListBO[$test.worker].username;
    console.log("BZ-LOG: username" + $test.username)
```

---

[17] This was done with a specific Boozang test, used more as an RPA (Robotic Process Automation) scenario than for testing.

```
    $test.password = $project.userListBO[$test.worker].password;
    break;
  default:
    console.log("BZ-LOG: don't know what to do with role: " + $parameter);
}
```

Set Variables

In this section we show the variables defined for later use.

```
//use the Golive shared library
@Library('apwide-jenkins-shared-lib') _

// _____Pipeline
Parameters_____
def agent_worker_name = env.AGENT_IMAGE?env.AGENT_IMAGE:"jenkins-agent-
boozang" //Jenkins agent Image (defined in Jenkins Configuration)
def debug=env.DEBUG?env.DEBUG:false // Force this pipeline agent in sleep
loop, enabling ssh inside this current agent where command are executed

// _____ Pipeline
Variables_____
def reportsDir = "/tmp/boozang/$JOB_NAME/$BUILD_ID" // Container folder
for reports
def lge3as255pDir = "/opt/data_unsecured/jenkins/boozang/$JOB_NAME/$BUILD_
ID" // Host folder for reports
def cucumberReport = 'results.json'
def imageName = "styrman/boozang-runner:"
def token = "xxxxxxxxx"  // Masked, to replace with your own oken
def baseurl = "http://eu.boozang.com"
def project = "5e60f3e3deb43b53367fb106"
def self = 0 //id used to isolate CI executions from local ones.
def group = "$BUILD_ID" //isolate concurrent boozang jobs
def env = env.BGENVIRONMENT //the environment is defined in the job
def jira_environment
def jira_version
```

We will use these variables in the following stages.

Define Job Parameters

The following code blocks define the parameters that can be set when launching the job. This is very important for a job that you will launch manually, and much less for nightly schedules.

```
pipeline {
    agent { label agent_worker_name }
    parameters {
        booleanParam(name: 'DEBUG',
                defaultValue: 'false',
                description: 'Parameter used to activate debug on pipeline,
                This parameter will print all job environment, and end your
                job in infinite loop allowing you to ssh inside it the
                debug commands or configuration'
                )
        string (name: 'TEST_ID',
                defaultValue: 'm74/t1',
                description: 'Suite or scenario ID, format mxx/txx '
        )
        string (name: 'BRANCH',
                defaultValue: 'master',
                description: 'Branch to be used for running the tests'
        )
        booleanParam(name: 'SMOKE_TESTS',
                defaultValue: 'false',
                description: 'Check to run smoke tests before the rest'
        )
        choice(name: 'WORKERS',
                choices: ['9','8','7','6','5','4','3','2','1'],
                description: 'Select the number of workers to use'
        )
        string (name: 'JIRALABEL',
                defaultValue: 'nista-acp-nightly-full',
                description: 'Attach a specific label to the Test Execution
                in JIRA'
```

```
        )
        string (name: 'JOB_DESCRIPTION',
                defaultValue: 'direct launch',
                description: 'Description to set for the build'
        )
        string (name: 'BZBASEURL',
                defaultValue: 'eu.boozang.com',
                description: 'Boozang base URL'
        )
        string (name: 'BZTOKEN',
                defaultValue: '555203d19a3caa582ea45ac9e6470eeb5e60f3e3deb
                43b53367fb106',
                description: 'Boozang token'
        )
        string (name: 'BZPROJECT',
                defaultValue: '5e60f3e3deb43b53367fb106',
                description: 'Boozang project'
        )
        string (name: 'BZIDE_RELEASE',
                defaultValue: 'Standard',
                description: 'Boozang IDE release used to run the job'
        )
        string (name: 'CONTAINER',
                defaultValue: '2.1.16',
                description: 'Container version used by the runner'
        )
    }
```

All these parameters give us great flexibility to use this pipeline for different purposes, and also adapt to Boozang releases in case of issues or beta features.

Set Build Information

When you work in a team, you might have several jobs running in your Jenkins project. It is a good practice to edit the build description so that you can find your build later and align also the other team members.

We decided to set the build description with a default test (one can change this in the parameters) and then the ID of the test launched plus the environment ID.

```
/*************************************************************************
        *  Set some information in the job description
 *************************************************************************
        stage('Set build info') {
            steps {
                script {
                    currentBuild.description = "${params.JOB_DESCRIPTION}
                    ${params.TEST_ID} Env: ${env}"
                }
            }
        }
```

Execute Smoke Tests

This is a step that can be skipped and is used to execute some smoke tests before launching the specified suite. It is useful when the suite launched is long, and you want to avoid failing all tests for an environment-related issue. In this case, you want to fail fast without running the rest of the pipeline.

In this stage we call the Boozang runner directly without any worker setup, since this is a quick test and does not need to run in parallel.

```
/*************************************************************************
        *  Launch the simple login tests on all the applications
 *************************************************************************/
        stage('Smoke connections') {
            when { expression { params.SMOKE_TESTS } }
              steps {
                script {
                    sh "docker run --rm  -v \"${lge3as255pDir}:/var/
                    boozang/\" -v \"${lge3as255pDir}/common:/var/
                    common/\" $imageName$params.CONTAINER --file-
                    smoke \"https://${params.BZBASEURL}/
```

```
                extension?token=${params.BZTOKEN}&env=${params.
                BGENVIRONMENT}#${params.BZPROJECT}/${params.BRANCH}/
                m74/t2/run\""
            }
        }
    }
```

Launch Boozang Workers and Master

The master-slaves concept has been introduced in section "Boozang Workers Setup in the Jenkins Pipeline."

One more thing to notice in the following stage is that we want to avoid having the same worker ID for jobs running in different environments. We therefore decided to use the following setup:

QA:

- Master key 1

- Workers keys 2-9

ACP:

- Master key 11

- Workers keys 12-19

```
/************************************************************************
        *  Launch the scenario/suite with distributed workers
 ************************************************************************/
        stage('Boozang distributed run') {
            steps {
                script {
                    echo "Setting up boozang slaves..."
                    def counter = 1
                    def worker_key = counter
                    def master_key = 1
                    if (env == '1') {
                        //spread workers id across environments
                        worker_key = counter + 10
```

```
    echo "Running on ACP"
}
else {
    echo "Running on QA"
}
echo "workers: $params.WORKERS"
Integer w = params.WORKERS as Integer
sh "mkdir -p ${reportsDir}"

while (counter < w) {
    counter++
    worker_key++
    echo "worker: $counter"
    echo "Launching worker with key:" + "${worker_key}"
    if (params.BZIDE_RELEASE == "Standard") {
        worker_url = "http://${params.BZBASEURL}/
        extension?token=${params.BZTOKEN}&en
        v=${env}&group=${group}&key=$worker_
        key&self=${self}#${params.BZPROJECT}/${params.
        BRANCH}"
    } else {
        worker_url = "http://${params.BZBASEURL}/
        extension?token=${params.BZTOKEN}&en
        v=${env}&group=${group}&key=$worker_
        key&self=${self}&ide=${params.BZIDE_
        RELEASE}#${params.BZPROJECT}/${params.BRANCH}"
    }
    sh "nohup docker run --name bg-worker$counter
     -e TZ=Europe/Paris --rm -v \"${lge3as255pDir}:/
    var/boozang/\" -v \"${lge3as255pDir}/common:/
    var/common/\" ${imageName}${params.CONTAINER}
    \"$worker_url\" > ${reportsDir}/boozang-
    worker_${worker_key}.log &"

    sleep(5)
}
```

```
echo "All boozang slaves started"
echo "Launching boozang master..."
if (env == '1') {
    master_key = master_key + 10
    echo "Running on ACP"
}
if (params.BZIDE_RELEASE == "Standard") {
    master_URL = "http://${params.BZBASEURL}/
    extension?token=${params.BZTOKEN}&env=${env}&grou
    p=${group}&key=$master_key&self=${self}#${params.
    BZPROJECT}/${params.BRANCH}/${params.TEST_ID}/run"
} else {
    master_URL = "http://${params.BZBASEURL}/
    extension?token=${params.BZTOKEN}&env=${env}&group=
    ${group}&key=$master_key&self=${self}&ide=${params.
    BZIDE_RELEASE}#${params.BZPROJECT}/${params.
    BRANCH}/${params.TEST_ID}/run"
}
try {
    sh "docker run --name bg-master -e TZ=Europe/
    Paris --rm -v \"${lge3as255pDir}:/var/boozang/\"
    -v \"${lge3as255pDir}/common:/var/common/\"
    ${imageName}${params.CONTAINER} \"$master_URL\"
    >  ${reportsDir}/boozang-master.log"
    echo "Well done, no errors!"
    currentBuild.result = 'SUCCESS'
}
catch (err) {
    echo "There were functional failures in the
    executed tests: ${err}"
    currentBuild.result = 'UNSTABLE'
}
        }
    }
}
```

Aggregate JSON Reports and Log Files

As previously mentioned, the aggregation of JSON files is necessary to send a single JSON to XRay to import results into a new Test Execution. We also aggregate the log files to be able to use the handy log formatter feature (see section "Log Files and the Log Formatter").

```
/***********************************************************************
        *   json reports aggregation
***********************************************************************/
      stage('Aggregate Cucumber json results') {
          steps {
              sh "sudo chown -R jenkins:jenkins ${reportsDir} &&
              cucumber-json-merge -d \"${reportsDir}\" -o \"${reportsDir}
              /${cucumberReport}\" && echo \$?"
          }
  }

/***********************************************************************
        *   Log files aggregation    *******************************/
      stage('Aggregate Log files') {
          steps {
              echo "Aggregating Log files..."
              script {
                  try {
                      sh "cat ${reportsDir}/boozang-*.log >
                      ${reportsDir}/merged-${group}.log"
                  }
                  catch (err) {
                      echo "Error executing the Aggregate Log
                      files stage"
                      currentBuild.result = "UNSTABLE"
                  }
              }
          }
      }
  }
```

Download and Execute RCA Script

The RCA script stage was already mentioned in section "Root Cause Analysis Report." We report the stage once more as follows for convenience.

```
/************************************************************************
        *   Root Cause Analysis
************************************************************************/
        stage('Perform RCA') {
            steps {
                echo "Analyze root causes..."
                script {
                    try {
                        sh "sudo apt-get -yq install jq"
                        sh "jq --version"
                        sh "sudo apt-get -yq install bc"
                        sh "bc --version"
                        sh "curl -o ${reportsDir}/generate_summary.sh
                        https://raw.githubusercontent.com/ljunggren/bz-
                        utils/main/scripts/generate_summary.sh"
                        echo "RCA script downloaded"
                        sh "chmod +x ${reportsDir}/generate_summary.sh"
                        echo "Rights adapted"
                        sh "${reportsDir}/generate_summary.sh
                        ${reportsDir}/${cucumberReport} > ${reportsDir}/
                        rca.txt | echo 'Script executed'"
                        sh "cp bz-report* ${reportsDir}"
                    }
                    catch (err) {
                        echo "Error executing the RCA stage"
                        currentBuild.result = "UNSTABLE"
                    }
                }
            }
        }
```

Publish Cucumber Reports

The stage to publish Cucumber reports via the Cucumber Report Jenkins plugin was already mentioned in section "Cucumber Reports." We report the stage once more as follows for convenience.

```
/**************************************************************************
        *  Collect the results with the cucumber report publisher plugin
        **************************************************************************/
    stage('Prepare Jenkins Cucumber reports') {
        steps {
            step([$class: 'CucumberReportPublisher',
                    buildStatus: 'UNSTABLE',
                    failedFeaturesNumber: 0,
                    failedScenariosNumber: 0,
                    failedStepsNumber: 0,
                    fileExcludePattern: "${cucumberReport}",
                    fileIncludePattern: "*.json",
                    jsonReportDirectory: "${reportsDir}",
                    pendingStepsNumber: 0,
                    skippedStepsNumber: 0,
                    mergeFeaturesById: true,
                    mergeFeaturesWithRetest: false,
                    undefinedStepsNumber: 0])
        }
    }
```

Get Currently Deployed Version

In this stage, via the APWide GoLive plugin,[18] we retrieve the version currently deployed in the test environment, be it QA or ACP. This will be used later on when importing results into Xray.

---

[18] https://github.com/apwide/apwide-jenkins-shared-lib

```
/***************************************************************************
        *  Get the IDIT version currently deployed on ACP
        ***********************************************************/
        stage('Get deployed version') {
            environment {
                APW_JIRA_BASE_URL = 'https://jira.tcsgroup.ch/'
                APW_JIRA_CREDENTIALS_ID = 'xxxxx'
                APW_APPLICATION = 'IDIT'
                APW_CATEGORY = 'ACP'
            }
            steps {
                script {
                    jira_environment = apwGetEnvironment()
                    jira_version = jira_environment.deployment.versionName
                    echo jira_version
                }
            }
        }
    }
```

Import Results into XRay

The import of execution results into XRay via the XRay Jenkins plugin was covered already in Chapter 14, "JIRA with Boozang via XRay." We report the stage once more as follows for convenience.

```
/***************************************************************************
        *  Upload cucumber results to Jira
        ***********************************************************/
        stage('Jira: Import execution results') {
            steps {
                step([$class: 'XrayImportBuilder',
                        endpointName: '/cucumber/multipart',
                        importFilePath: "${reportsDir}/${cucumberReport}",
                        importInfo: """{
                                        "fields": {
                                            "project": {
```

```
                                                    "key": "IDITS"
                                                },
                                                "summary": "$JOB_NAME build
                                                $BUILD_ID",
                                                "description" : "$BUILD_
                                                URL/cucumber-html-reports/
                                                overview-features.html",
                                                "labels": ["${params.
                                                JIRALABEL}"],
                                                "versions":  [{ "name":
                                                "$jira_version"}],
                                                "customfield_10516":
                                                ["IDIT_ACP"],
                                                "issuetype": {
                                                    "id": "10106"
                                                }
                                            }
                        }""",
                        inputInfoSwitcher: 'fileContent',
                        serverInstance: 'SERVER e427f454-1c58-44d0-
                        b99a-196bf141911b'
            ])
        }
    }
}
```

HTML Publisher

This stage was already shown in section "HTML Reports." We report it once more as
follows for convenience.

```
post {
        always {
            //publish worker logs
            publishHTML target : [allowMissing: false,
            alwaysLinkToLastBuild: true,
```

```
            keepAll: true,
            reportDir: "${reportsDir}",
            reportFiles: '**/*.log',
            reportName: 'Worker Logs',
            reportTitles: '']

            //publish json reports
            publishHTML target : [allowMissing: false,
            alwaysLinkToLastBuild: true,
            keepAll: true,
            reportDir: "${reportsDir}",
            reportFiles: '**/*.json',
            reportName: 'Cucumber Json files',
            reportTitles: '']

            //publish root cause report
            publishHTML target : [allowMissing: false,
            alwaysLinkToLastBuild: true,
            keepAll: true,
            reportDir: "${reportsDir}",
            reportFiles: '**/*.html',
            reportName: 'RCA report',
            reportTitles: '']

            script {
                if (params.DEBUG == true)
                    sh "sleep 999999"
            }
        }
    }
} //Pipeline end :)
```

This concludes the pipeline code and this chapter.

This working example is specific to our environment. However, I believe it can help a lot of readers to get ideas and solve problems.

Docker in Docker Setup

In our Jenkins setup, we have a dedicated linux host on a virtual machine, with a docker engine running on it. Jobs run on this slave but with a docker agent created on the fly,[19] and destroyed when the build is finished. The image is an Ubuntu image with a few more packages installed, hence a dedicated boozang-image.

In the dockerized Jenkins boozang-agent, we then execute the pipeline, which then launches the actual boozang master and workers.

In this "docker in docker" setup, a correct setup of the volumes is critical. The following picture summarizes the setup.

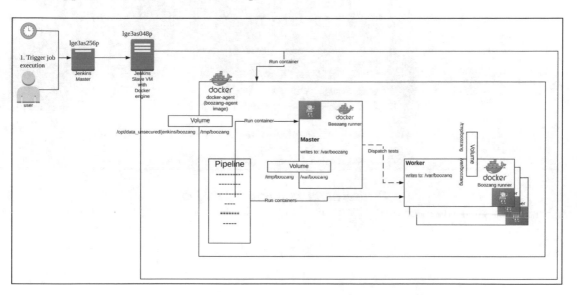

Jenkins Docker in Docker setup

The Boozang runner containers store report files in /var/boozang. We mapped this folder to /tmp/boozang on the Jenkins boozang-agent. In order to save those reports permanently, we then map the /tmp/boozang folder to a local folder on the physical host, where enough space is available.

It is worth mentioning that during remote executions via Jenkins, the currently active workers are visible in the UI. The following two screenshots have been taken at two different times during the execution of a scenario outline.

---

[19] This setup uses the docker plugin `https://plugins.jenkins.io/docker-plugin/`

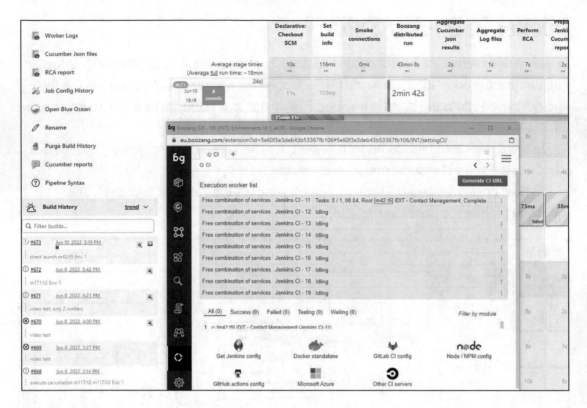

CI view at the beginning of the job

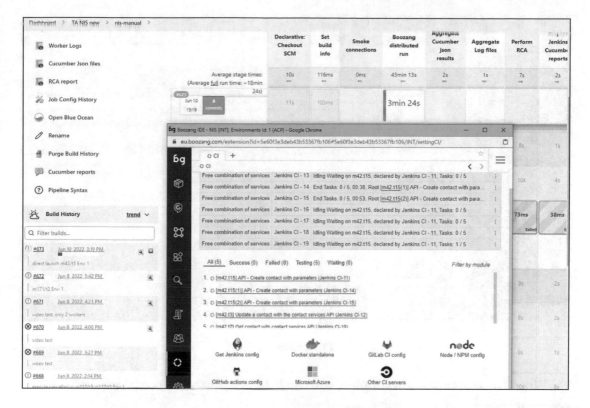

CI view during workers execution

While setting up your Jenkins pipeline, you might need to check directly on the containers what is happening. Especially to make sure that volumes are correctly mapped and that access permissions are correctly set.

If you are not too familiar with the Docker CLI, a tool like Portainer[20] can help. Without going into too much detail, Portainers allow you to see the images available, volumes and networks, and especially the running containers.

---

[20] www.portainer.io/

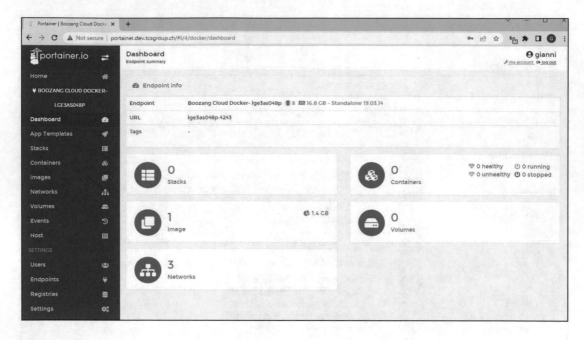

Portainer UI

When the containers are running, you can list them, enter the container shell, and see what is going on in case of issues.

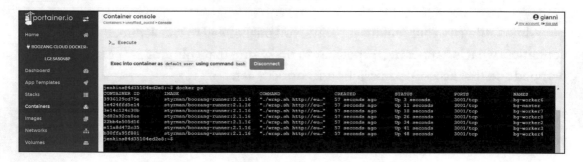

Boozang workers view in Portainer

CHAPTER 16

Boozang for Teams

In my house I am the boss, my wife is just the decision maker.

Working with a team increases productivity but brings new challenges.

This chapter covers all the Boozang features for collaborative work, but also some specific details on how to effectively collaborate in a Test Automation project.

© Gianni Pucciani 2023

G. Pucciani, *Boozang from the Trenches*, https://doi.org/10.1007/978-1-4842-9010-1_16

Team Collaboration

Boozang provides many features to make it well suited for team collaboration. Locking and especially branching provides all the necessary flexibility for concurrent work.

Besides Boozang features, keep in mind other collaboration and information sharing options.

In our project, we keep in Confluence some team rules like naming conventions, how-to articles, and other reference documentation. Besides this, we use a Slack[1] channel for the team, where we share quick and throwable information like temporary issues on the test environments or 1:1 conversations.

Gianni 10:14 AM
Hello, for the missing cucumber report on QA sequential job I created an impediment and ticket:
https://boozang.freshdesk.com/support/tickets/184

Gianni 11:13 AM
FYI I have added to the master branch directly some SAP authorization steps and environment data

A sample of Slack communication

Besides this we also practiced demo sessions on tasks done. The person who finishes a task (new scenarios, refactoring, CI work), before merging his work on the integration branch (see section "Working with Branches"), presents the work to the other team members and collects feedback. These periodic thirty minutes of screen sharing are very precious to catch issues, spot improvement opportunities, train team members, and share knowledge.

Explicit Lock

The explicit lock is the simplest way to avoid issues when working in a group without using the branching feature.

In this case, when you work on a Test, you can lock it to prevent other people from working on the same Test.

---

[1] https://slack.com/

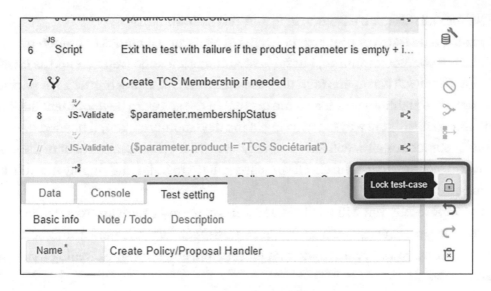

Lock test case button

Changes are shown in real times, so conflicts are quite unlikely to happen.

However, the explicit lock is just a first support for concurrent work. Whenever you scale up your team, you might want to consider creating branches, which is the topic of the next section.

Concurrent Development and Safe Refactoring with Branches

The explicit lock works fine as long as you do not have many tests and rarely work at the same time on the same items. A better way to work for a team is via version control, working locally on your own version and then publishing your changes and resolving possible conflicts.

This is a topic that is well known in software development, where version control systems (VCS) have been around since the 1970s.

Since 2005, when Linus Torvalds created it to manage the development of the Linux Kernel, GIT has been used with success by many small and large, local and distributed teams. We can say that GIT is today the standard de facto for version control, and it is a fundamental piece of a CI/CD pipeline.

If you are new to GIT, start from the official documentation (`https://git-scm.com/`) and then choose your favorite way of learning; resources on this topic are plenty. To understand the rest of this chapter, you should be familiar at least with the concepts of branching, merging, and conflict resolution.

What has all this to do with Boozang and Test Automation?

Boozang uses much of the same concepts as GIT when it comes to branching, merging, and conflict resolution, but for Test Automation code (represented as JSON data), not text files. This means for a user familiar with GIT, using branches in Boozang will be rather straightforward. It also means that in the software development life-cycle, it's possible to mirror the ways of working of the development team, if needed.

You, or somebody else, will also probably use GIT for the development of the system that you are testing. Hence the CI/CD pipeline will try to build and deploy the SUT from a GIT repository.

Most importantly you will want to use a version management approach to manage concurrent implementation of tests in Boozang. Especially while performing some refactoring tasks, you will want to do that in isolation, and continue creating new tests at the same time.

In the following sections you will see what Boozang offers in terms of version control and possible ways to use it.

Working with Branches

When you create your project in Boozang, the master branch is automatically created. All the new tests and test data are added to this branch.

The branch you are working in is shown next to the project name on top of the IDE:

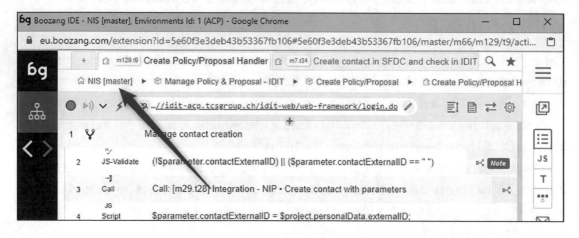

Branch display

When you click on the branch name, you can see all the currently active branches:

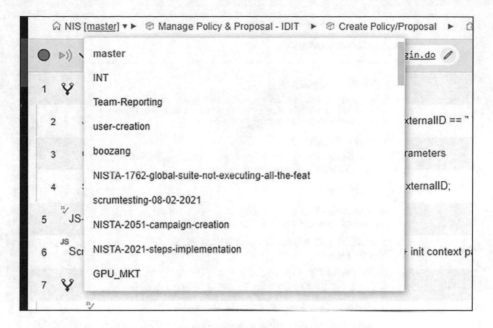

Branches display

The branch management is done via the Advanced Operations page:

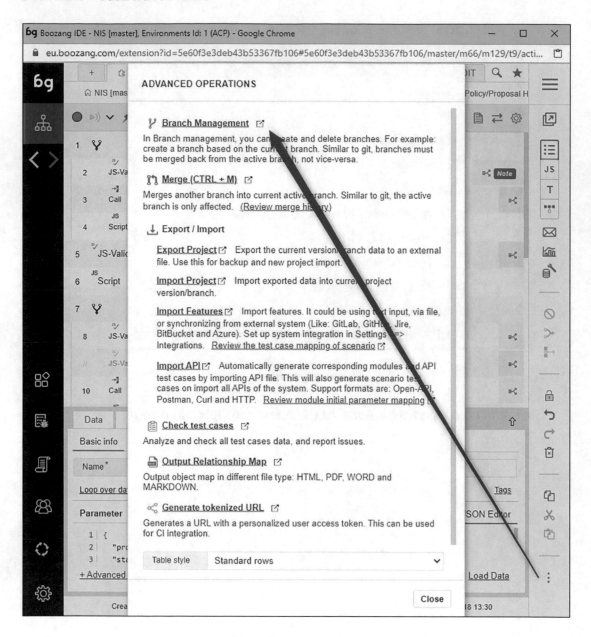

Branch management

The Branch Management option gives you the possibility to see all the branches and create new ones.

Branches details

When you create a new branch, you will have to specify the starting point (i.e., the source branch), a name and a description.

Once you create a new branch, the IDE will reload to switch on the new branch.

In this page you can also create a **milestone**. A milestone is nothing else than a backup that you can use to return to a previous state.

Using a Feature Branch Approach

The approach I suggest for concurrent work in Boozang is the classic feature branch approach.[2]

The approach you can use to follow a feature branch like approach in Boozang is the following:

1. John wants to improve an existing test case. He creates a new branch (let's call it "john-branch" for now) from the master branch and starts working on it.

---

[2] www.atlassian.com/git/tutorials/comparing-workflows/feature-branch-workflow

2. Julie wants to create a new test, but possibly interacting with existing tests that John is refactoring. Julie also creates her own branch ("julie-branch") starting from the master branch.

3. John has finished his refactoring; all the tests are passing on his branch. Julie has not finished yet. John goes on the master branch and merges the content of john-branch into the master branch. No conflicts are expected since nobody updated the master branch in the meantime. John notifies Julie that the refactoring is ready on the master branch.

4. Julie, from her branch, merges the content of the master branch into her branch. Here conflicts might happen if Julie and John modified the same item (test action or data). Julie can now resolve the conflicts (accept John changes or not).

5. Once conflicts are resolved, the new tests that Julie developed are now working together with the refactoring done by John, and all the existing tests are still working as expected. Julie can now safely go onto the master branch and merge the content of her branch into the master one.

Following this workflow allows people to safely work in parallel and keep the master branch clean and working as it should.

Branch Naming Convention

Here is the naming convention we used in our project, which is the standard when creating branches from JIRA and BitBucket:

<ISSUE-TYPE>/<NISTA-XXX>-<TITLE>

- **ISSUE-TYPE**: possible values:

  - **feature** for new developments.

  - **hotfix**: to fix the regression

- **XXX**: is the number of JIRA ticket associated with the work. Exp: **NISTA-123**

- **TITLE**: is the summary of the JIRA ticket of the auto test to implement

Examples:

- *feature/NISTA-123-endorsement-refactoring*

- *feature/NISTA-456-create-proposal*

- *hotfix/NISTA-789-fix-date*

Adding a Develop Branch

In many git workflows and in one of the most famous called Git-Flow (cite `https://nvie.com/posts/a-successful-git-branching-model/`), a new branch called "develop" is introduced.

The purpose of this branch is to add a quality gate between feature branches and the master.

In Test Automation, and with Boozang, this makes perfect sense since some time, the local execution might give different results than an execution within your CI tool. It is therefore desirable to integrate feature branches into the develop one, let your CI run on develop successfully, and only after that merge the content of the develop branch on the master one.

In this setup, the master branch will run your "official" or "production" tests via a "production" CI job. This job, when failing, should raise a big alarm. You will not want to have false positives in here.[3]

The develop branch instead will run all the finished work, and should have his own CI job. Failures on this job are tolerated, but must be fixed quickly.

Jenkins Setup

To complete the picture about the concurrent development workflow, here are the Jenkins jobs we use for executing our tests.

- **Master:** This is the job used to run nightly all the tests and check for regressions. This job is linked to the master branch. This job must stay as green as possible, and when read it should mean an SUT issue.

- **Develop:** This is the job used to run tests when they are ready and check if the execution from Jenkins runs as expected. This job will be launched manually with parameters because we might want to run and check just a subset of the tests. In this job we can tolerate failures, but they should be fixed with high priority.

---

[3] A false positive is a test that fails not because of a system bug but because of an error in the test.

Merging Process

The merge process in Boozang is available via the "Advance operations" menu.

It works in a pull mode, in the sense that you will have to

1. Place yourself on the target branch

2. Call the merge process to take the changes of another branch

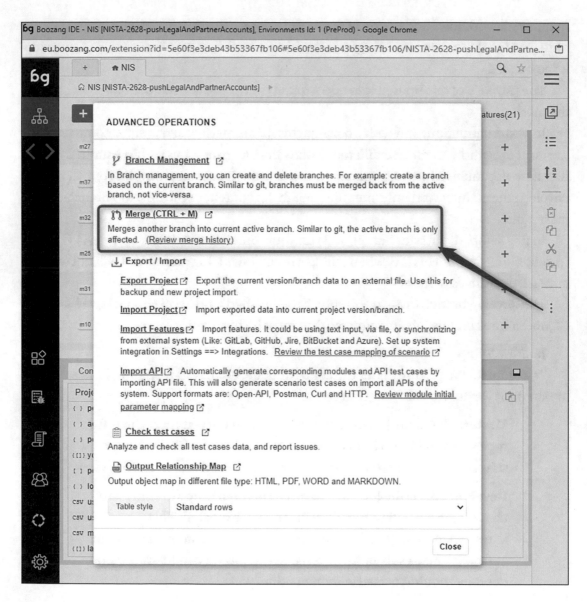

Merge process via the Advanced operations menu

To illustrate the merge process, I created a new branch, modified a test adding a note to an api action, and now trying to retrieve this change in the INT branch.

Once you select the target branch, Boozang will start analyzing the changes and will show you all the items that contain conflicts. In this simple case, no conflicts were found:

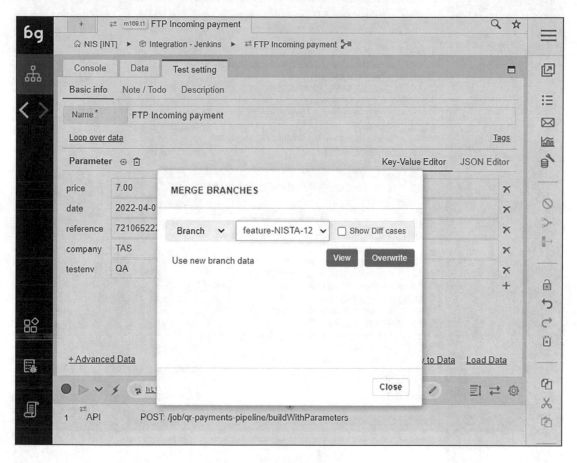

Merge process: branch selection, no conflicts

When a conflict is found, the merge window will display the test id containing the conflict up until the JSON details of what was changed.

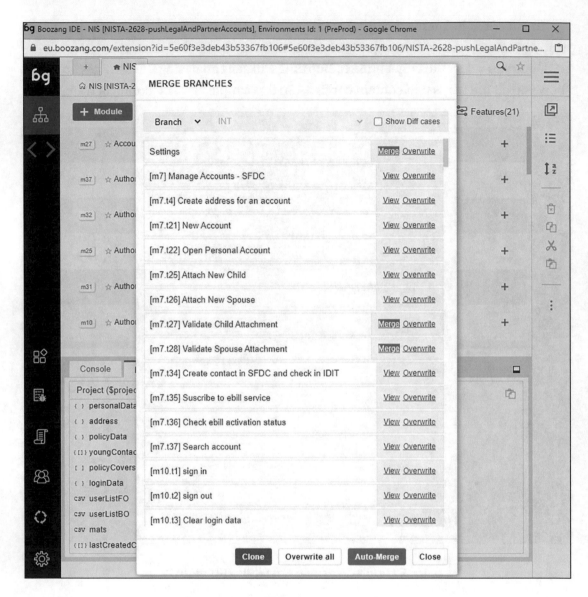

Merge process: changes

For each changed element you can see the content of the change and choose among two options:

1. **Overwrite:** The content of the target branch will overwrite the one of the current branch.

2. **Merge:** You will be prompted to select the changes you want to keep.

Tests Map

One more very useful feature that you can find in the Advanced operations menu is the Relationships map:

Relationships map

This option is available from any test or scenario in your project, and gives you the possibility to print a map of all the relations of your tests:

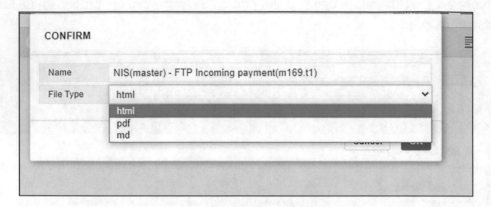

File type selection for the map

With several tests, you can check or uncheck some specific items to make the map smaller or focus on a specific item.

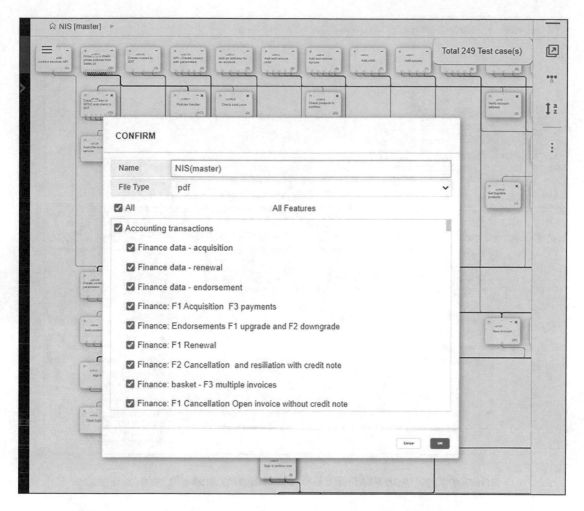

Generation of the relationships map from the root of the project

On a large project like ours, this process can take several minutes. The results will be a PDF file with a table of contents organized by module.

With the online map you can also analyze the relation between tests: by selecting a test, all the test upstream and downstream will be highlighted:

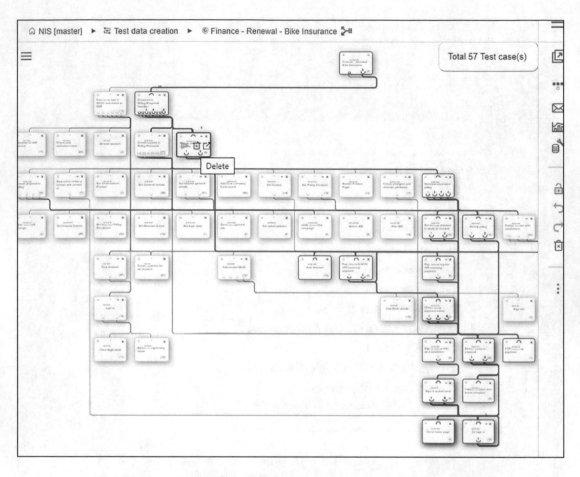

Relationships map with highlight of upstream and downstream tests

From a specific point in the tree, you can also open a popup with the details of the test:

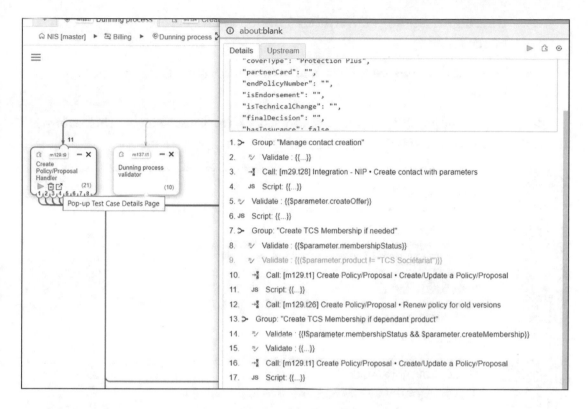

Popup Test Details

This map is very handy for two specific use cases:

- Onboarding new team members

- Finding duplications or unused items

Quality Control

When working on a large project, with a lot of automated scenarios and a group of
people collaborating, it is important to establish implementation policies and best
practices early on, but also to monitor the quality of the scenario implementation on a
constant basis.

This must be done at several levels:

- **Scenarios definitions**: The Gherkin steps should follow best
  practices (covered in Chapter 13, "Gherkin and Behavior Driven
  Development").

- **Data object naming conventions** (covered in Chapter 10, "Data Management")

- **Test size and reusability** (covered in Chapter 7, Main Concepts and Entities)

Boozang can support this activity with the "Check Test Case" feature. This feature is available in the Advanced Operations page:

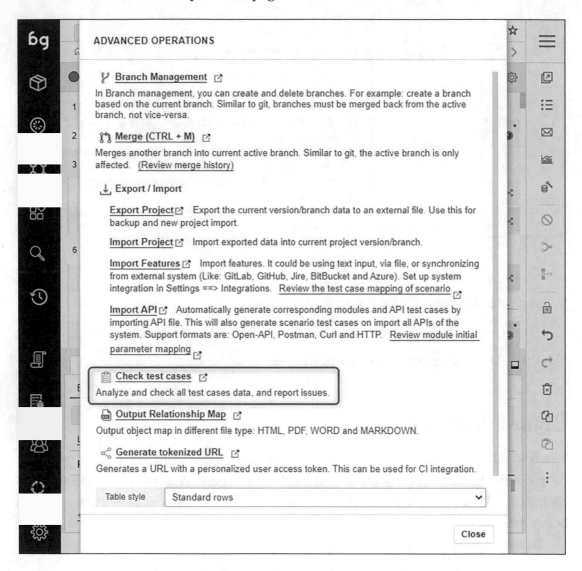

Check Test Cases option

The Check Test Case feature can be run from any object, be it a Test Case, Module, or the entire project.

There are several checks that can be done, and you can filter the view to see each of them separately. Some of them are shown as errors, others as warnings.

The issue list is shown in a summary tab and as well in a more detailed one (Issue list) where you can filter issues by type of check.

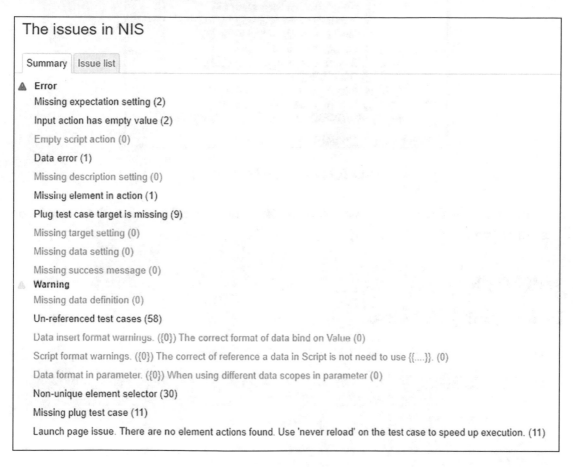

Issues summary

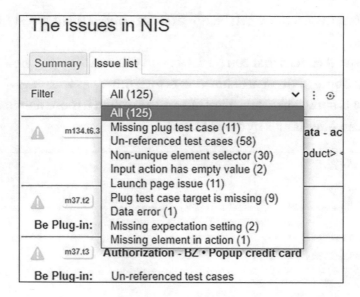

Issue list tab with all the checks

For all the checks, when you click on one issue, the IDE will switch to the concerned Test and action.

Warnings

Missing Plug Test Case

This check allows you to see the not yet implemented steps.

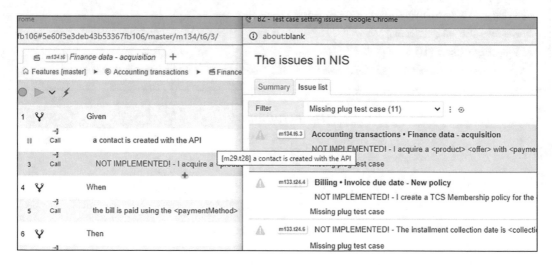

Not implemented step

Un-referenced Test Cases

This check tells you which Tests are not called by any upstream test. This is especially useful when using Gherkin scenarios: in this case no tests should appear as unreferenced. When using Gherkin scenario all Tests should be linked, directly or via an up-stream Test, to a Scenario step.

Non-unique Element Selectors

Another useful check is the "non-unique element selector" that can lead to flaky tests:

Non-unique selectors

Empty Input Values

Another important check that can lead to false positives is the "Missing expectation setting." It is shown as a warning because in some cases, like to clear a password field, this might be done with a reason.

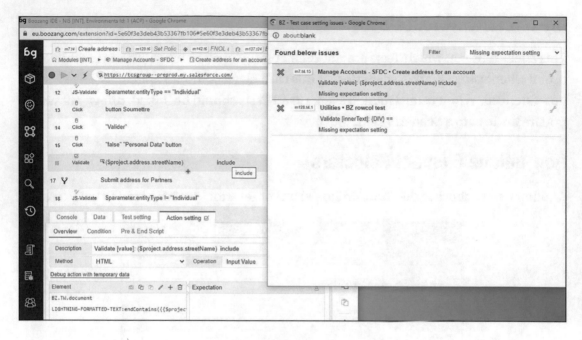

Empty input values

Launch Page Issue

As already mentioned in Chapter 7, "Main Concepts and Entities," when discussing the environment URLs, a common issue is not to set the correct launch page option.

Even if it is a warning, you should watch these issues carefully as they can impact the execution time of your Test Suite.

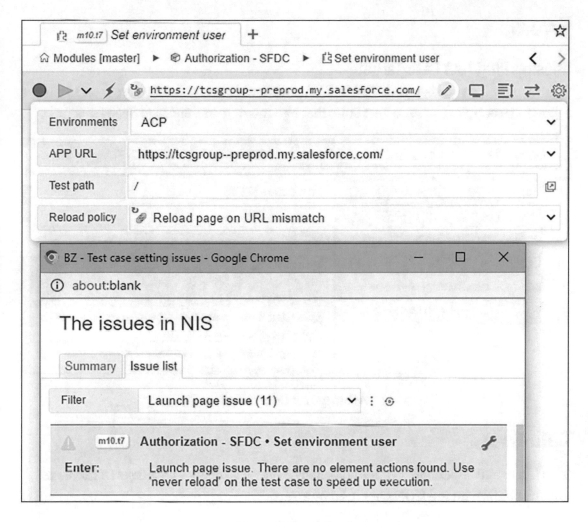

Launch page check

Errors

Missing Plug Test Case Target

This error helps you keep your Test Suite clean showing you invalid references. In the following example, you see a Test Suite that had missing references to Scenarios.

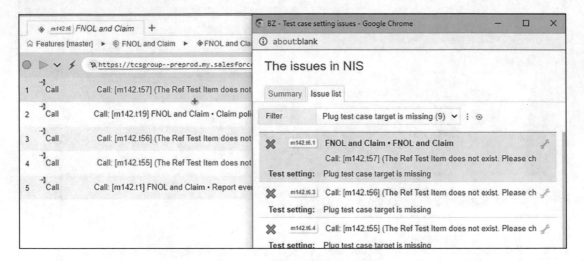

Missing Test Case target

Data Error

This is a useful check and it should normally have no issues. It will tell you if there are any problems with the JSON data used by a Test.

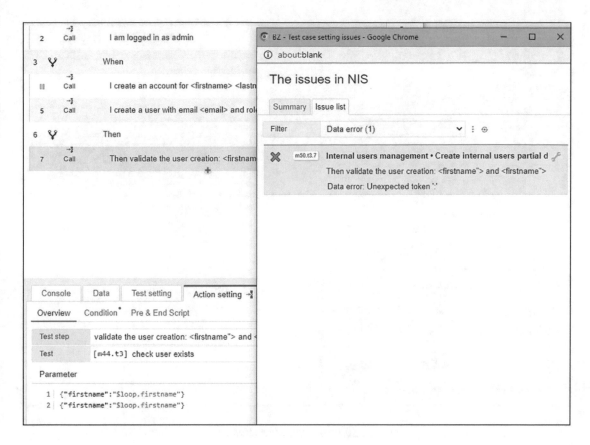

Data error

Missing Expectation Setting

Another useful check is to show actions where a validation on a web element has an empty expectation.

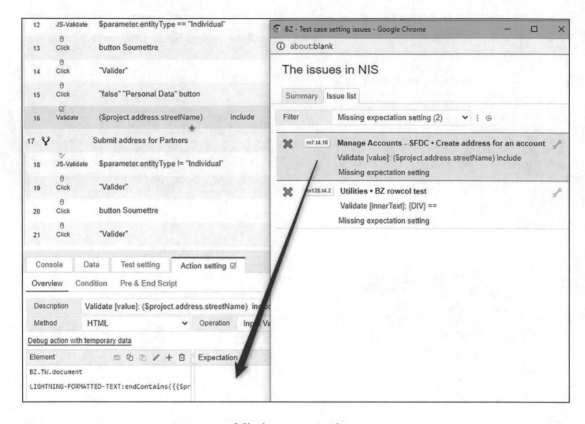

Missing expectations

Missing Element in Action

As last example, the missing element: this should normally show no issues. The following one in the example was artificially created to see how it looks in reality.

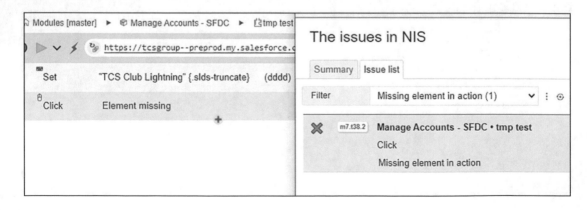

Missing elements

Our Main Learnings

As for every project that comes to an end, it is important to share some learnings.

Will I use Boozang in our next project? Certainly yes. From the time I selected this tool as our main Web automation tool, new features have been added, the stability and robustness increased, and the support has always been top of the class.

In terms of organization, having a dedicated automation team is certainly something I would recommend. However, there are certainly things I wish we could have done better.

The first one is the proximity of the automation team with the delivery team, both business analysts and developers. We did spend too much time retro engineering the scenarios and understanding the application flow. A more BDD-like approach would have certainly increased the efficiency.

The same proximity would have given us more confidence in our coverage.

The point where I feel we could have done much better is on the management of the test environments. Especially on the ACP (AKA PreProd), several activities were performed by different stakeholders, mainly UATs, performance testing, and data migration. Although Slack proved to be very useful to align all the stakeholders, proactive monitoring of these environments was missing mainly due to capacity and organizational constraints.

The integration with JIRA and XRay worked flawlessly, and it allowed us to increase the visibility and transparency of our work, presenting the progress and the coverage on a daily basis with the Scrum teams.

The Jenkins pipeline also worked well. It did go through several improvements at the beginning of the project, but after a few sprints it has reached a good degree of maturity and stability.

Some improvements can still be made concerning the concurrency of different Jenkins jobs. This is however due to some application constraints and the need to execute each Boozang worker with a separate test user.

Conclusions

I hope you enjoyed this read and most of all learned some new things for your professional activity.

My initial goal was to write a book "from the trenches" and not a plain user guide or theoretical testing book. I believe this goal was achieved by not only presenting Boozang but most of all how we used it in a real project. Of course, the recipes presented in this book might not apply to different contexts, but I believe that what was presented can still be useful to other testing folks.

It was not possible to show in detail all the features that Boozang offers; for this, you can always refer to the official Boozang documentation and their support channel. Whenever possible, I updated the screenshots to the latest IDE version.

Every feedback is always welcome, so feel free to reach out via my LinkedIn profile or via the book blog:

- `www.linkedin.com/in/gianni-pucciani-ab41705/`

- `https://boozangfromthetrenches.com/`

G. Pucciani, *Boozang from the Trenches*, https://doi.org/10.1007/978-1-4842-9010-1

APPENDIX

ROI Example for a Test Automation Initiative

Let's look at an example of a fictitious automation initiative where the SUT is in place and automated tests need to be developed to replace part of the manually executed regression tests.

Let's assume the following for our example:

- Licenses for the Test Automation tool cost 10K[1] per year.

- Training for the automation team costs 10K for 2 weeks.

- It will take 6 months to automate 80% of the regression test suite.

- Two FTEs working on the automation project, with an average daily cost of 1K per FTE.

- There are monthly releases, with 1 regression test cycle per release.

- Each regression test cycle run manually takes 3 FTEs for 5 days.

- The average cost of one FTE running manual tests is 1K per day.

- There are 20 working days in a month.

- Once the automated suite is in place, you will need 3 man-days[2] of maintenance effort per month.

The ROI formula we use is the following:

$$ROI = gain\ from\ investment \div cost\ of\ investment$$

---

[1] We do not specify the currency in all the costs.

[2] 1 man-day is considered an effort of 8h for one person.

© Gianni Pucciani 2023

G. Pucciani, *Boozang from the Trenches*, https://doi.org/10.1007/978-1-4842-9010-1

This calculation will not consider the time value of money; therefore, ROI calculation is done without incorporating the net present value concept.

The *gain from investment* is going to be the cost savings achieved on the testing activity.

To calculate this gain we will take a look at the costs with automation and costs without automation, over a period of 3 years, which is a reasonable time for most initiatives of this type and scale.

In case of no automation, the monthly costs are equal to running the entire suite manually; 3 FTE * 5 days * 1K = 15K.

In case of automation, the first month you will have the manual testing costs (15K), the licenses (10K), the training (10K), and the automation effort (20days*2FTEs*1K=40K) (which sums up to 75K).

To make the computation simple but realistic, let's say that for the first month there are no benefits since you are learning and setting up the tool. The following 2 months you manage to automate 10% of the tests each month, and then your efficiency increases to 20% per month.

So the cost with automation will be the automation effort (40K), plus the remaining manual effort (15K-10% for month 2 and 15K-20% for month 3, 15K-40% for month 4, 15K-60% for month 5, and 15K-80% at month 6).

On month 6 your automation work is complete, and for the following months you just have 3 man-days of effort per month needed for maintenance. Therefore after the sixth month, each additional month you are left with 20% of manual testing (3K) plus the automation maintenance (3K), for a total of 6K per month.

Month	1	2	3	4	5	6	7	8	9	10	11	12	...	24	...	36
Without automation	15	15	15	15	15	15	15	15	15	15	15	15	...	15	...	15
With automation	75	53.5	52	49	46	43	6	6	6	6	6	6	...	6	...	6

To correctly draw a graph you need to cumulate the costs.

Also, at month 13 and 25 the license renewal costs must be considered (remember it was 10K per year).

Month	1	2	3	4	5	6	7	8	9	10	11	12	...	24	...	36
Cum without automation	15	30	45	60	75	90	105	120	135	150	165	180	...	360	...	540
Cum with automation	75	128.5	180.5	229.5	275.5	318.5	324.5	330.5	336.5	342.5	348.5	354.5		436	...	518.5

Using the last table with the cumulative costs, we can draw the following graph.

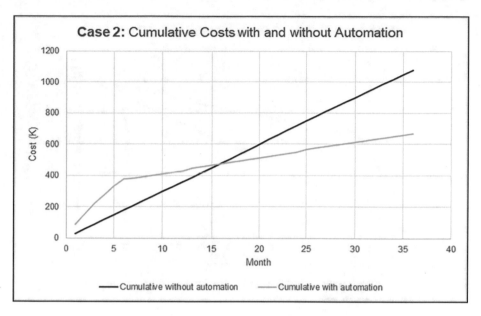

As you can see from the graph, the costs with automation start to be lower than the costs without automation around month 34. This is called the break-even point.

In this case, almost 3 years are needed for the automation initiative to be profitable. To calculate the ROI over 3 years, let's look at the costs with and without automation:

- Costs without automation: 540K

- Costs with automation: 518.5K

- **→ ROI = gain from investment / costs of investment = (540-518)/518 = 4.15%**

This was a simple example, and one could argue that the business case is weak.

But this is like comparing apples to oranges. With automation, you have added benefits. First of all, you can run all the regression tests nightly, rather than just once per release as you would do if you were to run them manually.

Therefore to make it more realistic and to have a similar quality objective, you could assume a scenario where you would run the manual tests 2 times for each release.

In that case, the costs without automation are 30K instead of 15K for each monthly release.

Adapting the table and resulting graph would look like:

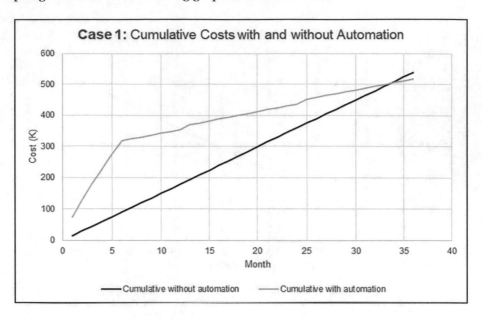

In this case, the break-even point is sooner, around month 16.
And the ROI over 3 years is

- Costs without automation: 1080K

- Costs with automation: 677K

- → **ROI = (1080-677)/677 = 62%**

As you see, the business case changes considerably, and we can push the scenario even further.

When using automation you find issues early on, while the fixing cost is lower.

To account for this you can assume that a certain percentage of issues discovered during UAT are now discovered during development, with little to none additional cost for fixing it.

Let's assume that, without Test Automation, 1 regression defect is spotted on UAT every other release. Over 1 year it makes 6 defects. Considering 2 days of effort for fixing a defect found in UAT (bug reporting, analysis, fix implementation, deployment, and retest), this means 12K saved each year, and 36K over 3 years.

Let's consider this and update the ROI:

- Costs without automation: 1080K + 36K = 1116K

- Costs with automation: unchanged, 677K

- → **ROI = (1116 - 677) / 677 = 83%**

Moreover, the manual test efforts you saved (12 man-days each month) will be reinvested in usability testing, or used on other value-add tasks.

Last but not least, the two team members that went from 15 boring days of manual regression tests to just 3 days will be much happier!

With these examples, I just wanted to illustrate how an investment that may initially seem worthless, in reality proves to be beneficial. Test Automation, both at the unit testing level and system level, is rarely a poor investment.

Sure, this type of analysis can and should be done in specific cases like

- Legacy applications with a limited lifetime

- Systems technologically complex where Test Automation might be challenging

- Systems where releases are not frequent and where regressions can be tolerated and quickly fixed

Aside from these specific cases, Test Automation should not be doubted: the question should be not if, but when, how, and to what degree.

In my experience, I have seen contexts where Test Automation was not applied from the beginning and manual testing effort was one of the reasons that slowed down release cycles and limited system evolutions. Other times, the Test Automation effort had to be justified and a formal ROI deeply questioned.

Luckily, in the NIS project, I was afforded a "good" context, where we do not question whether to apply Test Automation or not, but rather, how to do it in the most efficient way.

Index

A

Acceptance testing, 247
ACP environment, 13, 119, 270, 275, 309
API/GUI scenarios
    actions, 213, 214
    API calls, 212
    considerations, 214, 215
    meaning, 212
    PCAS application, 212, 213
    product acquisition step, 214
Automation team, 71, 72, 191, 253, 309

B

Behavior Driven Development (BDD),
    16, 37, 217
    COTS, 218, 219
    discovery, 218
    formulation, 218
    success factor, 218
Bind data, 99
Bookmarks, 97, 98
Boozang, 49
    API calls, 215
    API tests
        creation window, 204, 205
        empty module, 203, 204
        Google APIs, 205–207
        main items, 209
        NISTA module, 204
        parsing/validating, response
          object, 207, 208

architecture, 67
branch
    details, 289
    develop, 291
    display, 286, 287
    Jenkins, 291
    management, 287, 288
    master, 291
    milestone, 289
    naming convention, 290, 291
    Test Automation, 291
Chrome Extension, 64, 65, 69
client-server communication, 70, 71
concurrent development, 38
confirmation email, 57
data management, 37
ease of use, 36
edit project details, 62
feature branch approach, 289, 290
Gherkin/BDD, 37
GIT, 286
Git-Flow, 291
home page, 56
HTML fragment, 65
language-based element recognition, 37
location strategy, 122
merge process
    Advanced operations menu, 292
    branch selection, no conflicts, 293
    changes, 293, 294
    options, 294
possibilities, 64

© Gianni Pucciani 2023
G. Pucciani, *Boozang from the Trenches*, https://doi.org/10.1007/978-1-4842-9010-1

Printed in the United States
by Baker & Taylor Publisher Services